IMAGES
of Aviation

DELAWARE AVIATION

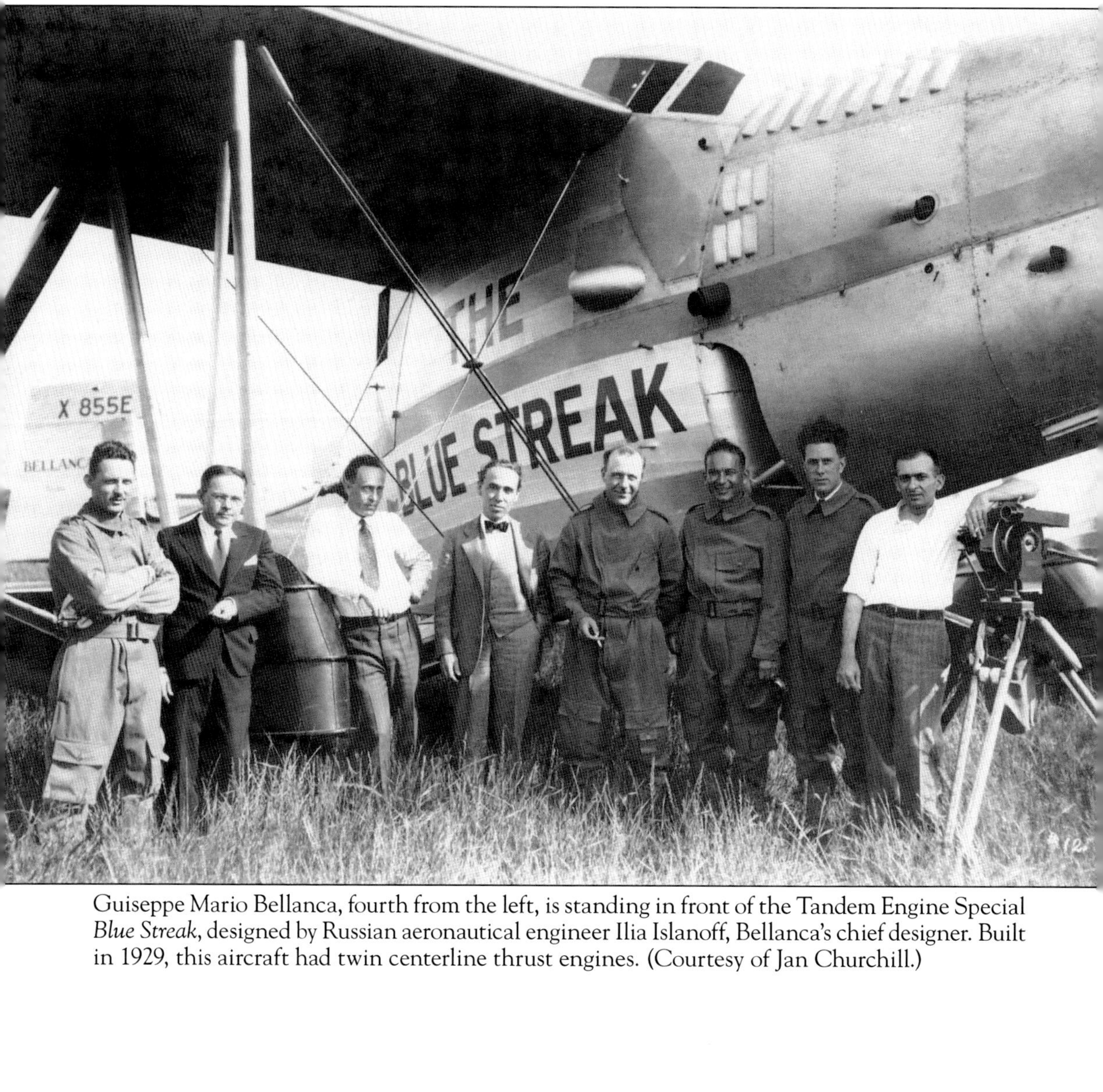

Guiseppe Mario Bellanca, fourth from the left, is standing in front of the Tandem Engine Special *Blue Streak*, designed by Russian aeronautical engineer Ilia Islanoff, Bellanca's chief designer. Built in 1929, this aircraft had twin centerline thrust engines. (Courtesy of Jan Churchill.)

ON THE COVER: This C-54, named *The City of Wilmington*, is pictured at Washington National Airport where it picked up the press (famous war correspondents) for a 45,000-mile world tour. The Air Transport Command (ATC) was so proud of local support that it painted the name on both sides of the C-54. The flight departed Washington, DC, on June 2, 1945, and returned on August 3, 1945. (Courtesy of Jan Churchill.)

IMAGES
of Aviation

DELAWARE AVIATION

Jan Churchill (ATP, CFII, USCGAUX) and
Brig. Gen. Kennard R. Wiggins Jr. (DE ANG Retired)

ARCADIA
PUBLISHING

ISBN 978-1-4671-2174-3

Published by Arcadia Publishing
Charleston, South Carolina

Printed in the United States of America

Library of Congress Control Number: 2013952071

For all general information, please contact Arcadia Publishing:
Telephone 843-853-2070
Fax 843-853-0044
E-mail sales@arcadiapublishing.com
For customer service and orders:
Toll-Free 1-888-313-2665

Visit us on the Internet at www.arcadiapublishing.com

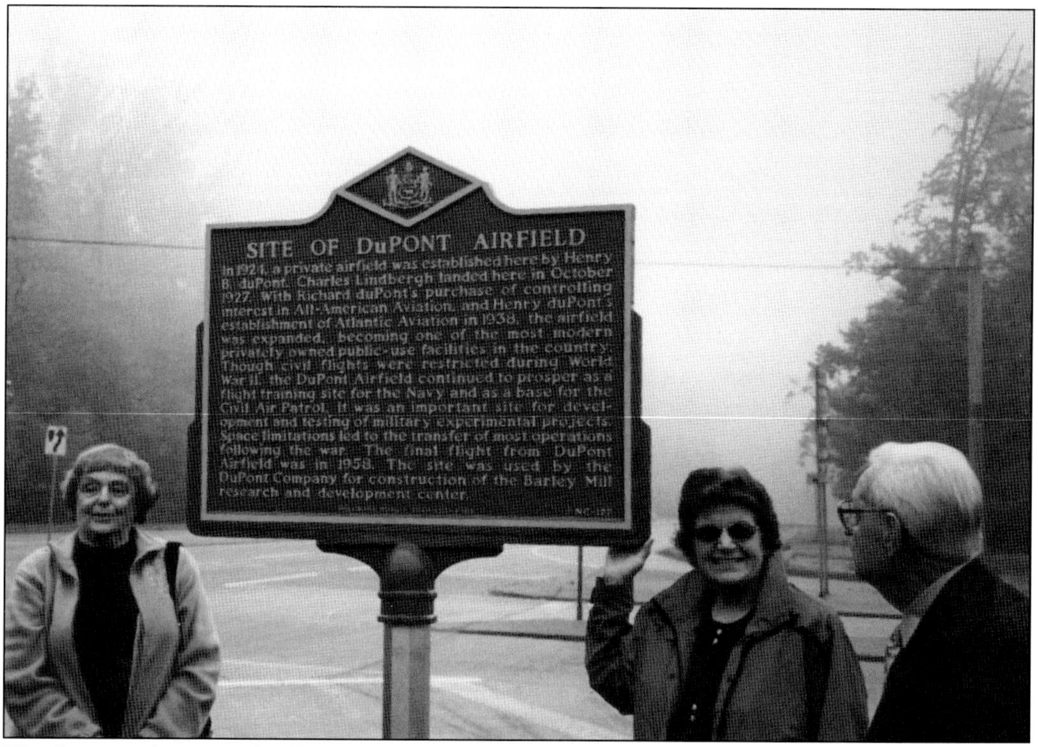

This historical sign marks the site of DuPont Airfield, established in 1921. During World War II, DuPont Airfield was used for training Navy pilots and was a Civil Air Patrol (CAP) base. The final flight from this airfield was on May 10, 1958. Today, this area is known as Barley Mill Plaza. Pictured here are, from left to right, Anne Eriksen, Jan Churchill, and Mike Guididas. All three are pilots. (Courtesy of Jan Churchill.)

Contents

Acknowledgments 6
Introduction 7
1. The Early Years 9
2. The War Years 27
3. Postwar 47
4. Air Shows and Events 83
Bibliography 127

ACKNOWLEDGMENTS

The authors would like to acknowledge with sincere gratitude the following organizations and people who share our love of aviation history. This book would not have been possible without their contributions. We owe a debt to the Air Mobility Museum, led by Mike Leister, who provided many images of Dover Air Force Base (AFB) as well as the archived images of Mike Frebert and the late George Frebert. We thank Caroline duPont Prickett and John Bonnell for their helpfulness with Summit Aviation. We are indebted to the Friends of Bellanca Airfield Museum and Frank Ianni as well as the Experimental Aircraft Association (EAA) Chapter 240 and the contributions of Hugh Horning and Reggie Thompson. We thank Robert McMahon and Charles Nabb of the Delaware State Police Aviation Unit. We are grateful to the Massey Air Museum, the Delaware State Archives, and the Delaware Military Heritage and Education Foundation as sources of many historic images.

We have used the following abbreviations in crediting our images: Air Mobility Command Museum (AMC), Adelaide Tinker (AT), Andrew Kondrach (AK), Bellanca Airfield Museum (BA), Caroline duPont Prickett (CduP), Charles Nabb (CN), Craig Wheel (CW), Dover Air Force Base (DAFB), Experimental Aircraft Association Chapter 240 (EAA), Delaware Military Heritage and Education Foundation (DMHEF), George J. Frebert (GF), Hugh Horning (HH), Jan Churchill (JC), Marge Matyniak (MM), Women's Army Corps (WAC), Women's Auxiliary Ferrying Squadron (WAFS), and Women's Air Force Service Pilots (WASP).

Introduction

For being a small state, Delaware has a very rich aviation history. It began with the *Delaplane* in 1910, marking the time an airplane first flew in Delaware.

As World War I approached, in 1917, Pierre S. duPont and John Jacob Raskob created a flying school for aviation cadets, called Delaware Aeronautical Company. It was located on Rascob's estate in Claymont along the Delaware River with three hangars and a bay for floatplanes. Student pilots had to apply to the US Aviation Corps for admission to the flying school. On June 26, 1917, the cadet pilots flew a mock attack on Wilmington, dropping leaflets enticing recruits for the National Guard to enlist in the Delaware Regiment.

Henry Belin duPont Jr. was impressed by the world records set by immigrant Giuseppe Mario Bellanca. When Bellanca needed his own airplane factory, Henry duPont wanted him in Delaware and made this possible by purchasing a large farm in New Castle for the Bellanca Aircraft Factory. The land included Delaware River frontage for floatplanes.

Grass fields sprang up all over Delaware. Henry duPont's own DuPont Airfield was the first private-use airport. The first public-use airport was Biggs Field, on the Stockton Farm in New Castle on property owned by the Trustees of New Castle Common. The first public demonstration of the ability to pickup mail at night was at Wilmington's Bellanca Airfield with pilot Holger Hoiriis, a Danish immigrant, on October 29, 1939. Hoiriis was a test pilot for Air Services, Inc., and the Bellanca Aircraft Factory. Alexander, John, and Mary Biggs were the operators of the big grass field that was marked with a large white circle. The field was used from 1922 to 1957, in part by US Army biplanes. The airfield was closed during World War II, from 1941 to 1945. It was sold in March 1959 for the Penn Acres Development.

J. Allison Buck ran Bucks Airfield from 1928 to 1933, incorporating his business as Delaware Flying Service. His field was located between Minquadale and Farnhurst, across from the Delaware State Hospital, on property now known as Gracelawn Cemetery. From 1932 to 1937, there was a small field, called Skycroft Field, north of Wilmington between Shipley and Weldin Roads with a 1,300-foot grass strip; Maurice Paschall owned it. Benedict Airport was seven miles north of Wilmington along Foulk Road. This location held dealerships for Piper and Seabee airplanes. Another small grass strip, called Pilots Haven, was located near Christiana.

The Point Breeze Flying Club operated a grass strip on Naaman's Road. There were small fields at Red Lion in Bear, Lovett Airport near the University of Delaware, and Cherry Island Airfield with one hangar rented by William and Johnny Ward from 1938 to 1941. Throughout the rest of Delaware, small grass landing strips were available on many farms.

In 1930, the Department of Commerce Airport Directory listed Bellanca Field–Wilmington Airport as a 3,800-by-2,000-foot sod field with its name painted on a hangar roof. It was Airfield No. 65 along the New York-to-Atlanta airway, with two grass runways. The airfield was operated by Richard D. Morgan for Air Service, Inc., in a new hangar built across the field from the Bellanca Aircraft Factory in New Castle. Later, the Bellanca Aircraft Factory built a paved runway.

Dr. Lytle S. Adams, who had invented a unique airmail pickup system, chartered All American Aviation as a Delaware corporation on March 5, 1937. This led to the nation's first feeder airline, which was developed in Delaware. By the late 1930s, All American Aviation called itself "Airways to Everywhere." Headquarters were in Wilmington while the maintenance and repair work was done at DuPont Airfield on the Lancaster Pike. By January 1944, airline route 49F included Wilmington and extended from New York to Washington, DC. Later, All American Aviation became Allegheny Airlines and ultimately US Air.

The first public demonstration of the ability to pickup mail at night was at Wilmington's Bellanca Field with pilot Holger Hoiriis, who was inducted into the Delaware Aviation Hall of Fame in 2009. On October 29, 1939, Stinson airplanes practiced airmail pickups at Irenee duPont's estate in Granogue.

All American Aviation and Richard C. duPont were very significant. The airmail pickup system they developed put Delaware in the forefront of this technique. DuPont played a big part in glider pickup, a valuable technique in World War II. All American abandoned the airmail pickup in 1949, replacing the Stinsons with Beechcraft and Douglas DC-3 passenger airplanes. After the war, All American Engineering had a test facility at the Georgetown Airport in the 1950s.

The Civil Air Patrol had an important part in World War II locating enemy submarines just off the East Coast. In addition to the unit at DuPont Airfield, Civil Air Patrol Base Two was located at Rehoboth Beach. A Sikorsky S-39, owned by CAP major Hugh R. Sharp Jr., was flown by CAP major Sharp and CAP pilot Edmund I. Edwards, 20 miles offshore to rescue a pilot whose plane had crashed in the Atlantic Ocean. Sharp and Edwards devised a means to tow the crippled plane with its wounded pilot to safety. Pres. Franklin D. Roosevelt presented Sharp and Edwards with the Army Air Medal for the rescue of a downed airman at sea. They were the first civilians to receive this honor.

Other early airfields included Dover Municipal, Smith Field, Jenkins Airfield, Harrington Airfield, Milford Airpark, Dover Airpark, Delaware Airpark, Sunglo Airfield (near Dover), Chandelle Estates, Henderson Airfield, Rehoboth Beach, and Bridgefield Airfield.

Two of the largest aviation organizations in the world hosted events in Delaware. The Aircraft Owners and Pilots Association (AOPA) initial international conventions were held at Rehoboth Beach Airfield in 1947, 1948, and 1949, with over 500 aircraft flying into the big grass field. The Experimental Aircraft Association (EAA) sponsored local chapters and fly-ins in Delaware.

In 1983, Delaware was the only state in the United States without airline service, so the government subsidized the attempt to provide airlines. A Civil Air Terminal was built on Dover Air Force Base for airline use. Four different subsidized airlines were unable to make this plan economically feasible.

Flight Safety International constructed its own building at New Castle County Airport for a jet simulator training center, which is attended by pilots from all over the world. Eventually, the Delaware River and Bay Authority assumed a long-term lease to run New Castle County Airport. Centrally located in the busy Northeast Corridor, New Castle had been for many years the only major commercial, business airport in Delaware. Later, Georgetown received funding to enlarge its airport as more businesses located there. Today, airplanes operate from New Castle County Airport, Dover Air Force Base, and Georgetown to destinations all over the world—"From Delaware to Everywhere."

One

The Early Years

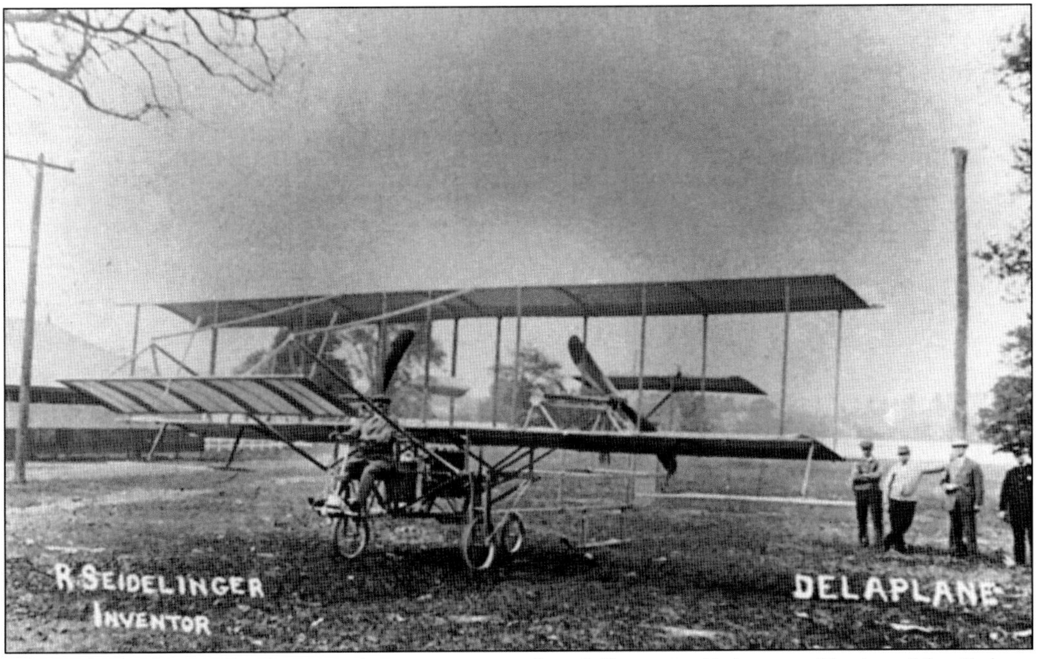

The *Delaplane* was the first airplane constructed and flown in Delaware. Designed by Robert Seidelinger, it was first flown by Edward Bloomfield on October 21, 1910, at Wawaset Park in Wilmington, sponsored by the Wilmington Aero Club. (GF.)

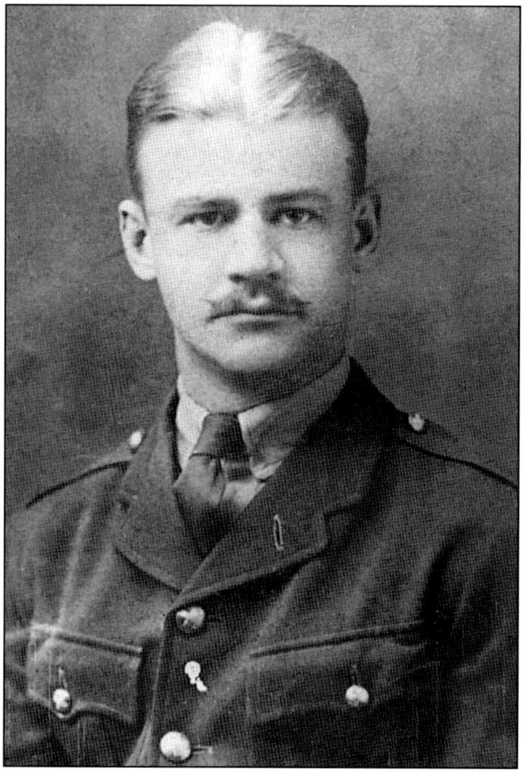

Shown here is Lt. William Pricket, flight observer and gunner during World War I, who joined many others from Delaware in serving his country. They included James Allison O'Daniel of Newark, who was killed in action. (GF.)

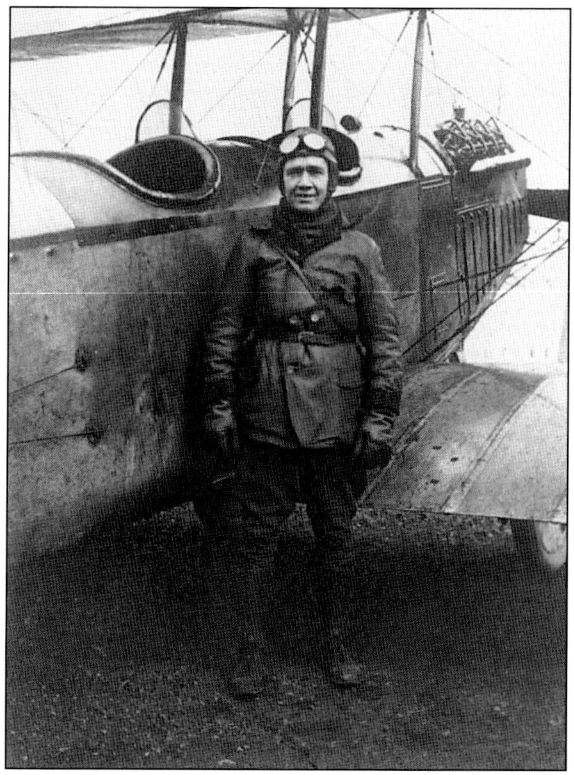

Here, Walter Willoughby Josephs is a flying student in this Curtiss JN-4 "Jenny" at the Delaware Aeronautical School in 1917 in Claymont. Pierre S. duPont, Irenee duPont, and John Jacob Raskob formed this flying school, called the Delaware Aeronautical Company, for aviation cadets. (GF.)

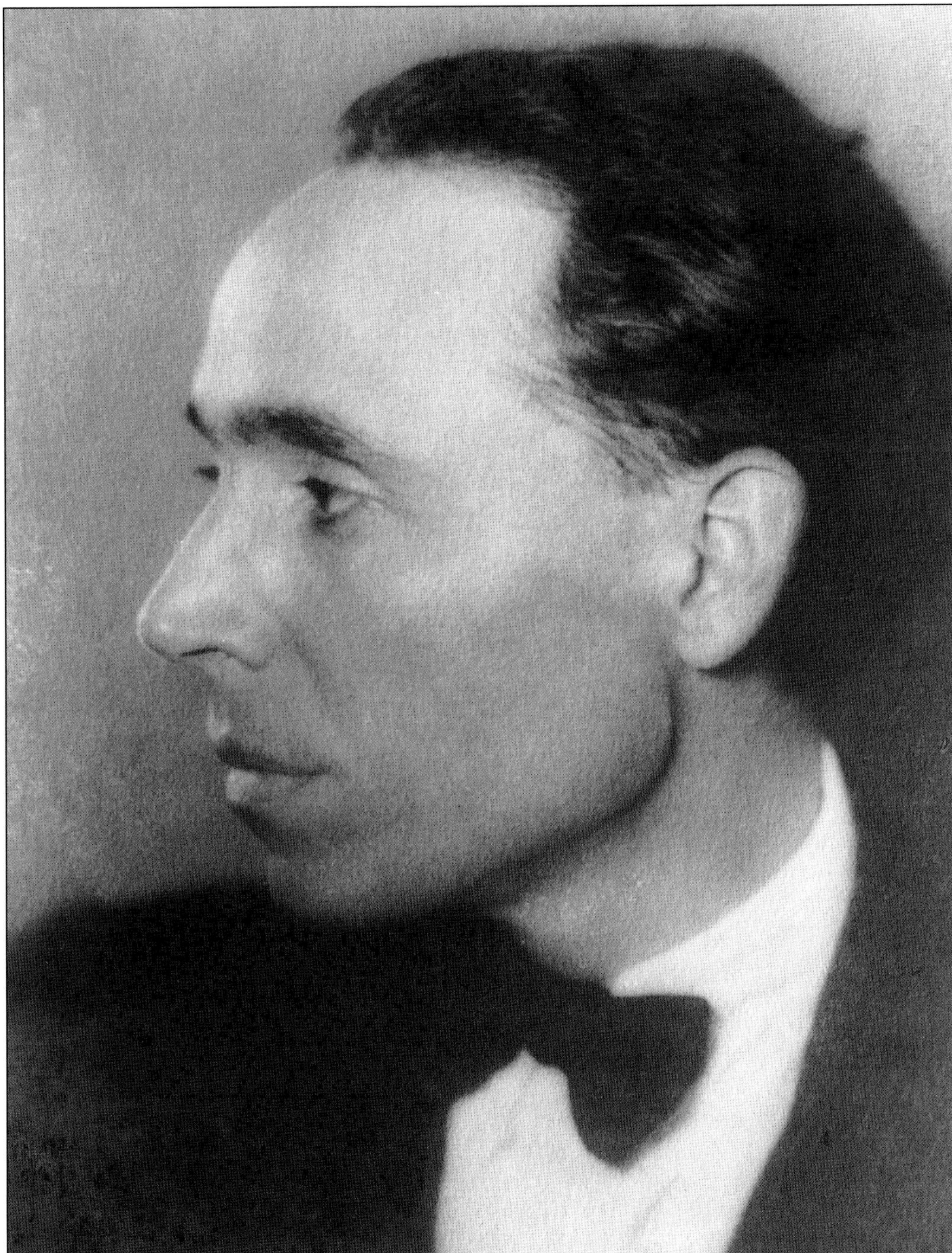

Giuseppe Mario Bellanca (1886–1960), originally from Sicily, arrived in the United States in 1912 and opened a flying school in New York. His reputation grew, and by 1927, Henry Belin duPont Jr. spearheaded a drive to bring Bellanca to New Castle. The 360-acre Spring Garden Farm, which included 1,100 feet of waterfront on the Delaware River for floatplanes, was purchased for $37,215. The formal opening of the Bellanca-Wilmington Airport was on October 6, 1928. (JC.)

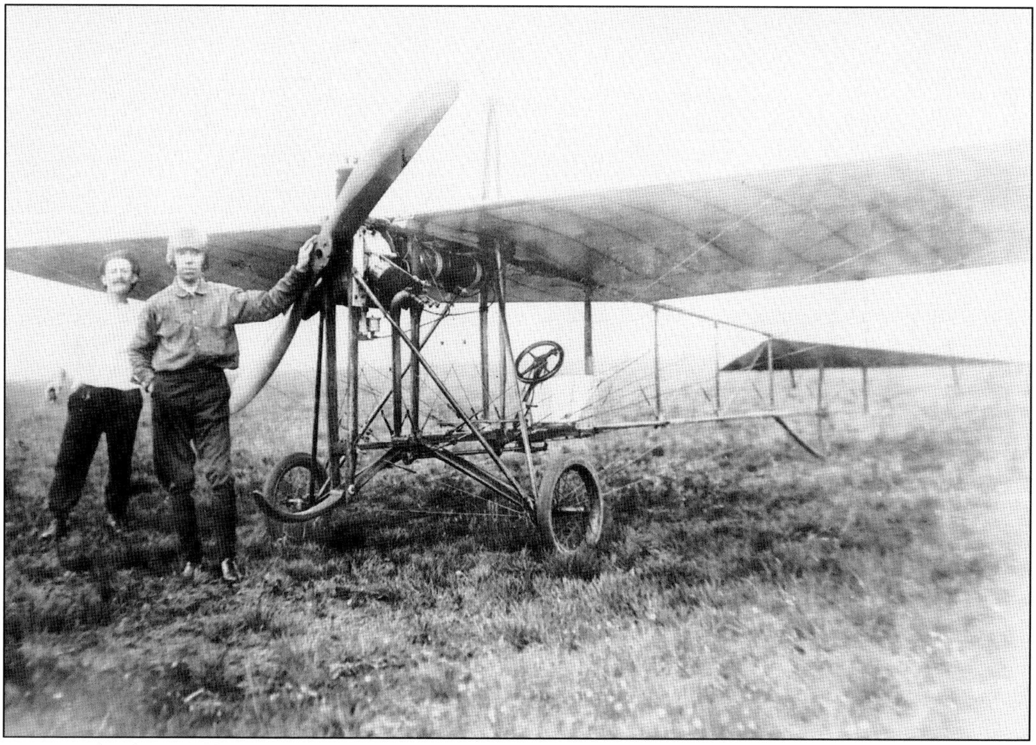

Here is the first Bellanca airplane. Note there is no fin or rudder. (JC.)

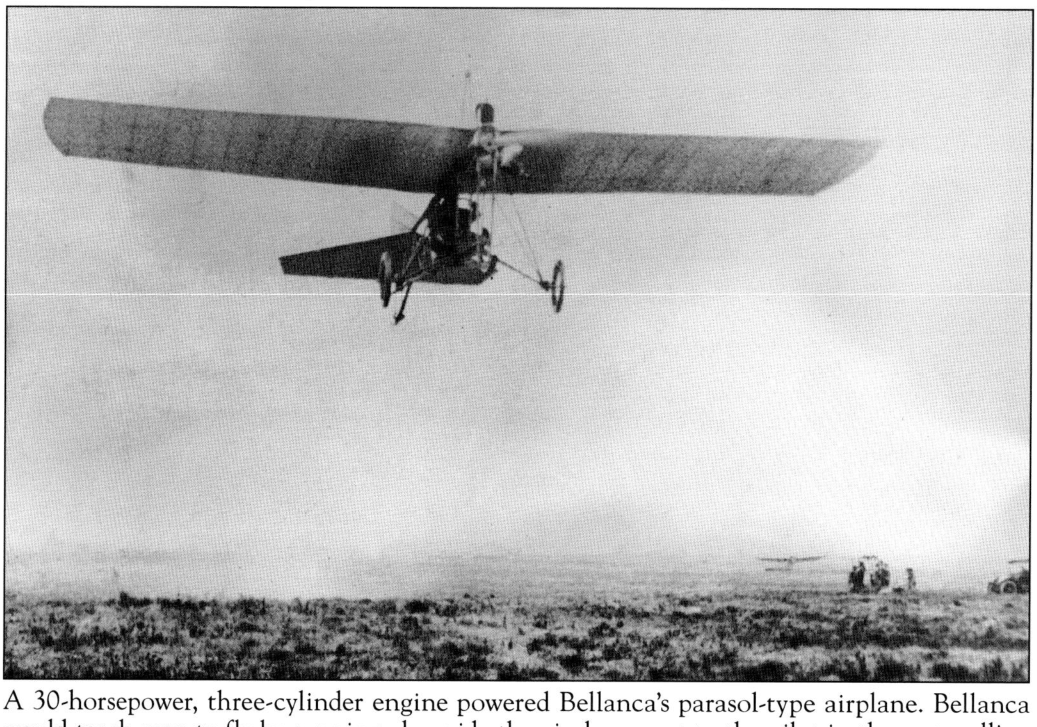

A 30-horsepower, three-cylinder engine powered Bellanca's parasol-type airplane. Bellanca would teach men to fly by running alongside the airplane next to the pilot in the seat, yelling instructions. (JC.)

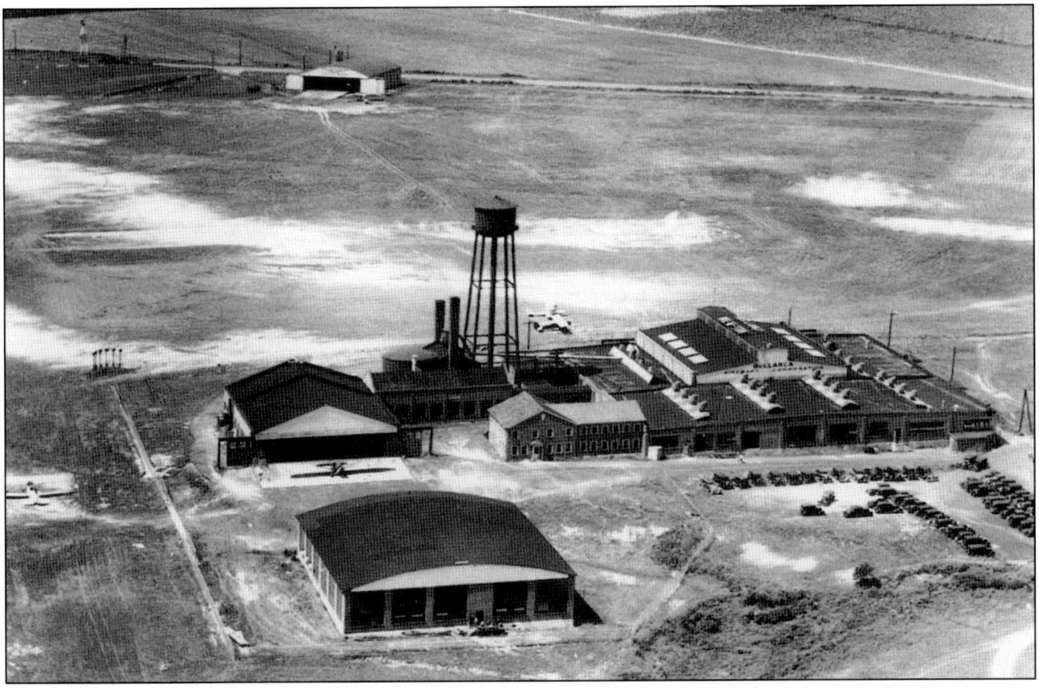

Pictured is the Bellanca Aircraft Factory in New Castle with the Air Service hangar in the distance. The airfield was five miles southwest of Wilmington with a 3,800-foot sod runway and Bellanca-Wilmington painted on a hangar roof. (JC.)

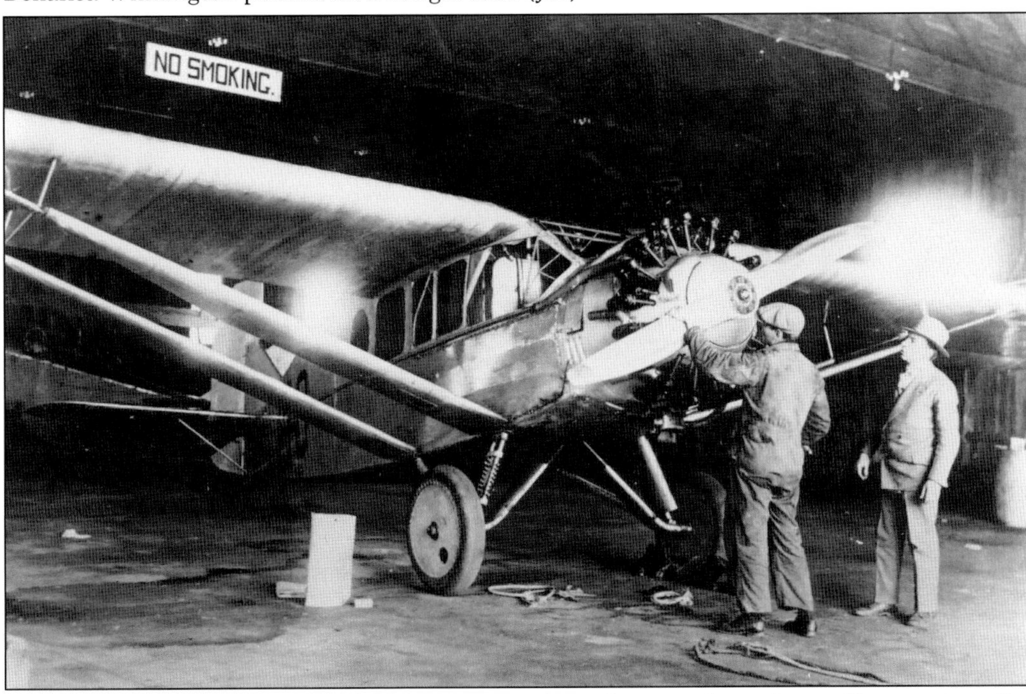

Bellanca's *Columbia* is shown before the Townsend speed ring and metal propeller were installed to increase performance. The plane was constructed of duralumin tubing welded together. The wings were made with very small pieces of wood, giving them great strength. (JC.)

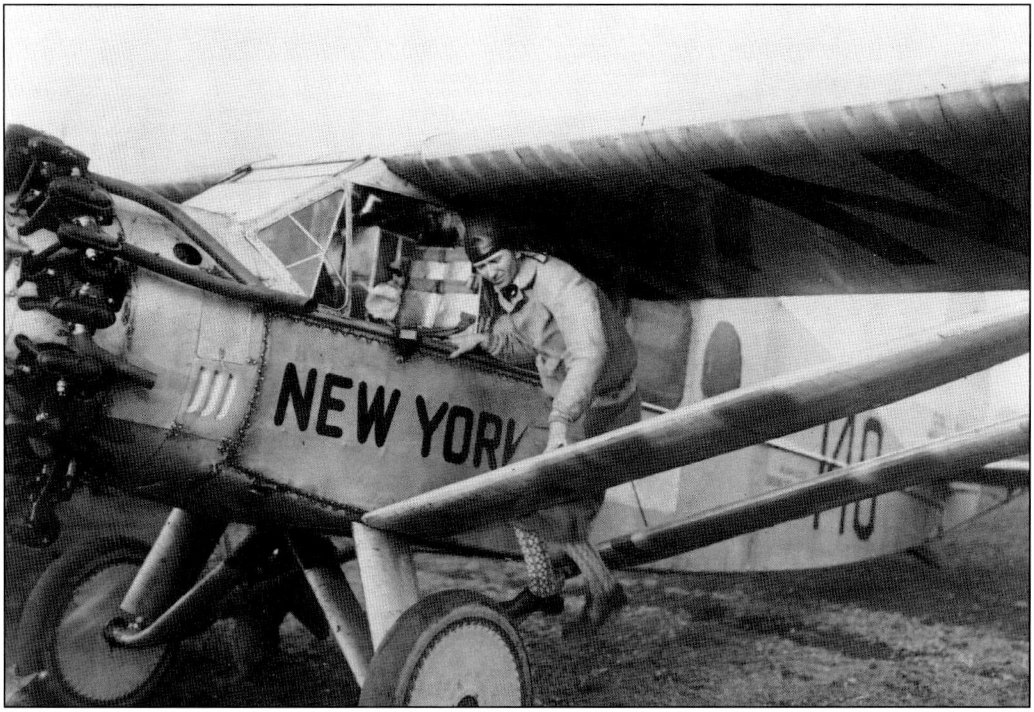

Clarence Chamberlain is shown climbing into the cockpit of this Bellanca Aircraft named *Columbia* just before he and Charles A. Levine took off from Roosevelt Field for a nonstop flight to Eisleben, near Berlin, Germany, setting a world-record nonstop flight of 3,911 miles. (JC.)

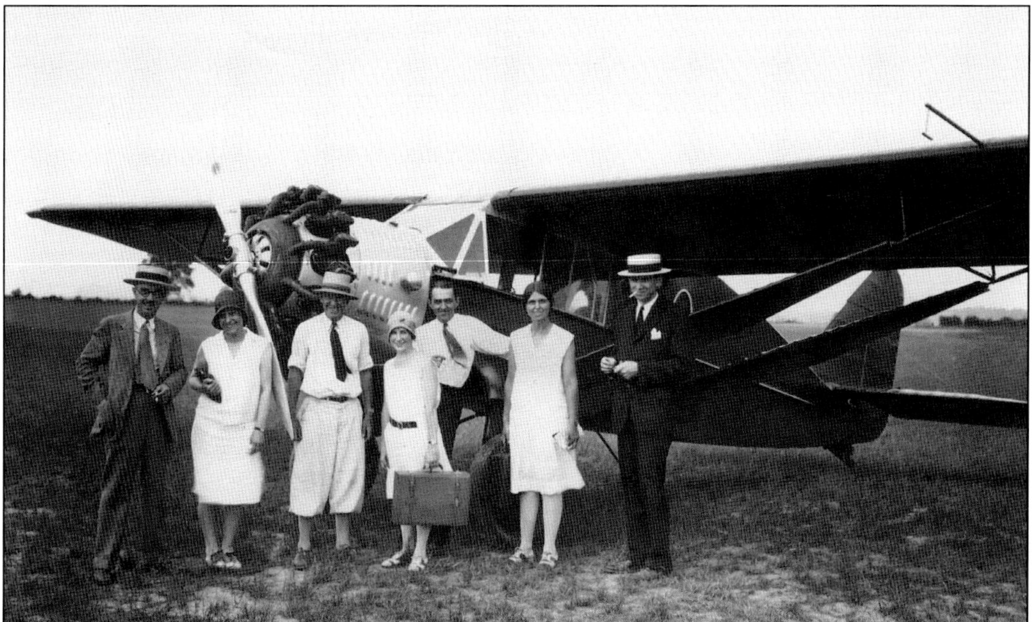

This aircraft is a Bellanca CH-300 powered by a nine-cylinder Wright J-6 of 300 horsepower in this high-wing monoplane. Only a few of these humpbacked gear J-6 series were built. Shortly thereafter, the gear was made more conventional and wider. (JC.)

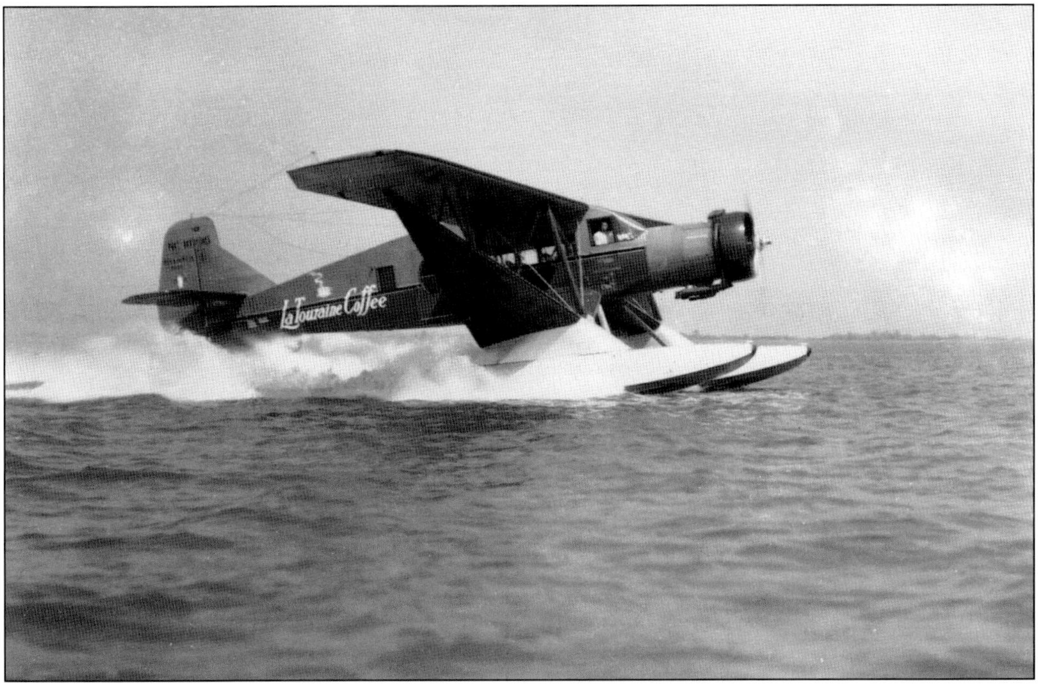

Landing on the Delaware River, this Bellanca floatplane, No. NC10796, was sold to the La Touraine Coffee Company. It was later upgraded as Model 66-67 when the La Touraine Coffee Company returned it for a larger engine. (JC.)

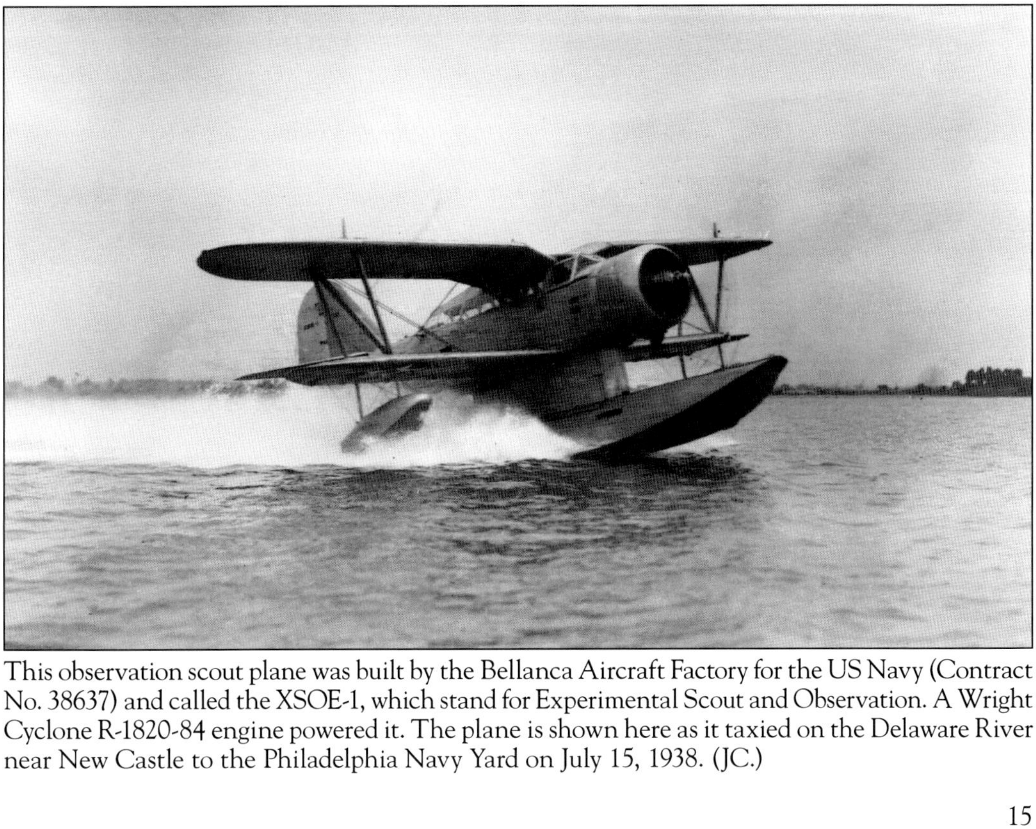

This observation scout plane was built by the Bellanca Aircraft Factory for the US Navy (Contract No. 38637) and called the XSOE-1, which stand for Experimental Scout and Observation. A Wright Cyclone R-1820-84 engine powered it. The plane is shown here as it taxied on the Delaware River near New Castle to the Philadelphia Navy Yard on July 15, 1938. (JC.)

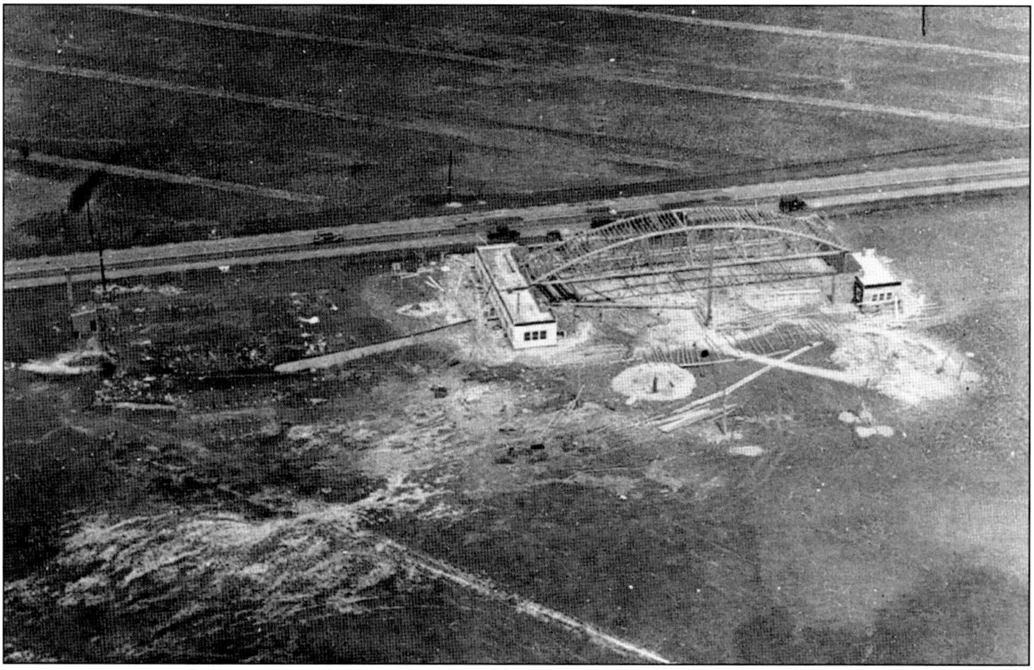

The Air Service hangar at Bellanca Airfield was built in the 1930s. It consisted of block wood measuring 60 by 130 feet plus appendages at each end. Three fan-type trusses, right out of the architectural textbook for that era, support the roof. (JC.)

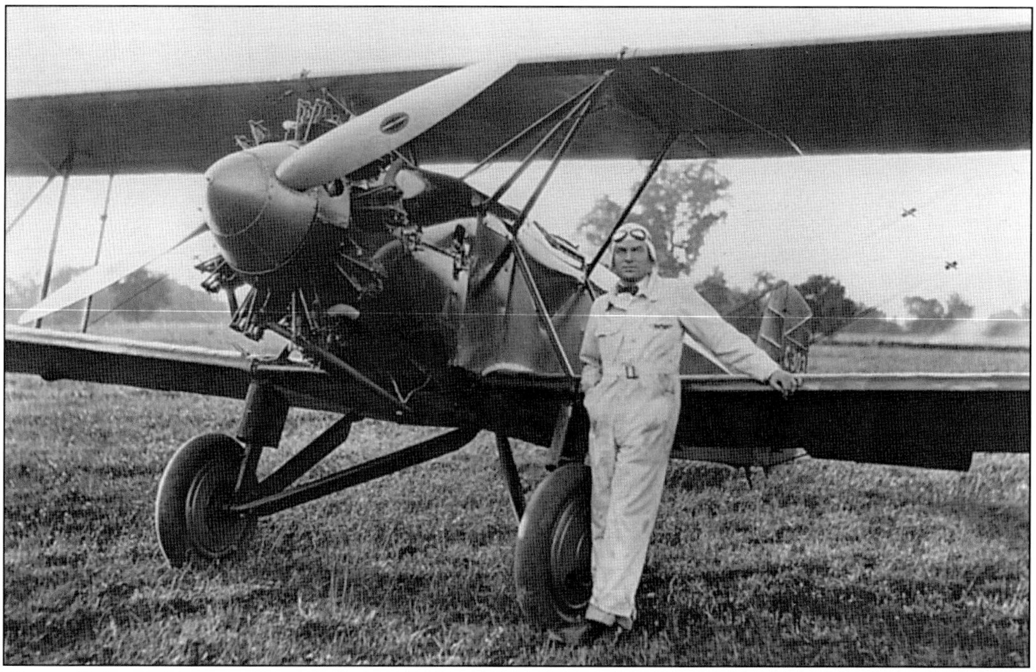

Henry Belin duPont (1898–1970) and his 1927 Buhl Airster are pictured at DuPont Airfield. The Buhl Verville J4 Airster ushered in a new era in aviation history as the first to earn and receive the new Approved Type Certificate, which was a "certificate of airworthiness" issued by the Department of Commerce under the Air Commerce Act of 1926. (GF.)

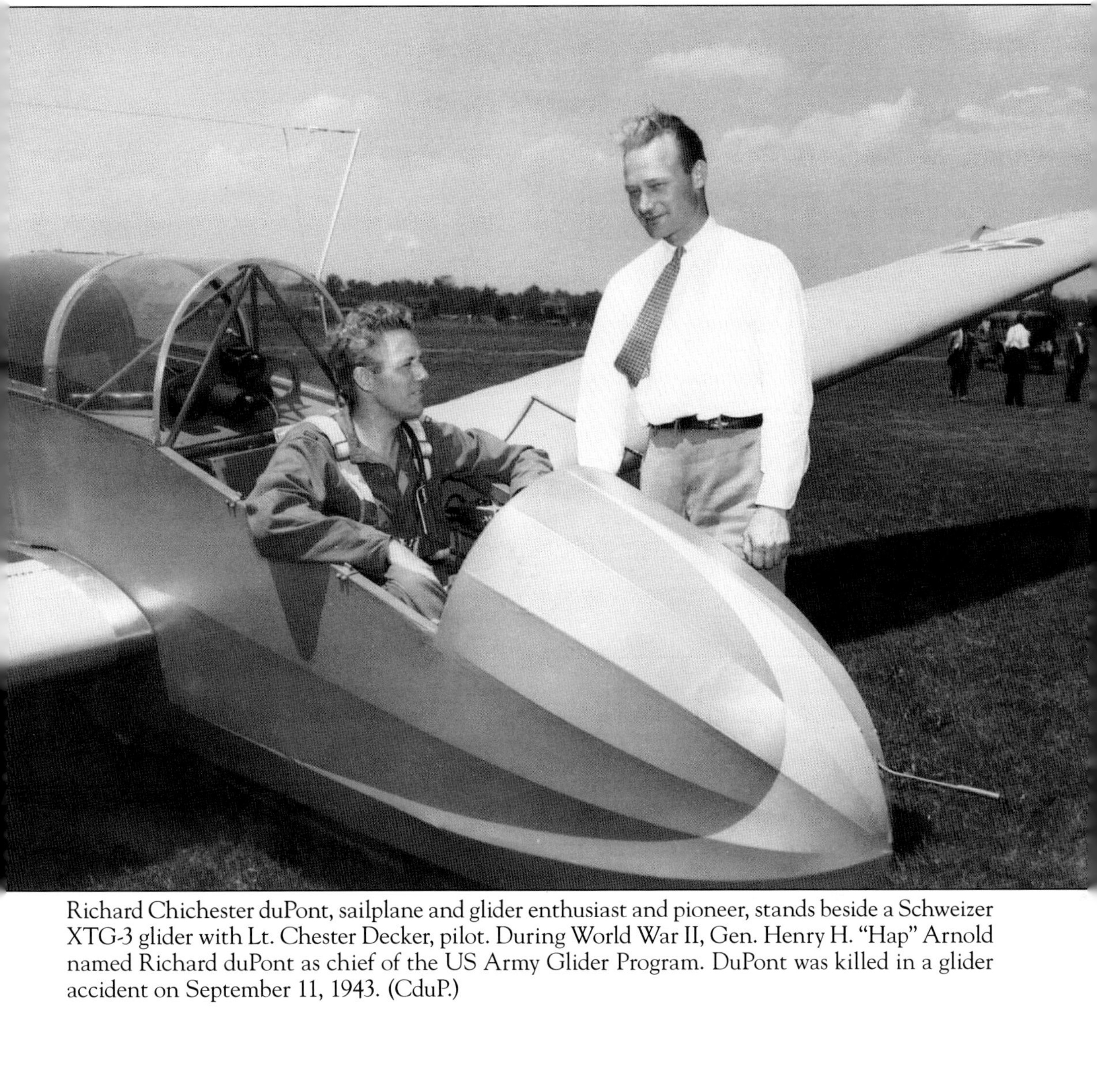

Richard Chichester duPont, sailplane and glider enthusiast and pioneer, stands beside a Schweizer XTG-3 glider with Lt. Chester Decker, pilot. During World War II, Gen. Henry H. "Hap" Arnold named Richard duPont as chief of the US Army Glider Program. DuPont was killed in a glider accident on September 11, 1943. (CduP.)

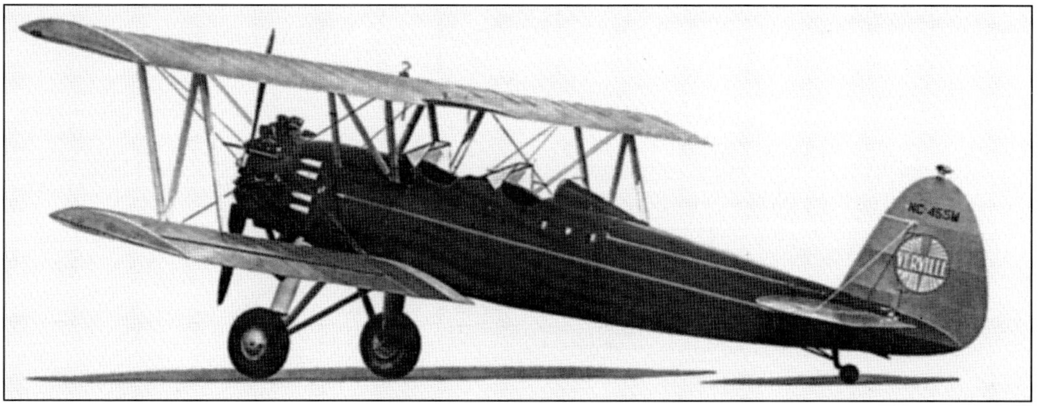

This Verville Sportsman (ATC-323), manufactured by the Verville Aircraft Company, was owned by Henry Belin duPont Jr. Fred Verville was an aeronautical engineer whose company sold four Sportsman biplanes to the Army Air Corps as trainers in 1929. (GF.)

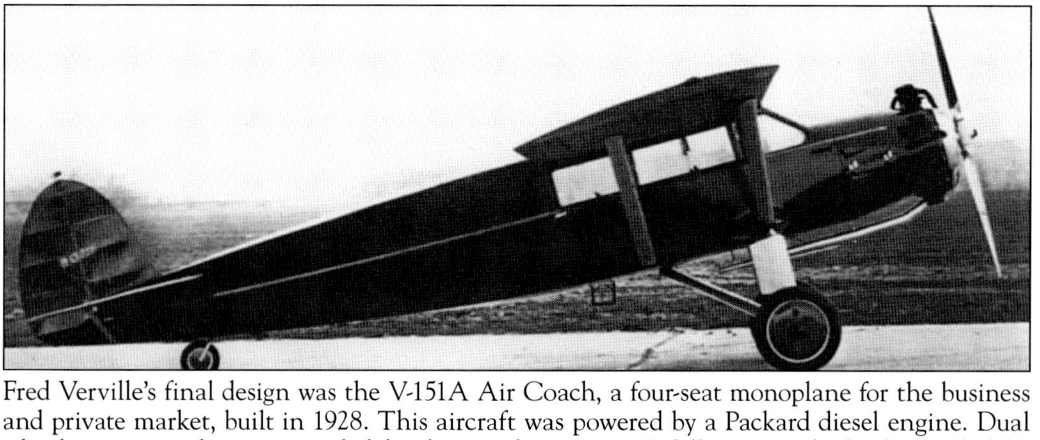

Fred Verville's final design was the V-151A Air Coach, a four-seat monoplane for the business and private market, built in 1928. This aircraft was powered by a Packard diesel engine. Dual wheel-type controls were provided for the two front seats. A full caster tail wheel provided for better ground maneuverability. (GF.)

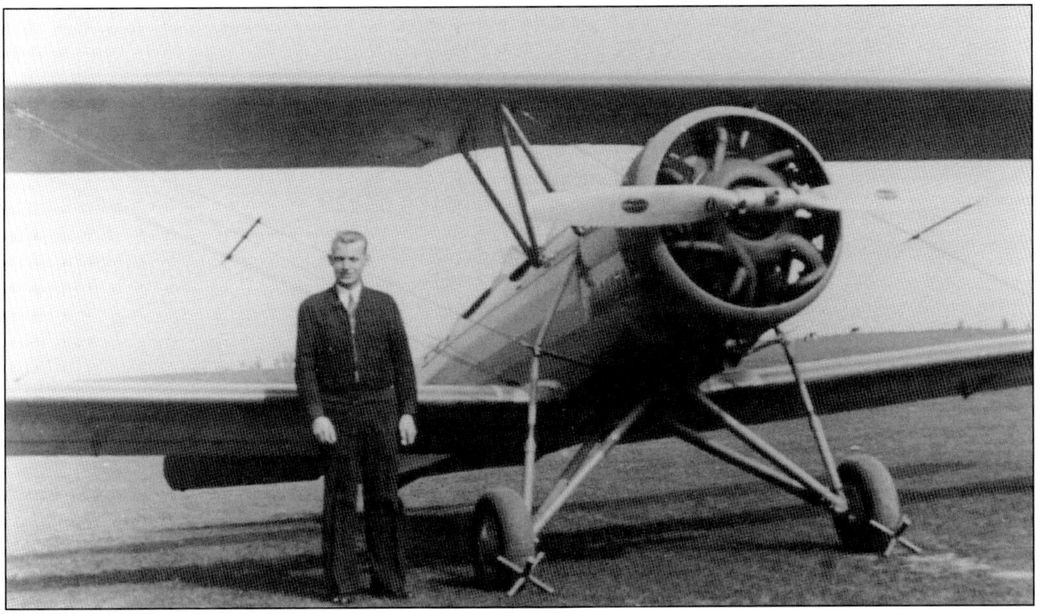

Frank R. Guididas, at 16 years old, worked at the Bellanca Aircraft Factory. He is pictured here with his favorite airplane. During World War II, he worked as a quality control inspector for All American Engineering Company. After the war, he established the flight department for Atlantic Aviation Company at the New Castle County Airport. He was chief pilot for several types of jet airplanes. (JC.)

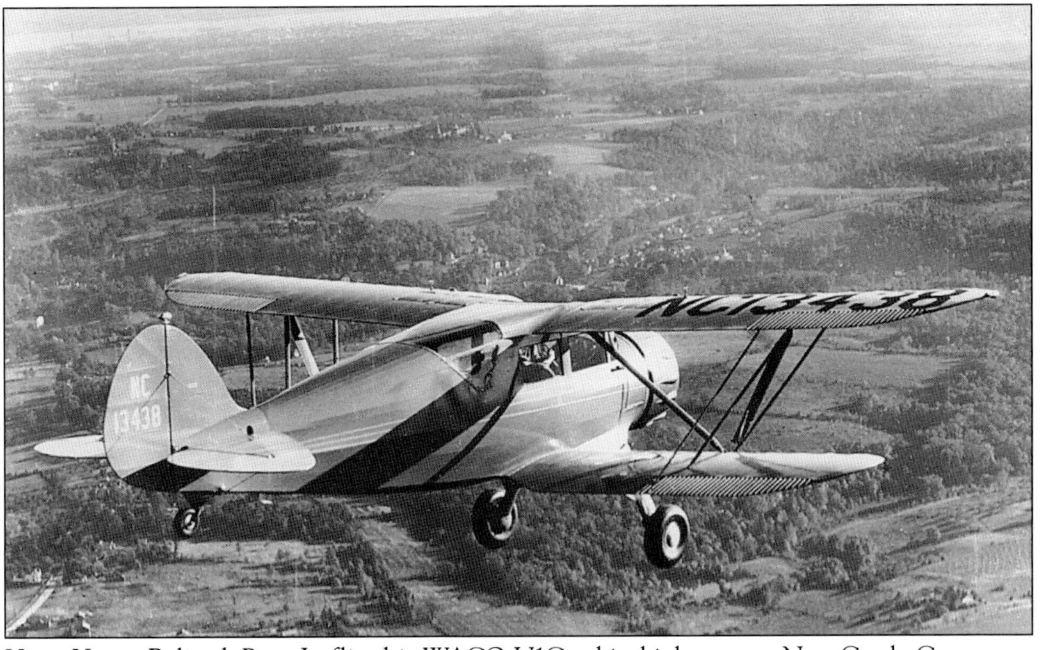

Here, Henry Belin duPont Jr. flies his WACO U1C cabin biplane over New Castle County on October 14, 1933. Many improvements were incorporated in this 1933 model, which was powered by a 210-horsepower Continental engine. This cabin-type biplane, which seated four, sold faster than it could be built. DuPont was the first to own a WACO U1C, and he took advantage of the fact it could easily be converted to floats for water landings. (GF.)

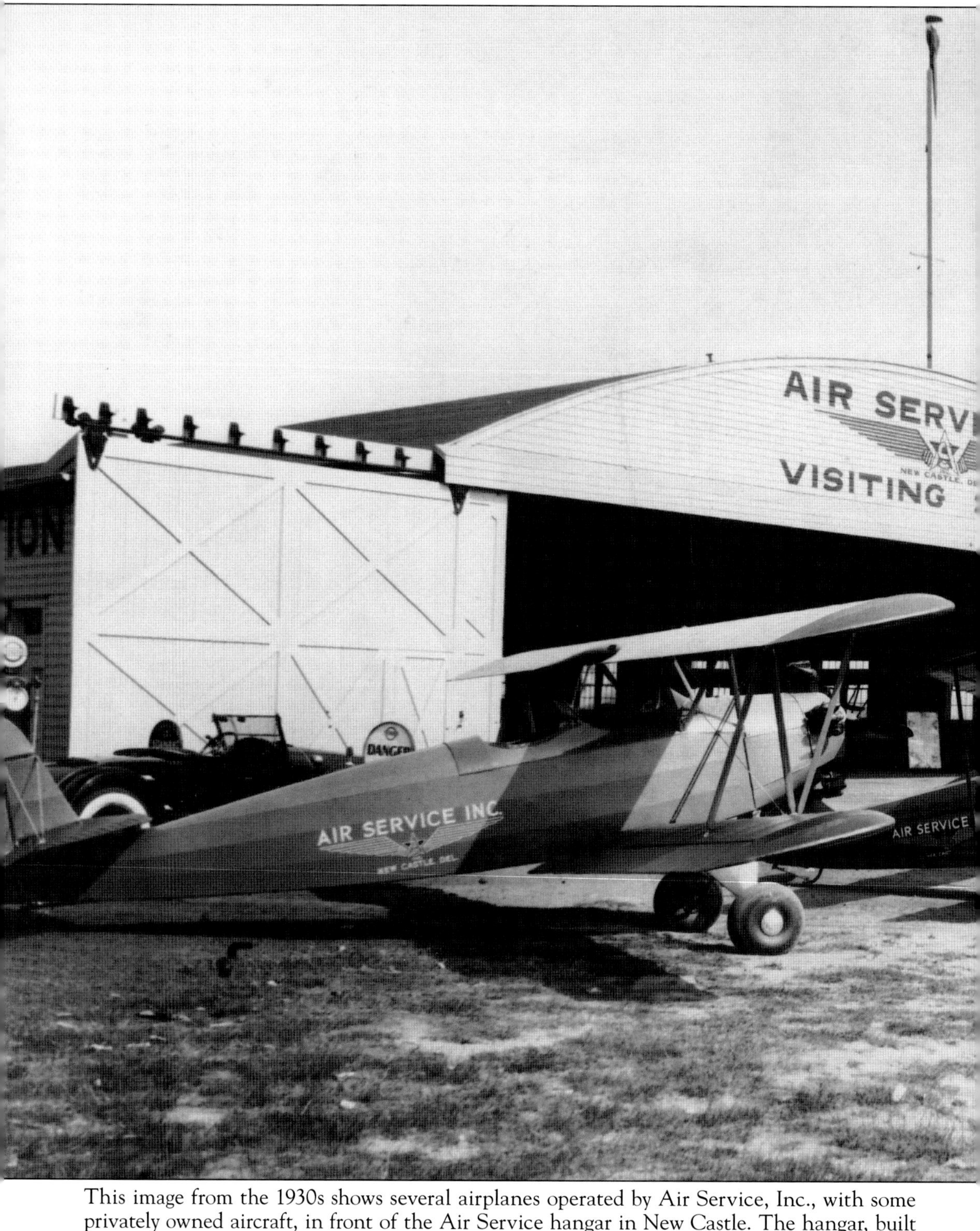

This image from the 1930s shows several airplanes operated by Air Service, Inc., with some privately owned aircraft, in front of the Air Service hangar in New Castle. The hangar, built in the 1930s, used three fan-type trusses. It was located across the grass field from the Bellanca

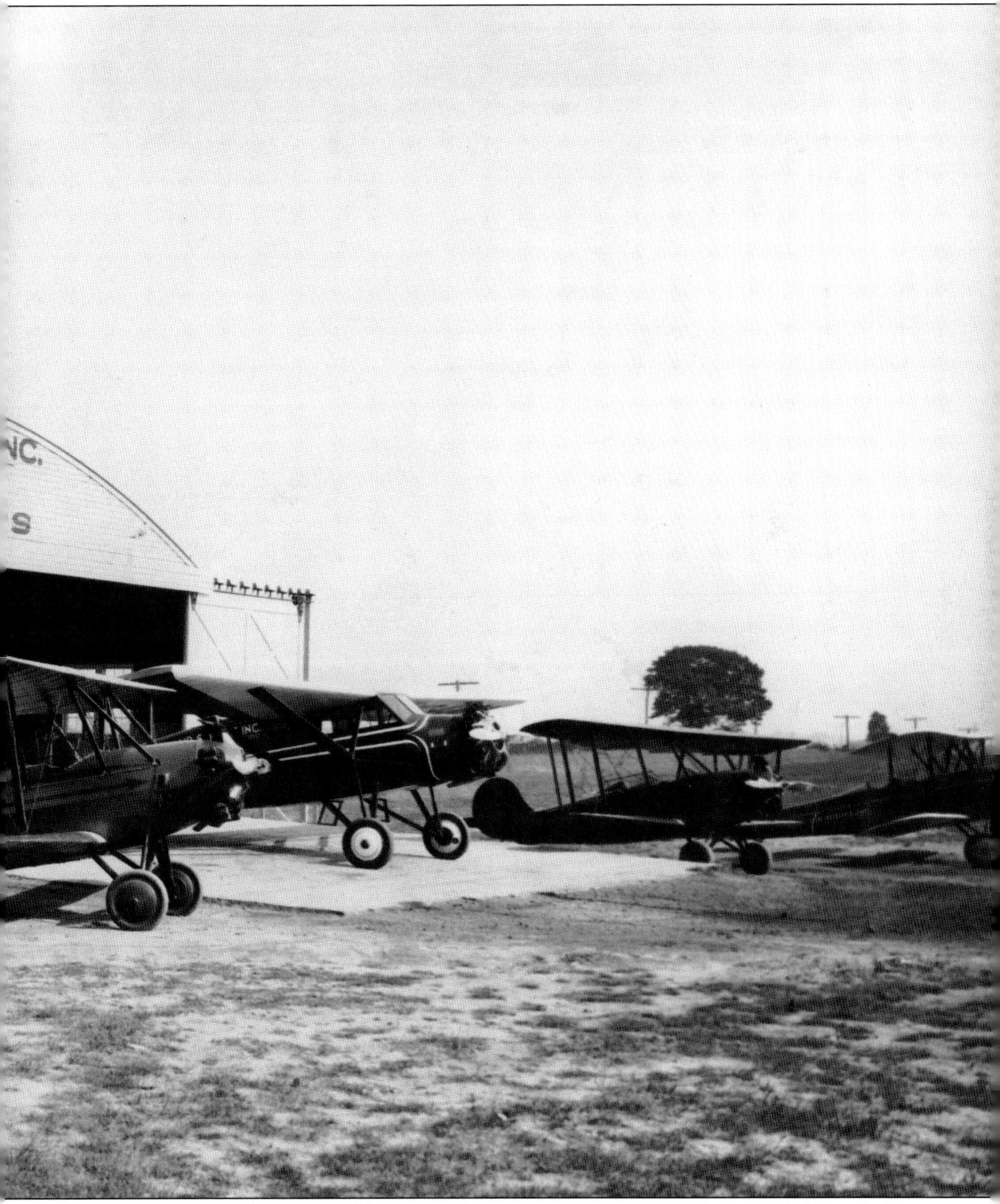

Aircraft Factory. Today, the building is used as a museum for Bellanca memorabilia and also displays the Delaware Aviation Hall of Fame. (JC.)

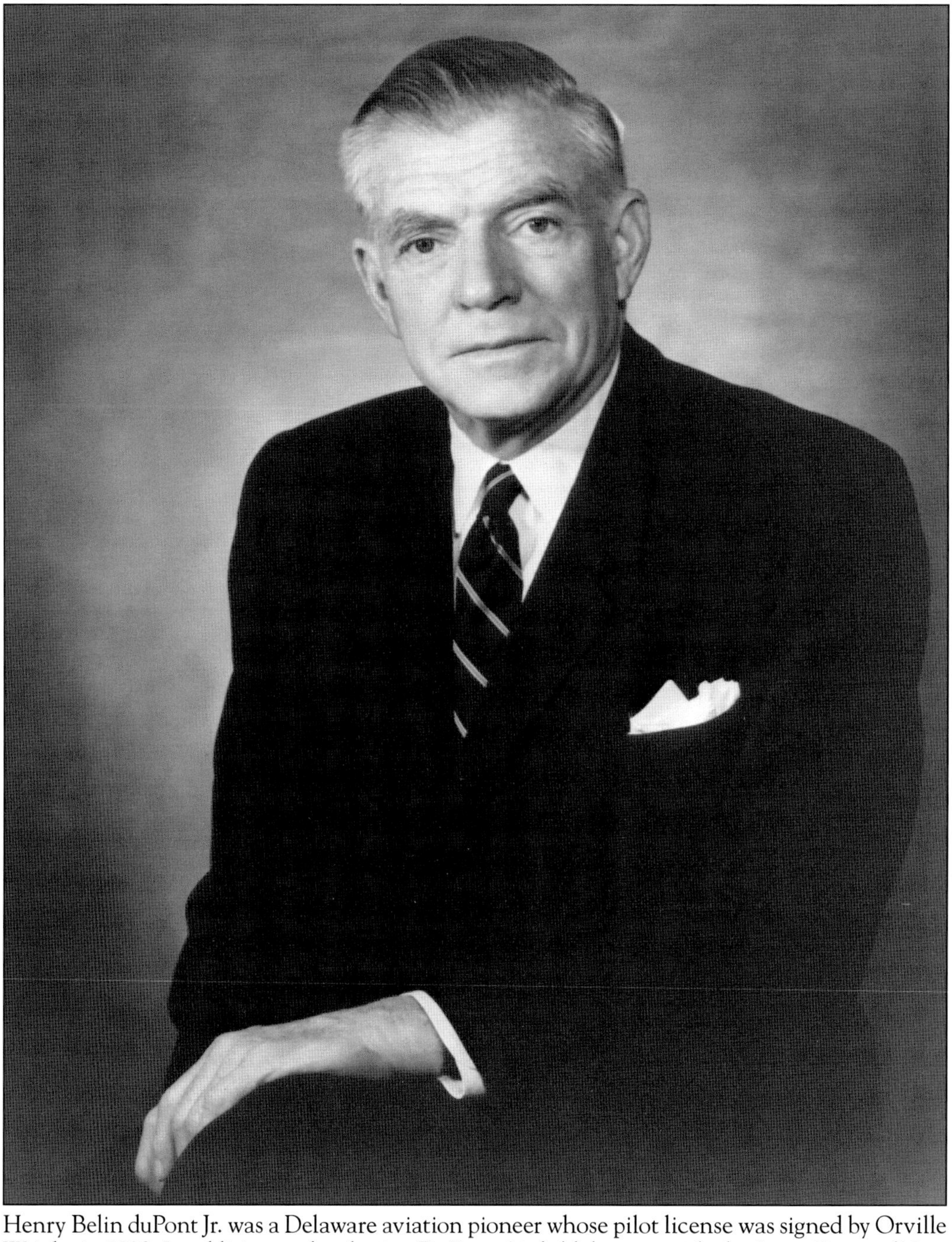

Henry Belin duPont Jr. was a Delaware aviation pioneer whose pilot license was signed by Orville Wright in 1923. In addition to developing DuPont Airfield, he met with the Levy Court of New Castle County in 1940 to explain the need for a larger airport. Subsequently, the county took title for the land that became New Castle County Airport as a public-use airfield that would be adequate for defense purposes if the war in Europe intensified. (JC.)

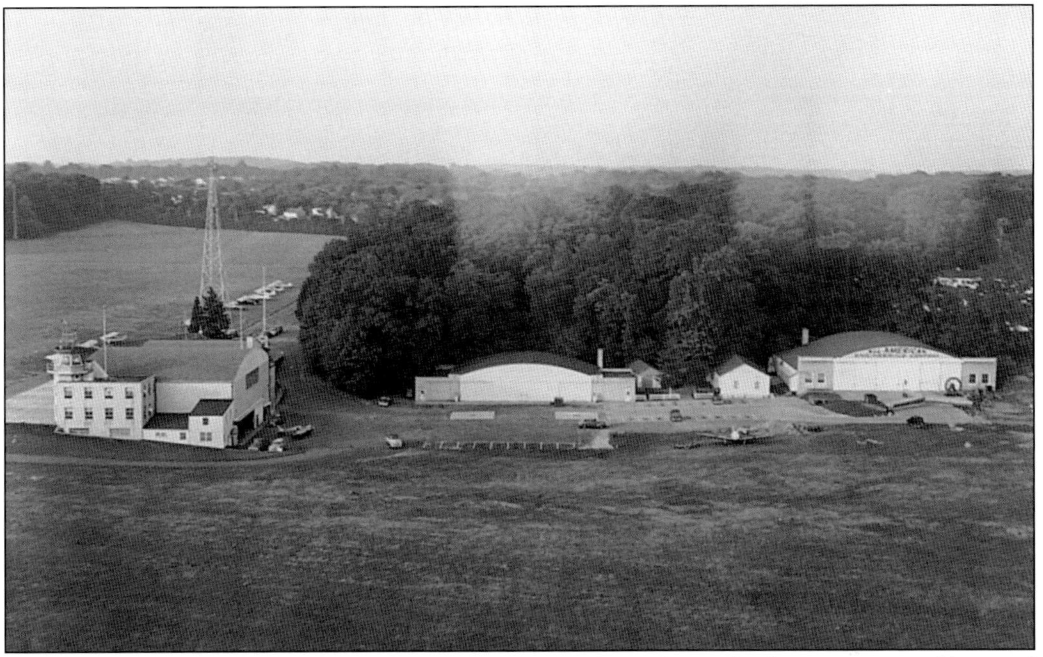

DuPont Airfield began with an 1,800-foot grass runway and a single wooden hangar on part of Ann and William duPont's farm. Opened for public use in 1928, brick-and-steel hangars were built and landing lights were installed, making DuPont Airfield the first lighted airport in Delaware. To the far right is the All American Engineering Company building. This image dates from about 1951. (GF.)

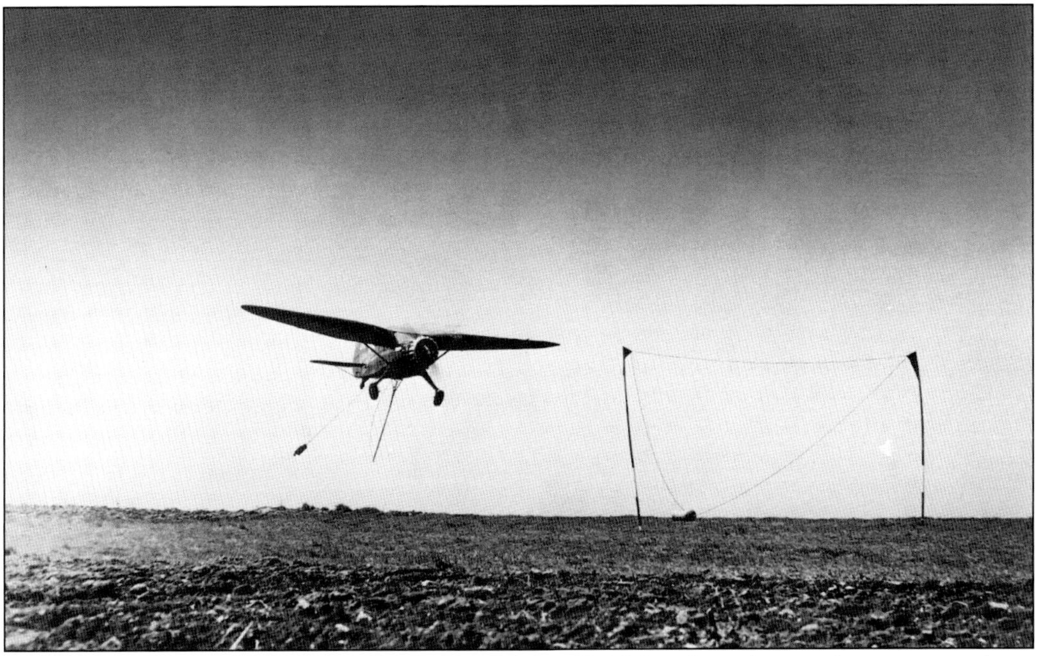

All American Aviation Company's Stinson Reliant SR-10C pickup plane is shown approaching a station with the trailing bag of mail about to be delivered. All American Aviation provided this service for six years to 118 towns and cities in Delaware, Pennsylvania, New York, Ohio, Kentucky, West Virginia, and the District of Columbia. (JC.)

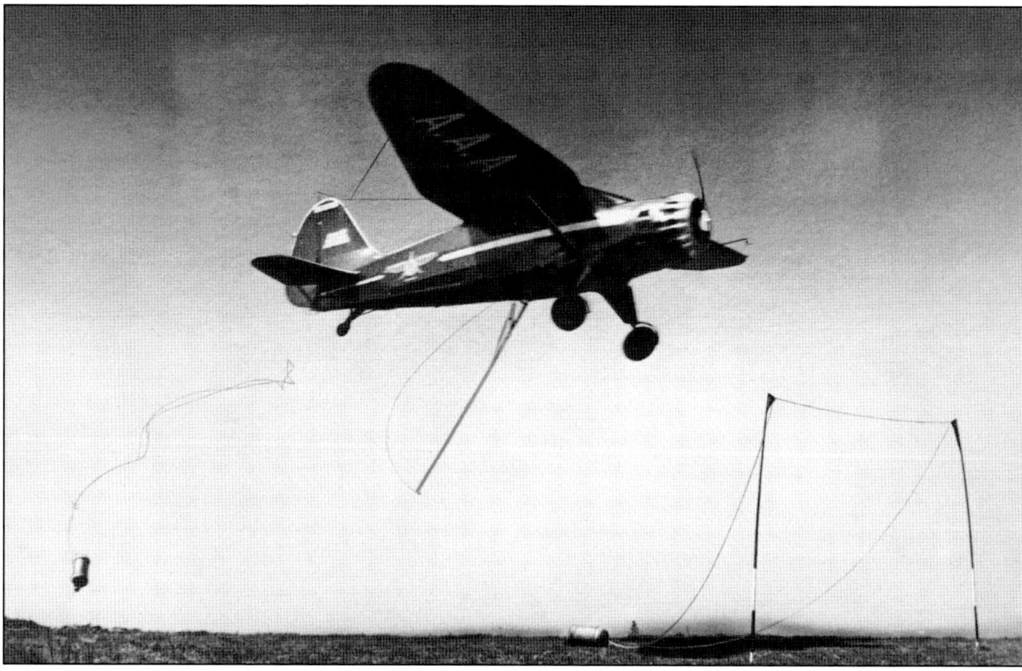

All American Aviation Company's Stinson Reliant SR-10C, with "AAA" painted under the wing for recognition from the ground, has just released the inbound airmail bag as it approached the poles for a pickup of another mailbag. (JC.)

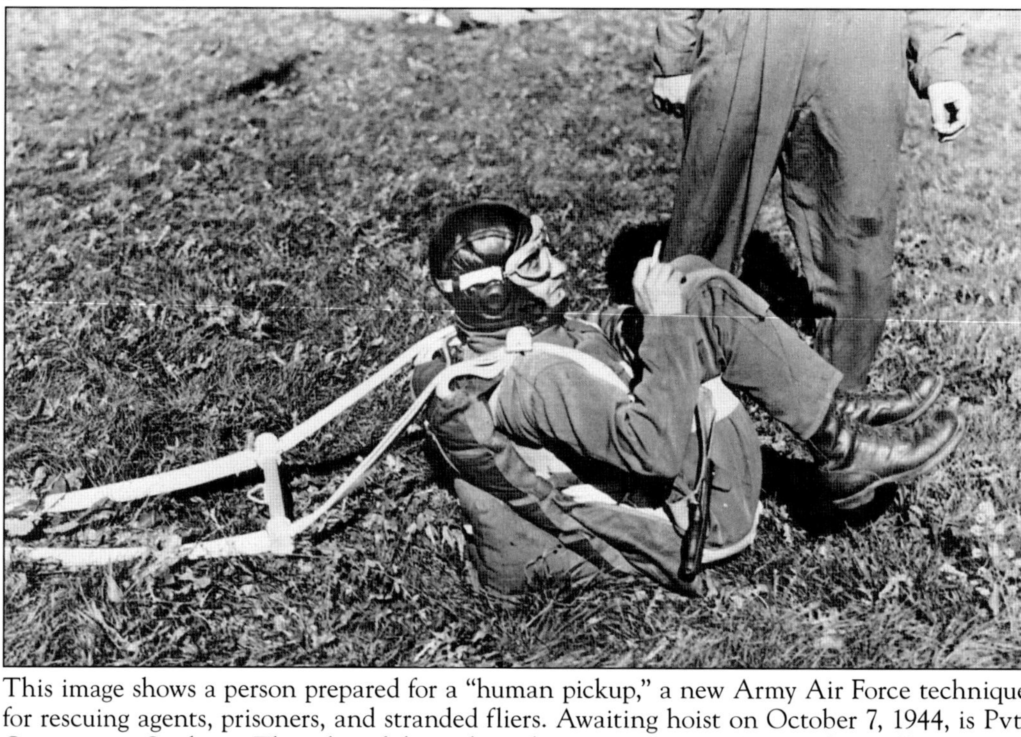

This image shows a person prepared for a "human pickup," a new Army Air Force technique for rescuing agents, prisoners, and stranded fliers. Awaiting hoist on October 7, 1944, is Pvt. Constantine Stiakatis. The pilot of the pickup plane was Norman S. Benedict. All American Engineering developed the system. (JC.)

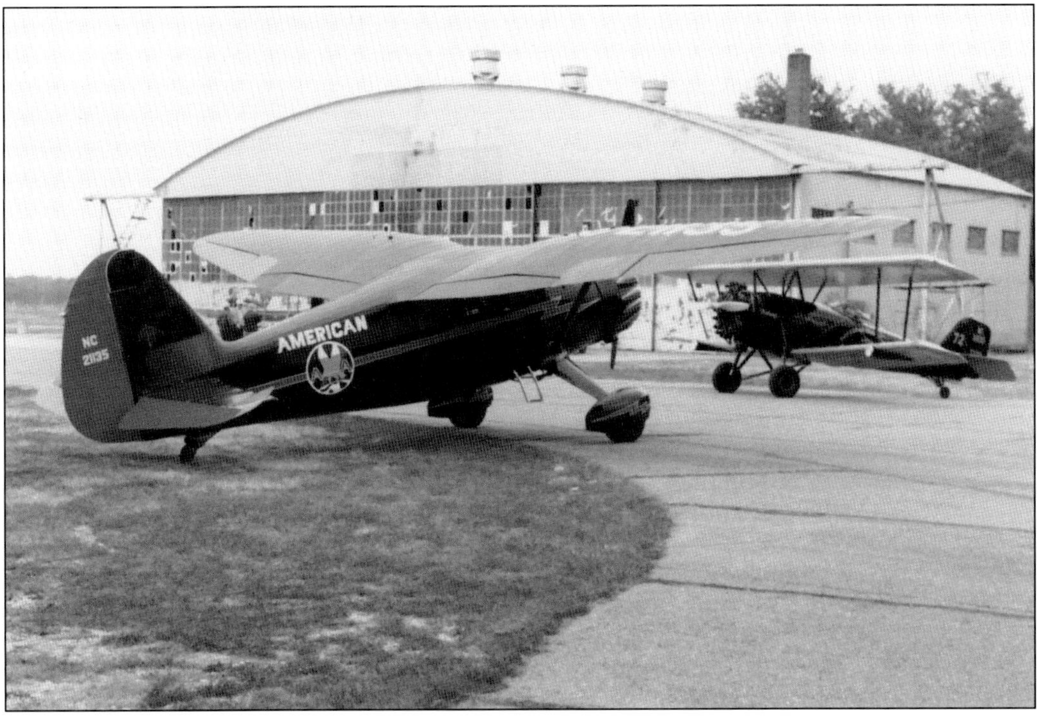

All American Engineering used the gull-wing Stinson Reliant for airmail pickup. The SR-10 Stinson was a masterpiece of classic styling. A Lycoming 260-horsepower R-680-D5 engine powered this high-winged cabin monoplane. All American Engineering used three SR-10Cs for airmail pickup. This impressive airplane had a relatively high price tag due to its versatile performance. (CduP.)

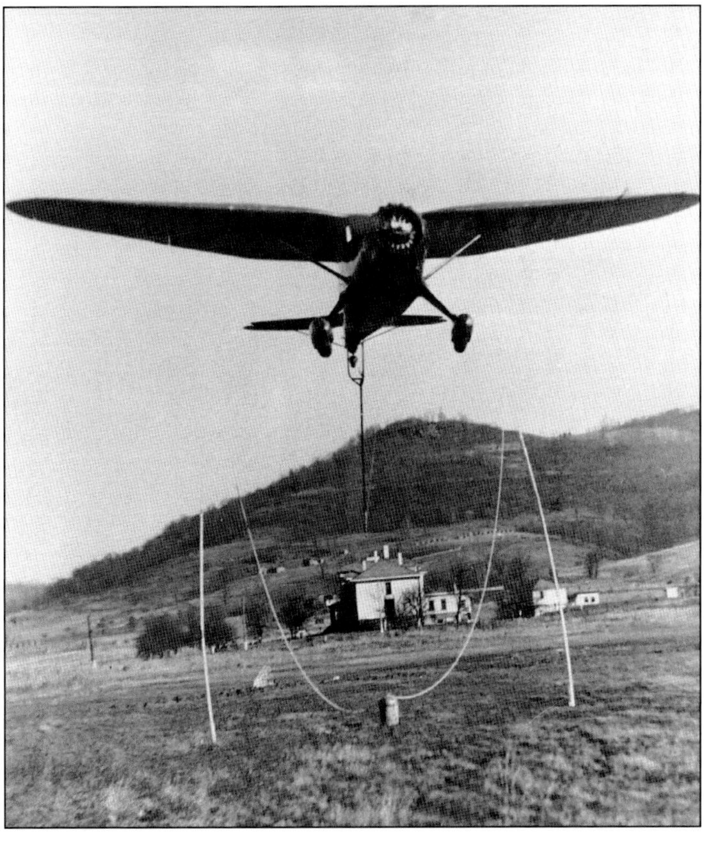

This image shows the drop hook about to snatch the mailbag deposited by the local post office. Two steel poles, 54 feet apart, were painted bright orange and yellow. (JC.)

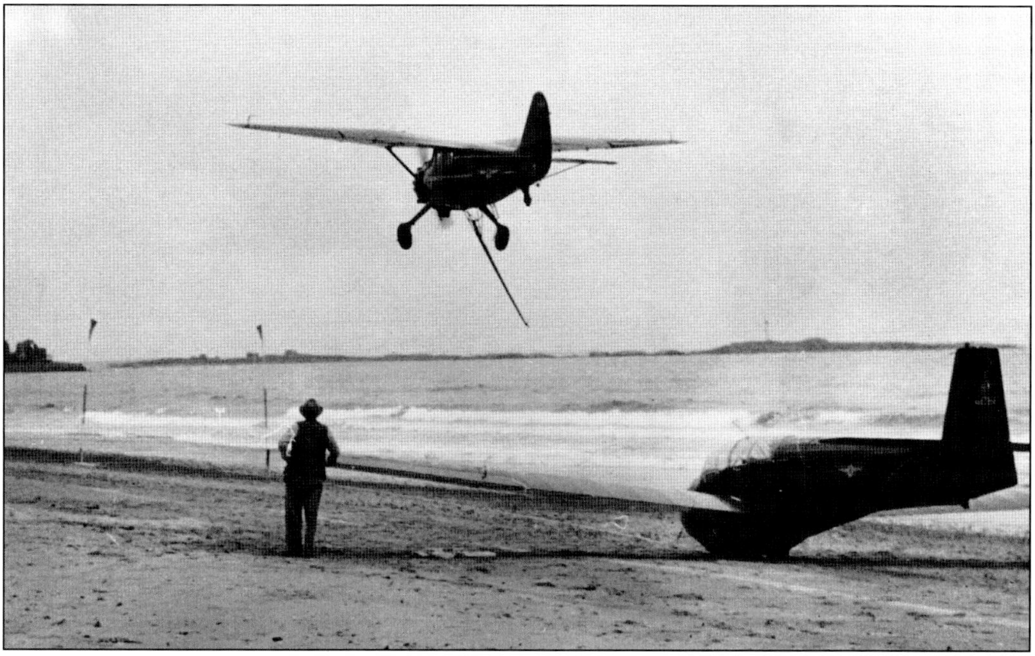

Richard C. duPont worked with his All American Engineering Company to determine if the pickup equipment could be used to tow gliders. This image shows a small plane, with its engine and propeller removed, being picked up on the beach next to the Delaware River by a Stinson SR-10F. (JC.)

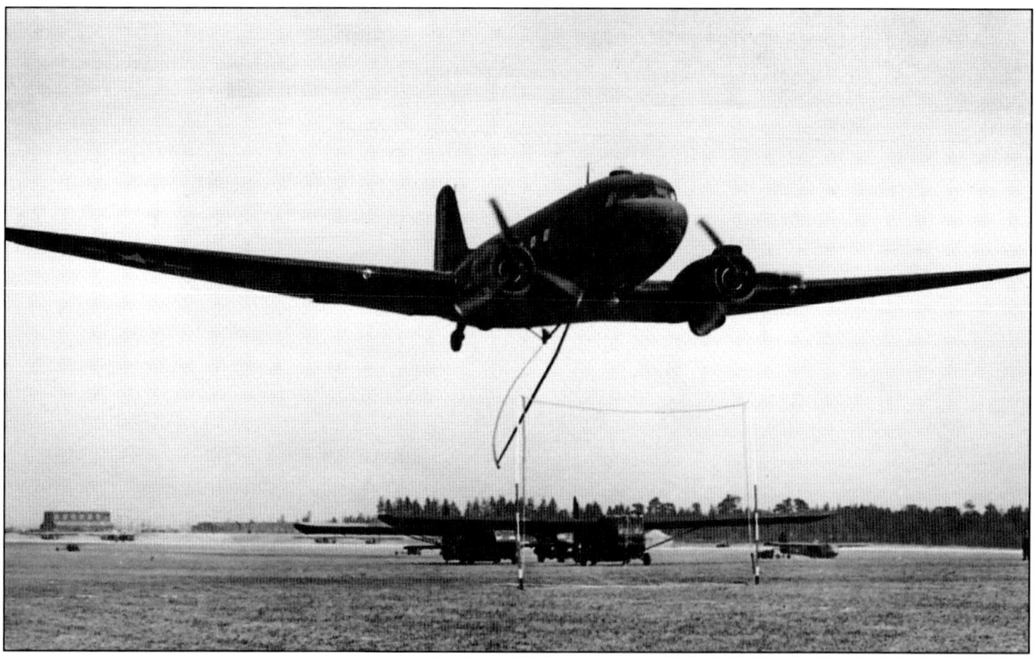

This Douglas C-47 shows the drop hook that will pick up a glider. All American's engineers, headed by Arthur B. Schultz, strengthened the mechanism and adapted it to the larger aircraft to be flown by the US Army Air Corps. This technology was very important for the Allied invasion of Europe in World War II. (JC.)

Two

THE WAR YEARS

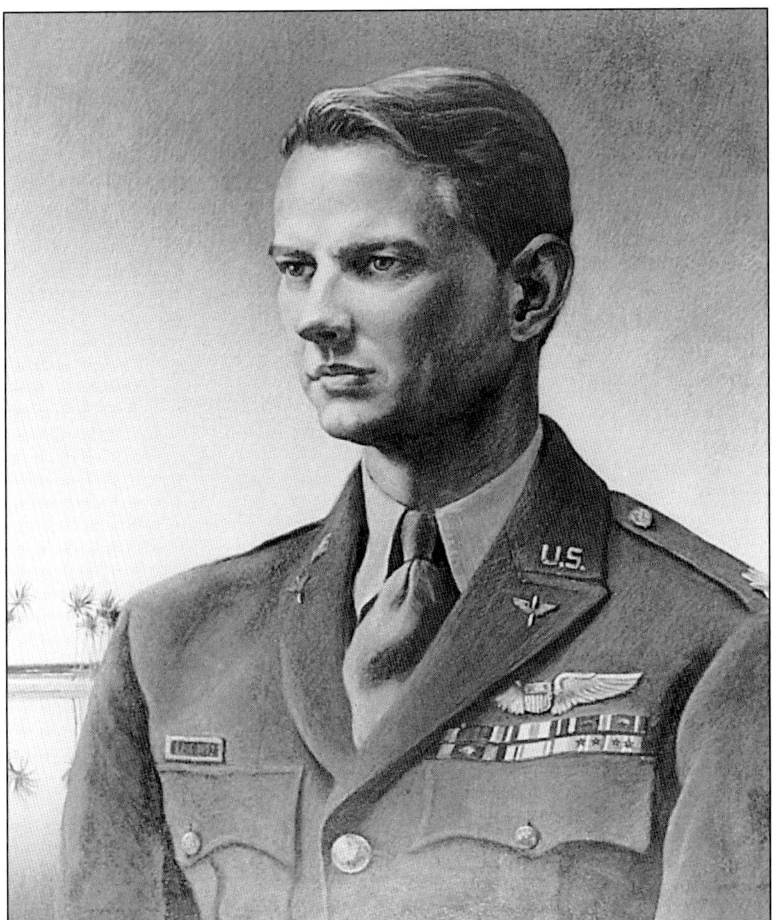

Maj. George Welch of Wilmington was a World War II flying ace and a Medal of Honor nominee for his exploits at Pearl Harbor, downing four Japanese aircraft on December 7, 1941. He was also an experimental pilot after the war. Welch is known for allegedly being the first pilot to unofficially break the sound barrier (two weeks before Check Yeager) in the prototype XP-86 Sabre. Welch was inducted into the Delaware Aviation Hall of Fame in 2001. (GF.)

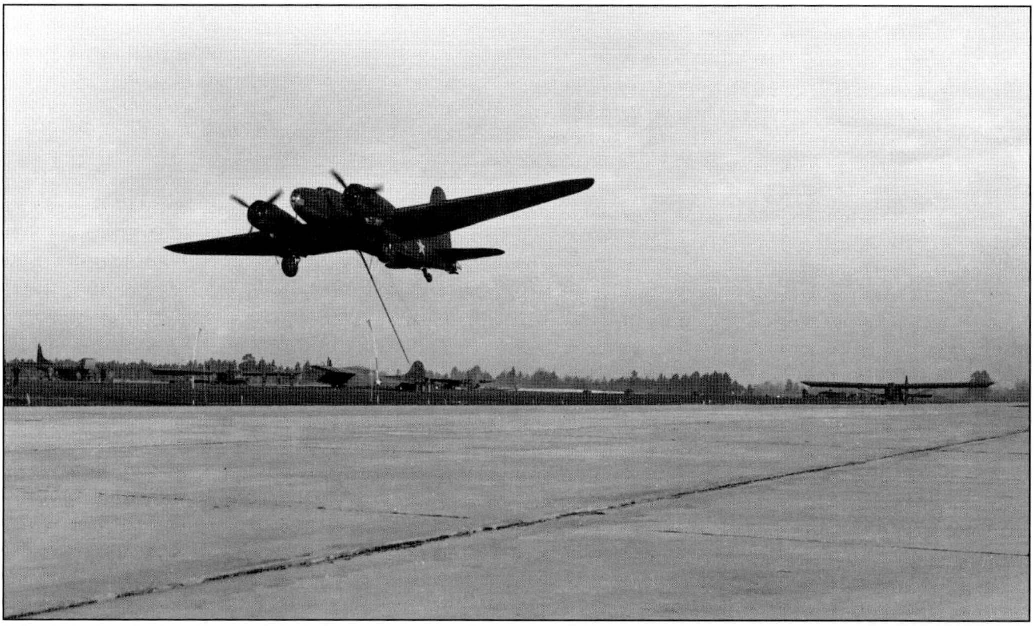

This image shows a twin-engine US Army B-23 Dragon bomber with a large glider in tow, getting ready to lift the glider off the ground. After success with this Douglas-built bomber, Douglas C-47s were used for glider pickup. Eventually, an 80-by-80-foot hangar was built at DuPont Airfield to continue progress on this pickup system that was so vital in World War II. All American's work was classified, restricted, or secret during wartime. (JC.)

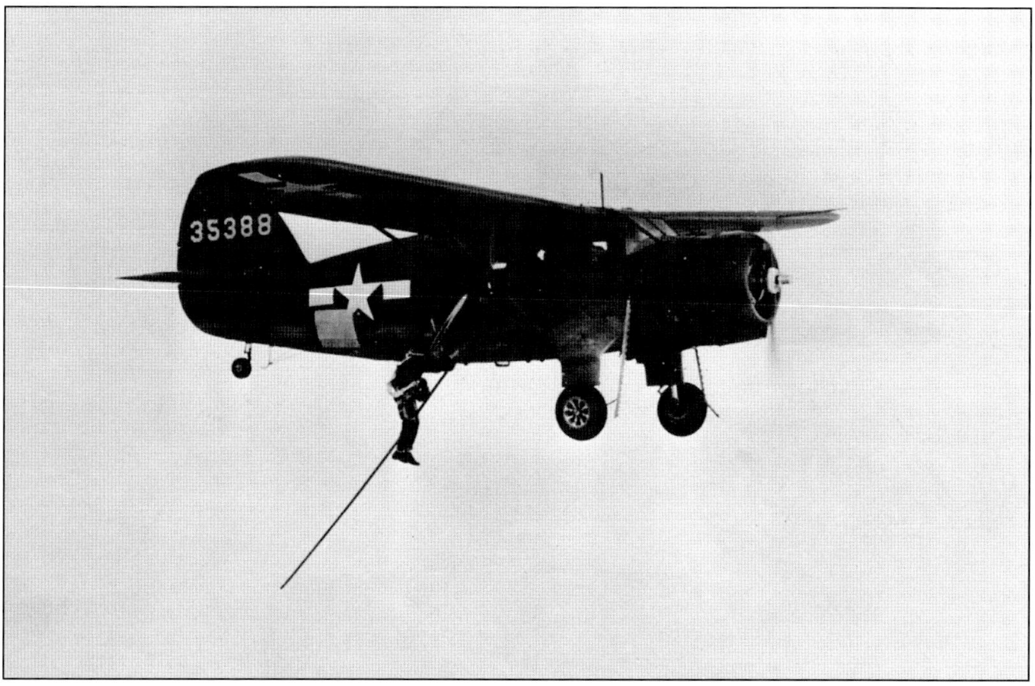

Here, S.Sgt. H.C. Conway shinnies up the glide pole through the slipstream to a C-64 airplane. J-edged blades in front of the fixed gear would cut the loop if the plane was too low for pickup, so that the plane's landing gear would not get tangled in the loop and cause injury to the man waiting. (JC.)

New Castle Army Air Base is pictured in 1943. This aerial image shows two of the runways, a hangar, and some hard stands for parking airplanes. A hard stand was a parking space reinforced by concrete so that airplanes would not sink into the dirt. New Castle Army Air Base had a very high water table, which meant hard stands were used during the war. (JC.)

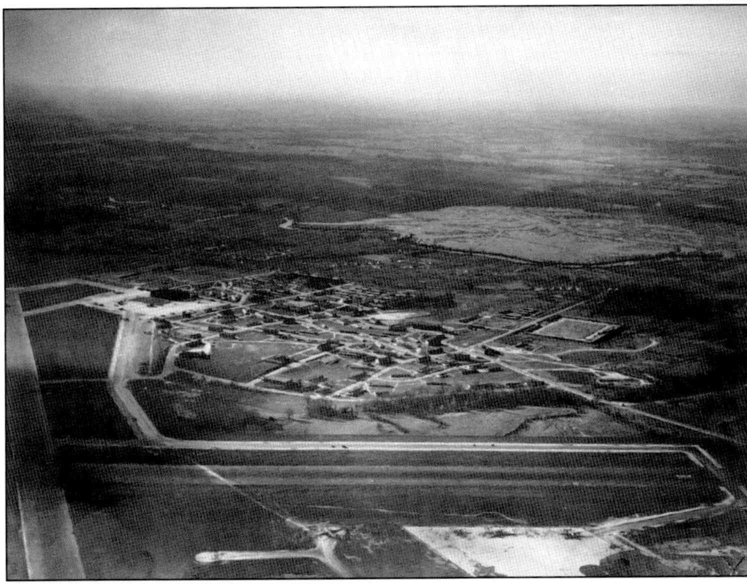

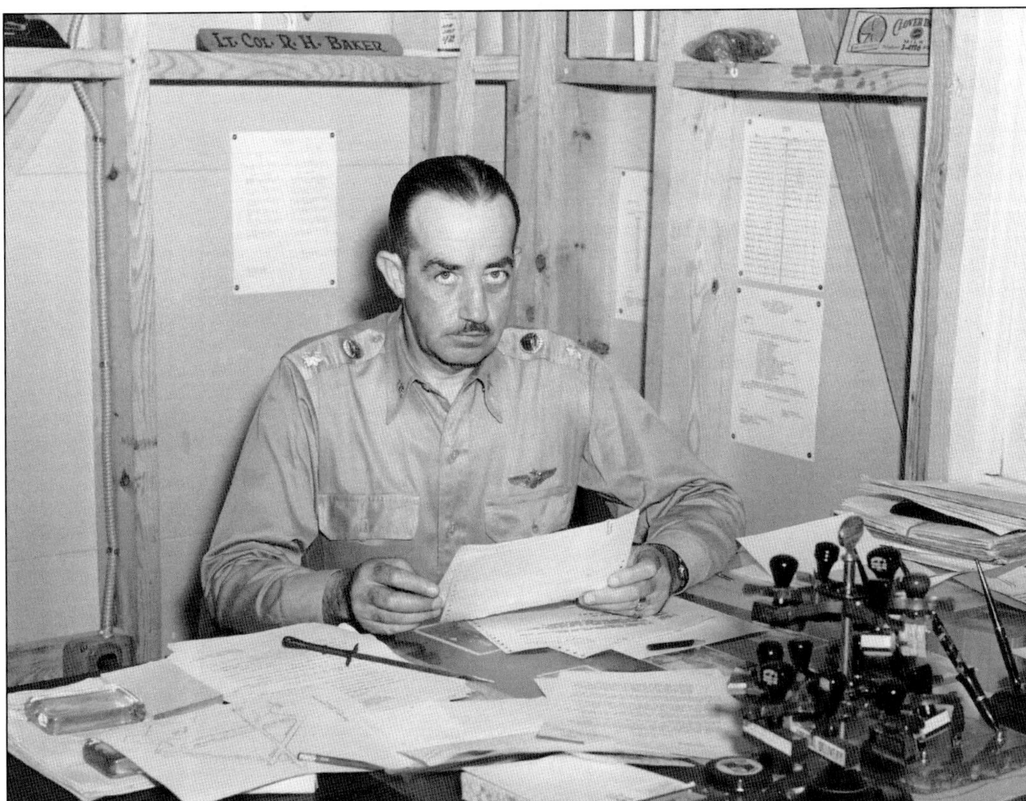

This image shows Lt. Col. Robert H. Baker at his desk at New Castle Army Air Base. As commanding officer of the Northeast Sector of the Air Transport Command, Baker recommended that Army Air Forces, 2nd Ferrying Group, Domestic Wing move to New Castle because it had outgrown Logan Field, near Baltimore, Maryland. On May 29, 1942, the 2nd Ferrying Group, Ferrying Division, Air Transport Command was activated at New Castle Army Air Base. (JC.)

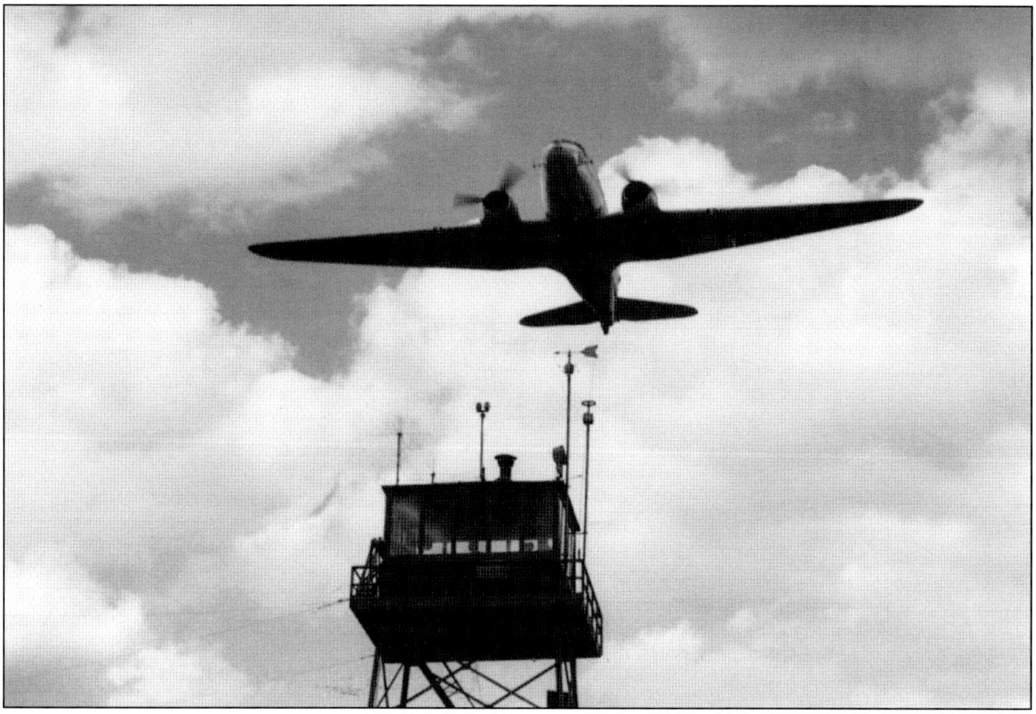

An Army Air Force C-47 flies over the control tower at New Castle Army Air Base in 1944. The tower had glass windows, providing the air traffic controllers with views in all directions. (JC.)

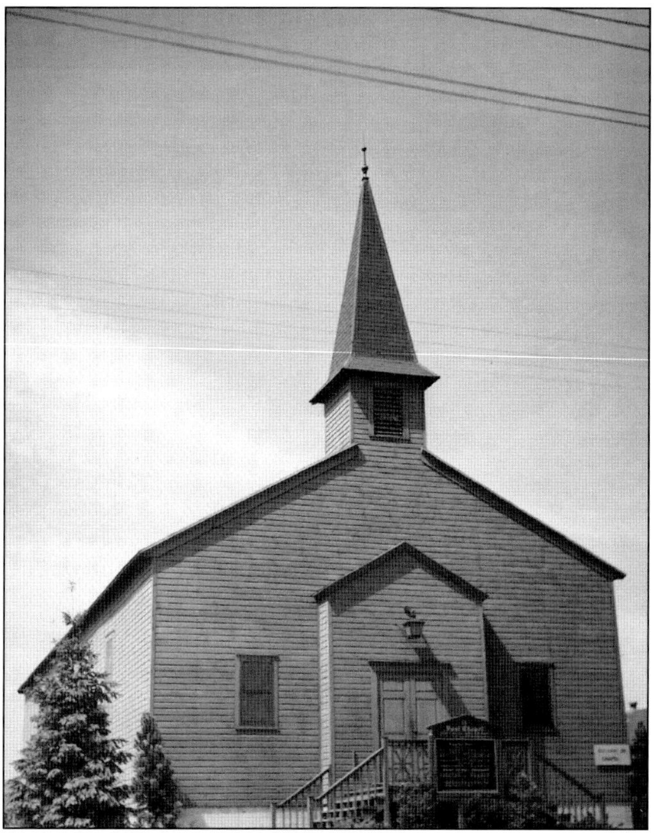

At New Castle Army Air Base, the chapel, Building No. 39, was constructed in September 1942. The first service was held on October 11, 1942. After that, services were held each week for all denominations. (JC.)

A Women's Army Corps (WAC) member, pictured here at the top of the control tower, is talking in a flight of P-47 Thunderbolts and assigning the planes their positions. The WACs were responsible for getting each plane down safely as well as regulating takeoffs and direction of flights. In addition to transmitting recent weather information, the WACs also handled radio and telephone apparatus, including transmitting Morse code. Quarters for the 150 WACs assigned to the 2nd Ferrying Group were located on the base. (JC.)

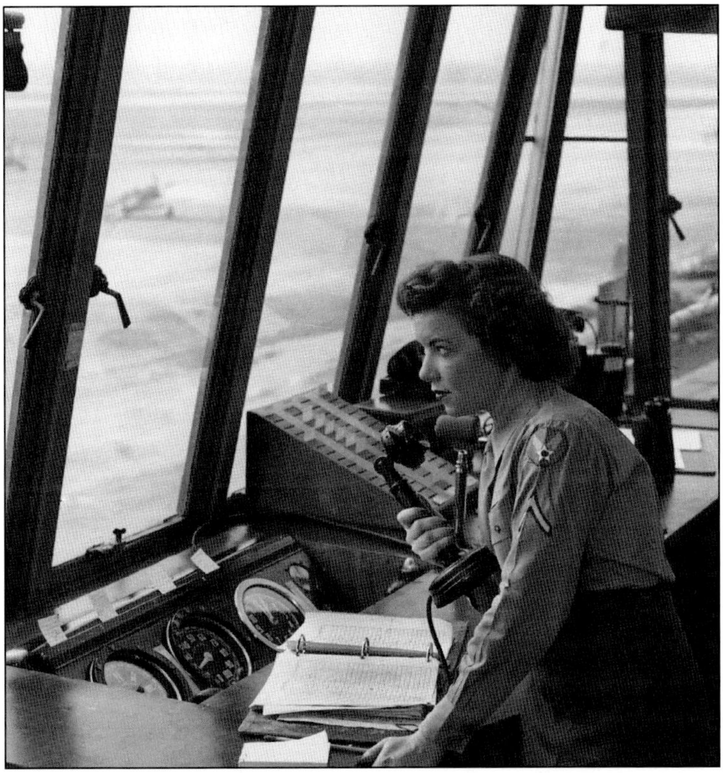

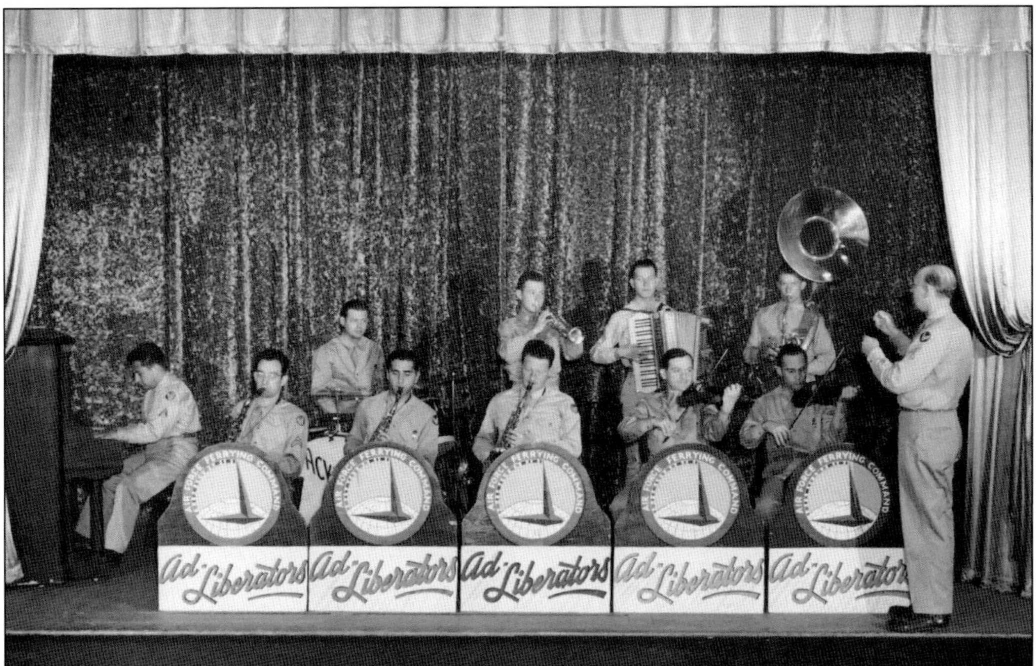

Here, the Ad Liberators Band gives a performance on D-Day, June 6, 1944. New Castle Army Air Base had a theater in Building No. 41 for the noncommissioned officers' club. With a seating capacity of 300, this building had other uses, such as the required orientation classes. (JC.)

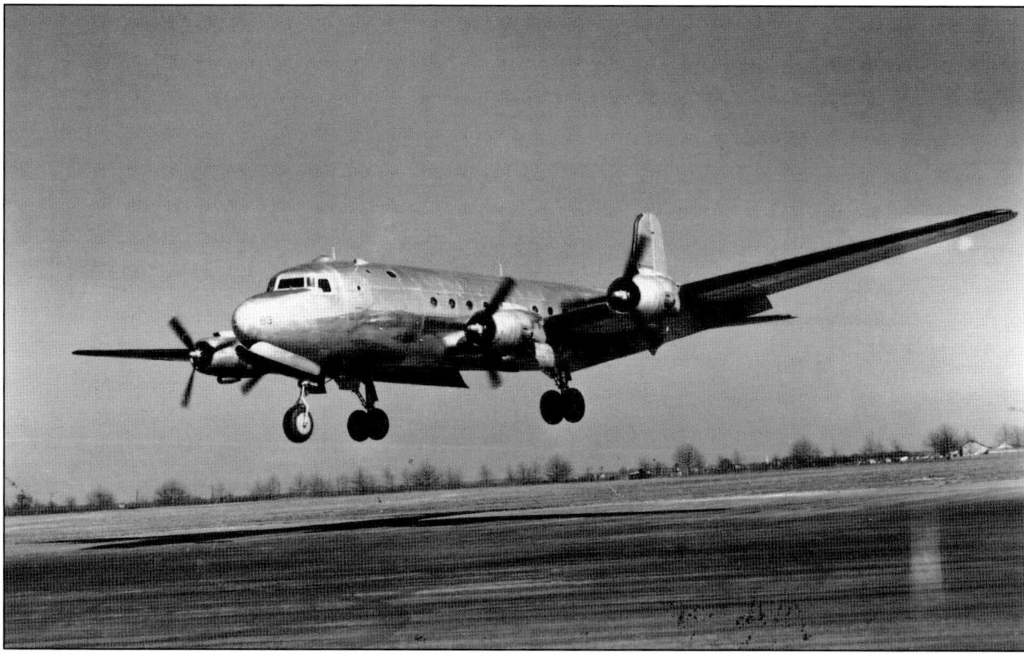

A Douglas C-54 Skymaster of the 2nd Ferrying Group is depicted landing at New Castle Army Air Base on March 28, 1944. The C-54 was used on a powerful new lifeline that was established in February 1944, providing trips taking supplies to and from Chabua, India. The basic round-trip from New Castle Army Air Base to Chabua was 22,588 miles. This effort was called "the Crescent Caravan." (JC.)

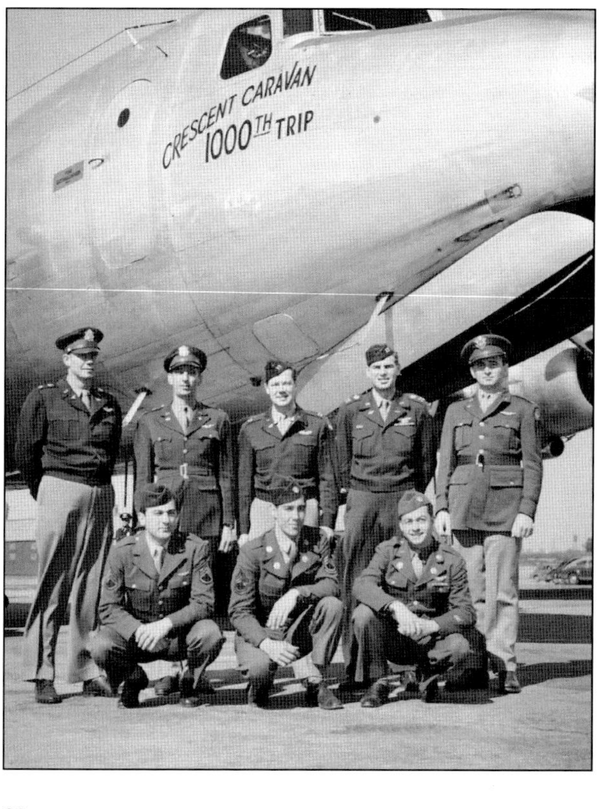

The Crescent Caravan crew poses in front of a C-54 following their 1,000th successful trip. The Crescent Caravan began its worldwide service on February 6, 1944. The route was crescent shaped over three continents as it formed the world's largest aerial freight and passenger service. (JC.)

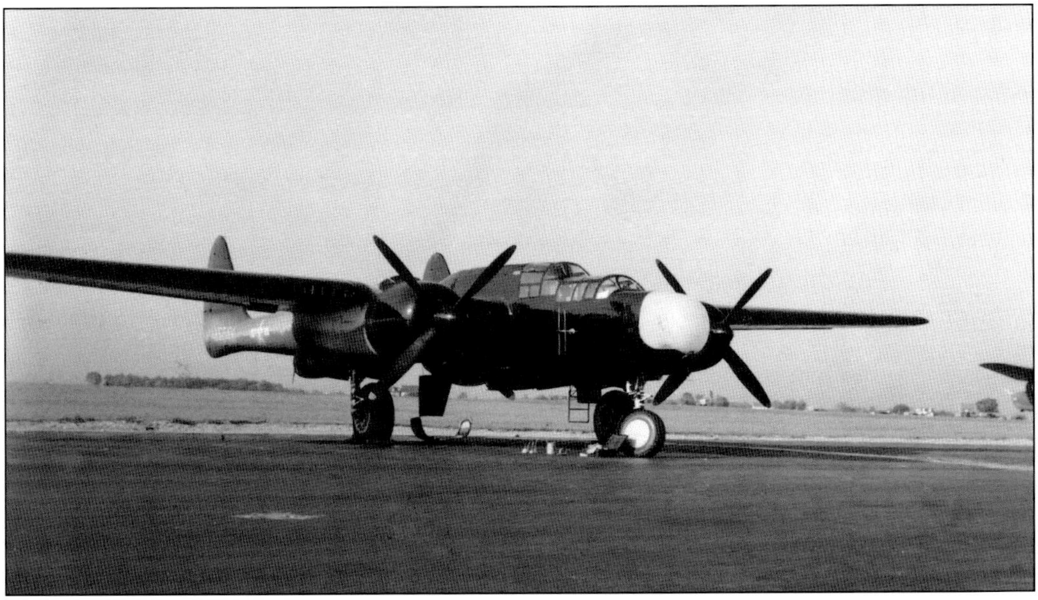

A P-61 Black Widow, assigned to the 552nd Army Air Force Base Unit, 2nd Ferrying Group at New Castle Army Air Base is standing on the ramp at the base on May 8, 1944. (JC.)

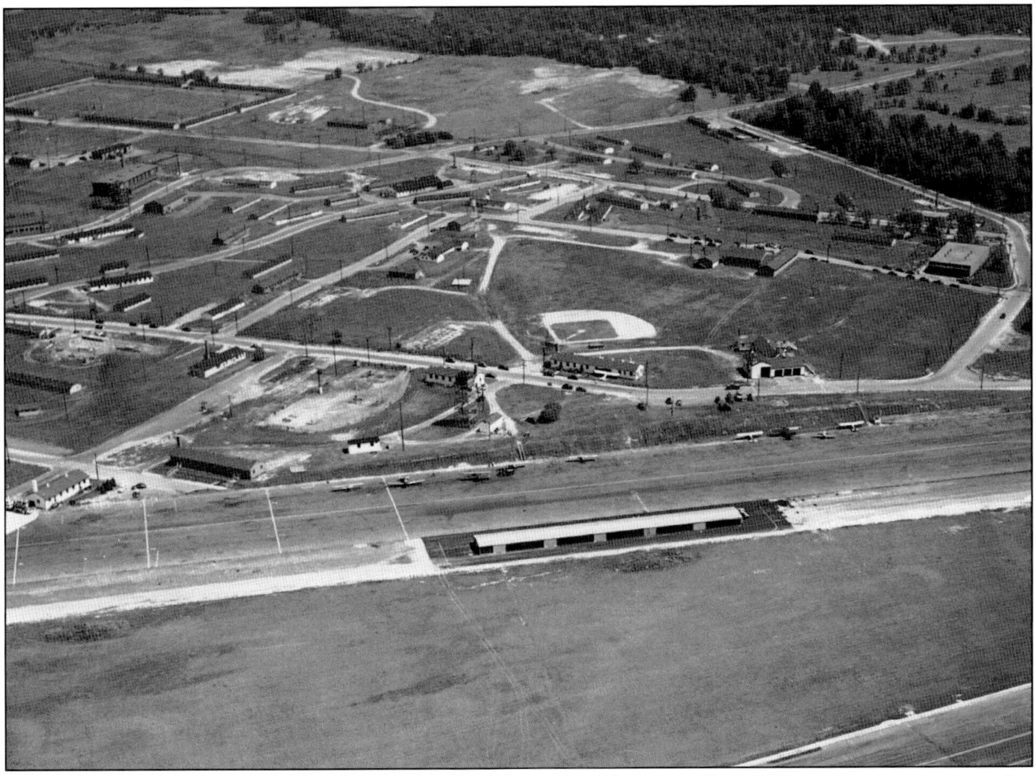

This aerial view shows part of New Castle Army Air Base in 1943. There is a runway in the foreground, and the control tower is in the middle of the picture. The buildings to support the base, constructed by the US Army Corps of Engineers, were laid out in a maze of twisted roads and oddly placed buildings to guard against possible enemy bombing attacks. (JC.)

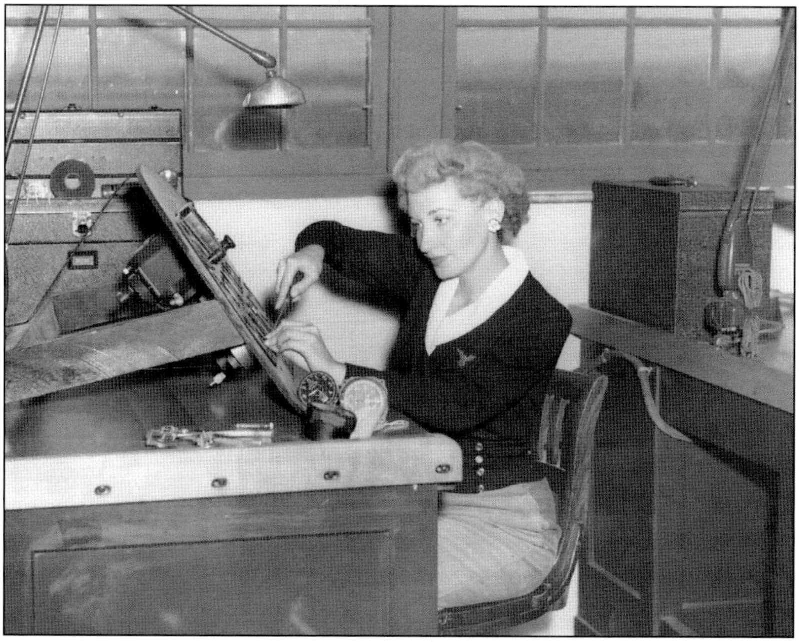

Jane Jenkins worked at New Castle Army Air Base during World War II. An important job she performed was installing instruments on cockpit panels for Army aircraft in 1944. (JC.)

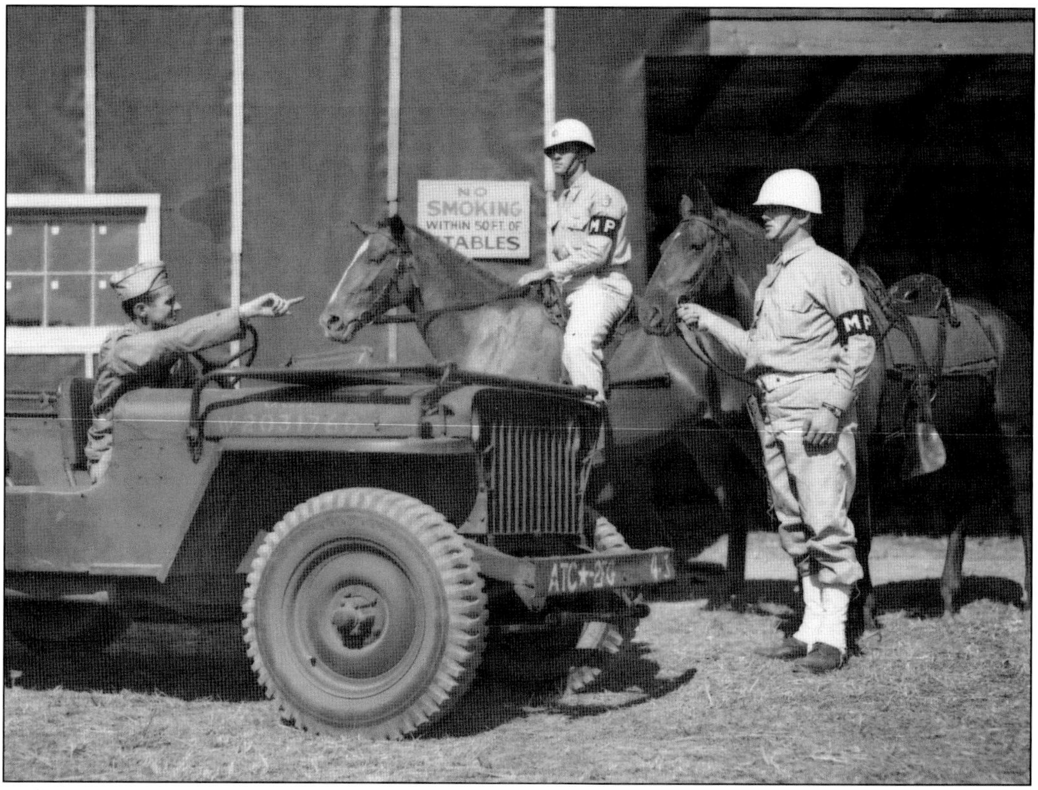

Military Police (MPs) on horseback patrolled New Castle Army Air Base with the 891st Guard Squadron, organized by Capt. Charles A. O'Connor. Activated July 28, 1942, the 891st had 19 riders and 20 horses to patrol the perimeter fence during the day. At night, they had a dog patrol with 8 dogs and 17 men. Jeeps with two-way radios provided communications. (JC.)

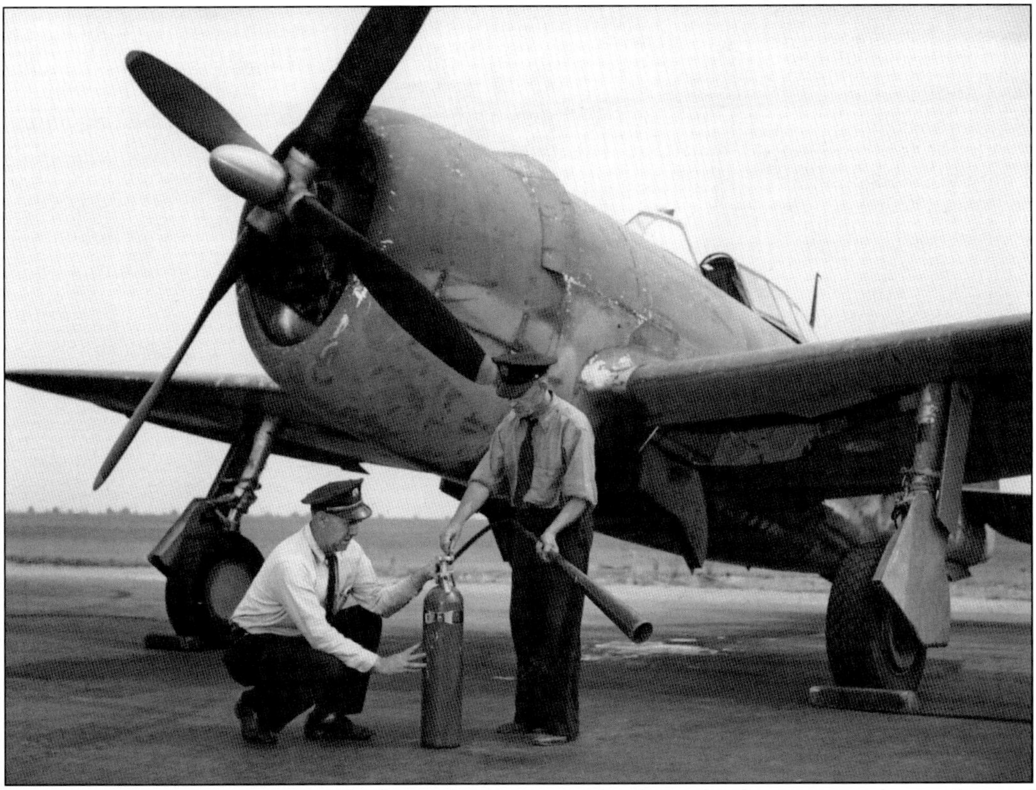

Here, two firemen at New Castle Army Air Base are checking the fire extinguisher in front of a P-47 fighter airplane. This extinguisher contains liquid carbon dioxide and can extinguish a blaze in 15 seconds. (JC.)

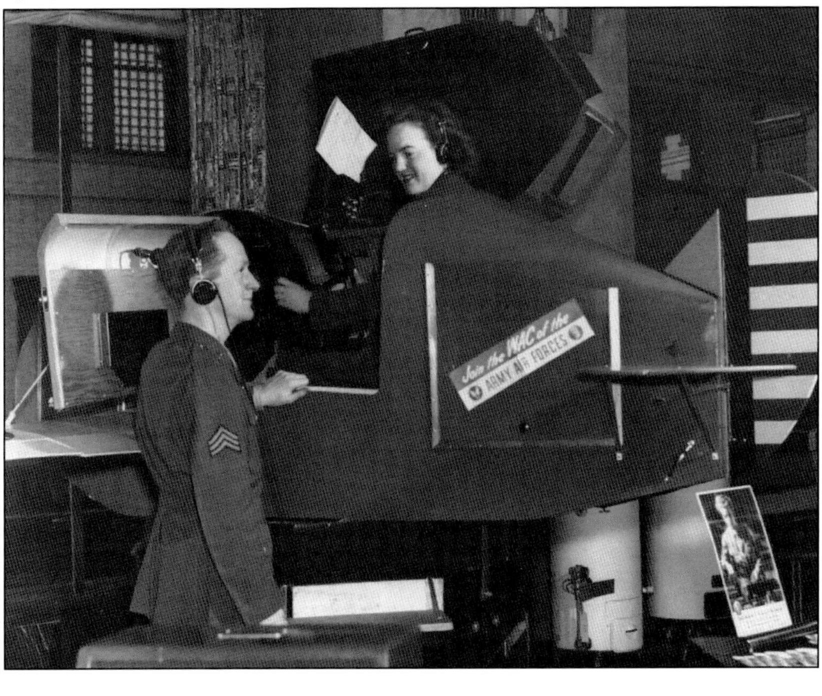

The Link Trainer is pictured at New Castle Army Air Base in 1942. Pilots were trained to fly on instruments while enclosed in this machine. The ability to fly solely on instruments, in case of bad weather, was essential to a pilot's training. (JC.)

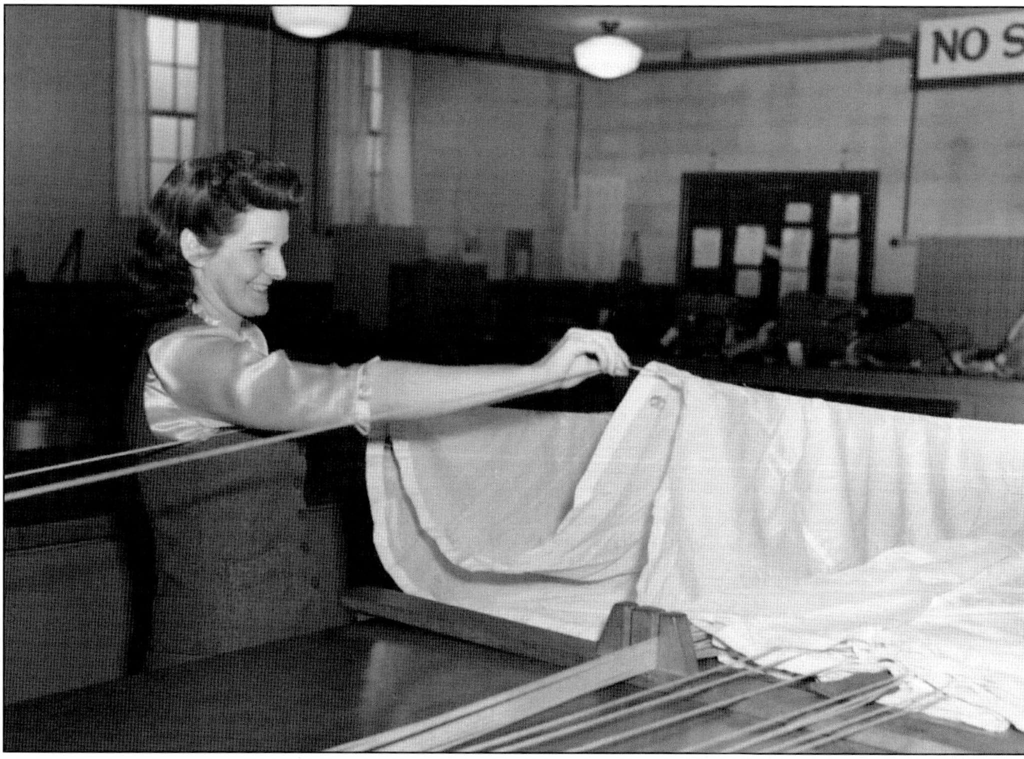

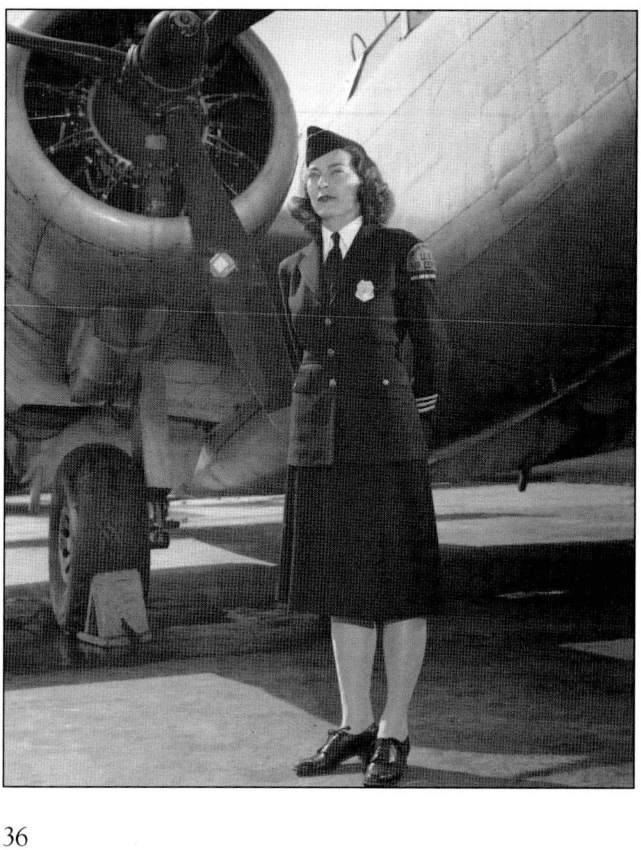

The parachute shop, which opened Memorial Day 1942, was a vital place on New Castle Army Air Base. Three women assisted Sgt. R.B. Stevenson as parachute riggers. By September 1942, repacking chutes was done on a regular basis, even if the parachutes had not been used. The women also worked as aircraft mechanics. (JC.)

Civil Guard Blanche Schaffer stands guard by an Army C-47 at New Castle Army Air Base during World War II. The Douglas C-47 was equipped with an autopilot and other advancements, which made it a workhorse for many military needs. The crew consisted of pilot, copilot, navigator, and flight engineer. (JC.)

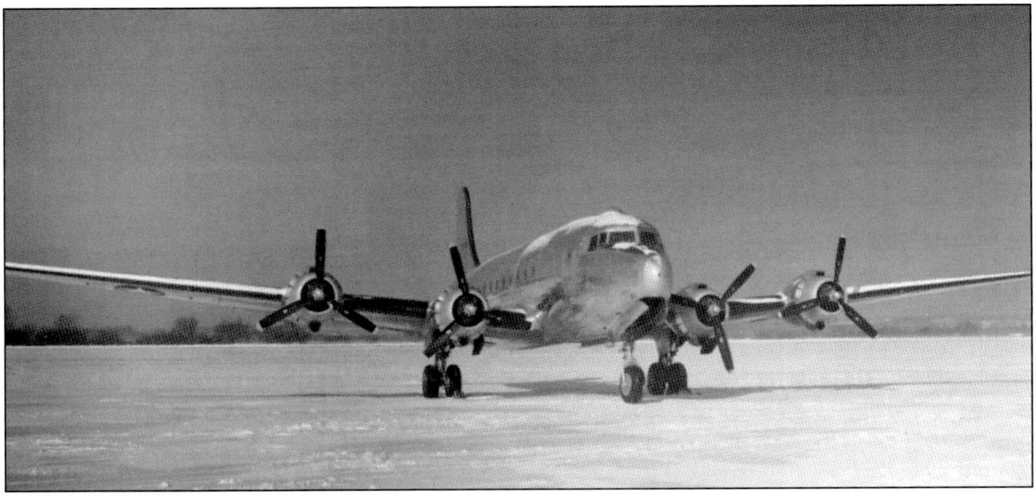

This is the C-54 airplane that set a record in 1944 flying to Orly, near Paris, France, and then back to New Castle Army Air Base. New Castle was a RON (remain overnight) stop for wounded personnel returning from Europe. The base hospital was enlarged to care for the wounded before they traveled to their hometowns. (JC.)

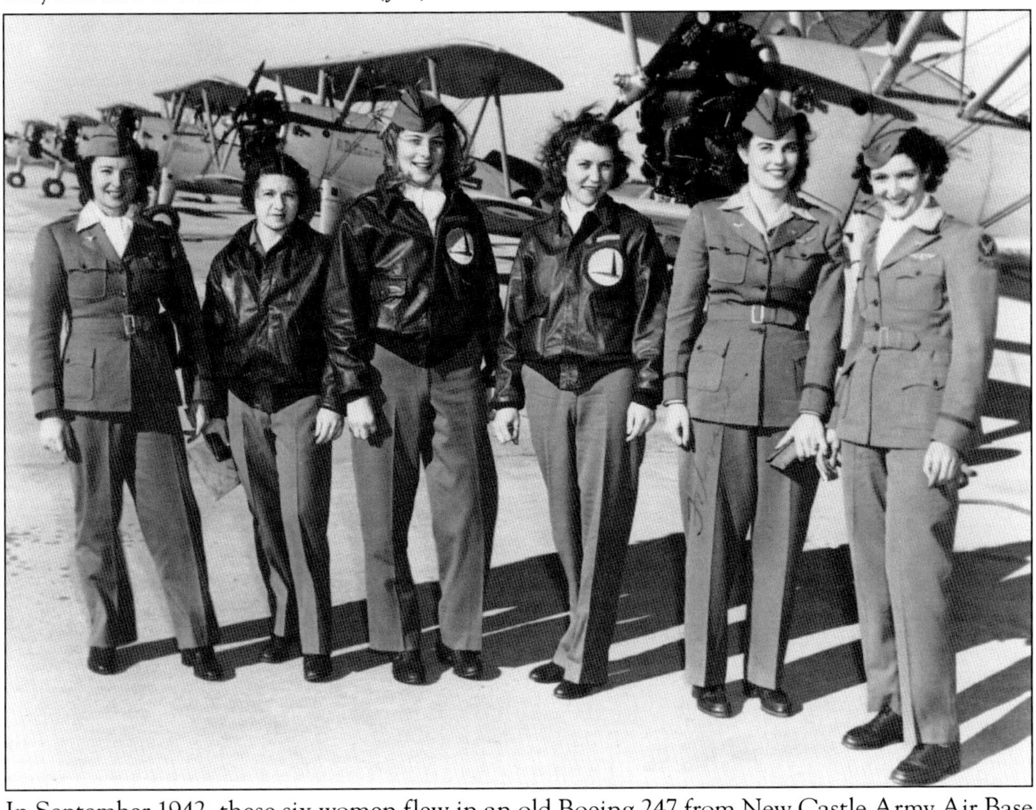

In September 1942, these six women flew in an old Boeing 247 from New Castle Army Air Base to the Piper Aircraft Factory in Lock Haven, Pennsylvania. From there, they ferried six small Piper Cubs to Mitchel Field on Long Island, New York. Pictured are, from left to right, Katherine Rawls Thompson (Olympic swimming champion), Phyllis Burchfield, Nancy Batson, Delphine Bohn, Florene Miller, and Teresa James. (JC.)

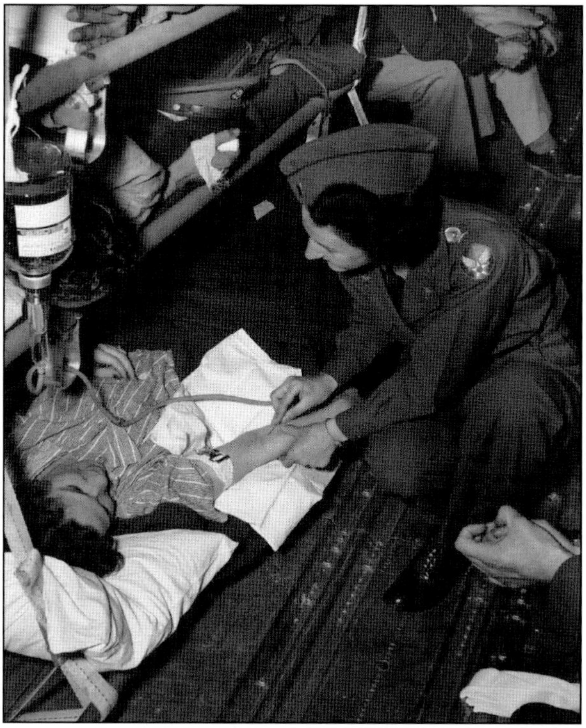

On May 4, 1945, eight Crescent Caravan C-54s brought 144 wounded casualties from Europe to New Castle Army Air Base, the largest air evacuation up to that date. This image depicts 2nd Lt. Ann Markowitz, 2nd Ferrying Group flight nurse, administering blood plasma to 2nd Lt. Mary Harvey, an Army nurse. New Castle Army Air Base was designated as an alternate port of evacuation when the weather was too bad for landing at Mitchel Field, Long Island, New York. (JC.)

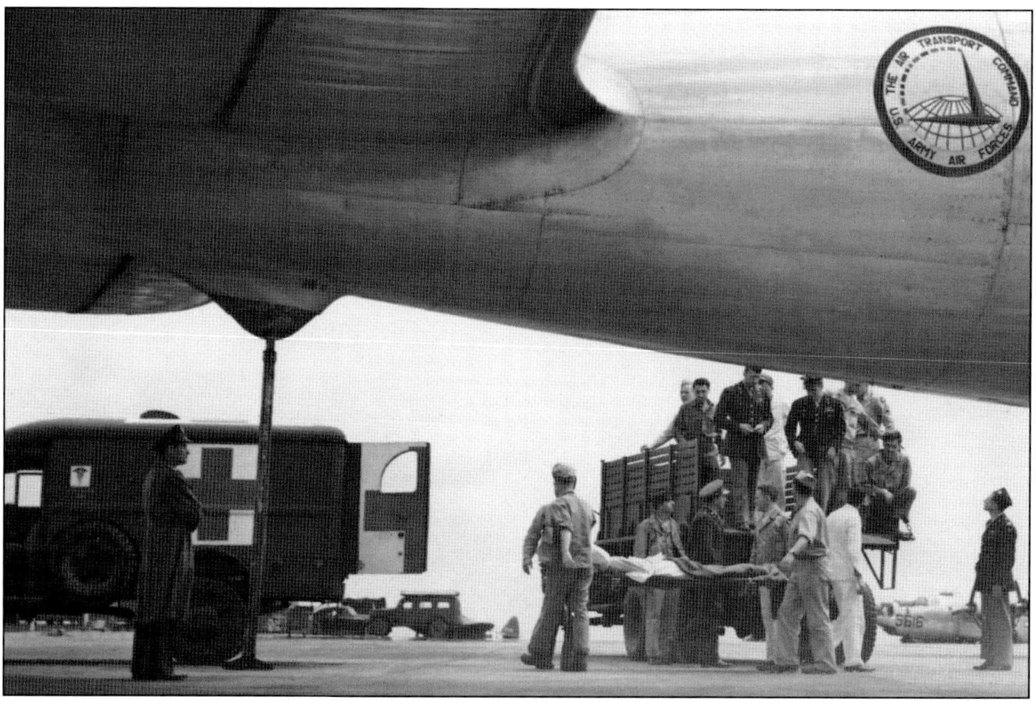

By January 1945, New Castle Army Air Base was a port of debarkation, receiving air evacuation patients from Europe on C-54s. The patients were strapped on canvas cots, with three or four to a stack inside the airplane. The litter patients were transported by truck to one of the four wards at the base hospital. (JC.)

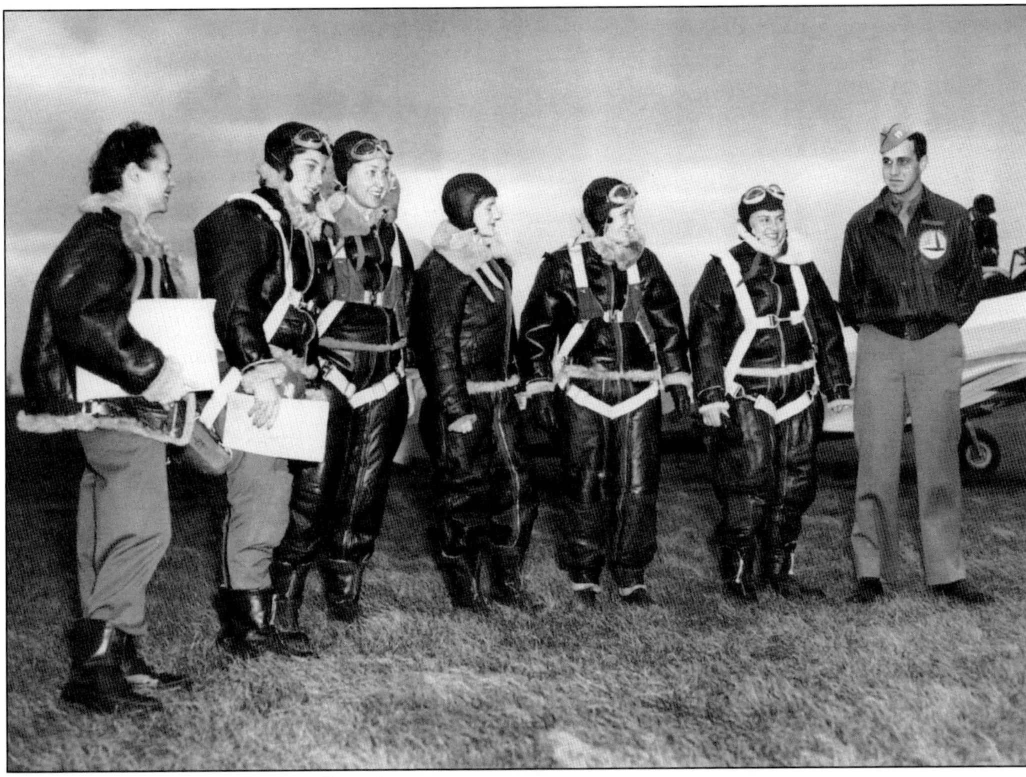

This image shows a pilot briefing for the first Fairchild PT-19 trip from the factory at Hagerstown, Maryland, given by the operations officer, Captain Franks. The women pilots had flown from New Castle Army Air Base to Hagerstown, Maryland, for their ferry flights to Mitchel Field, Long Island, New York. (JC.)

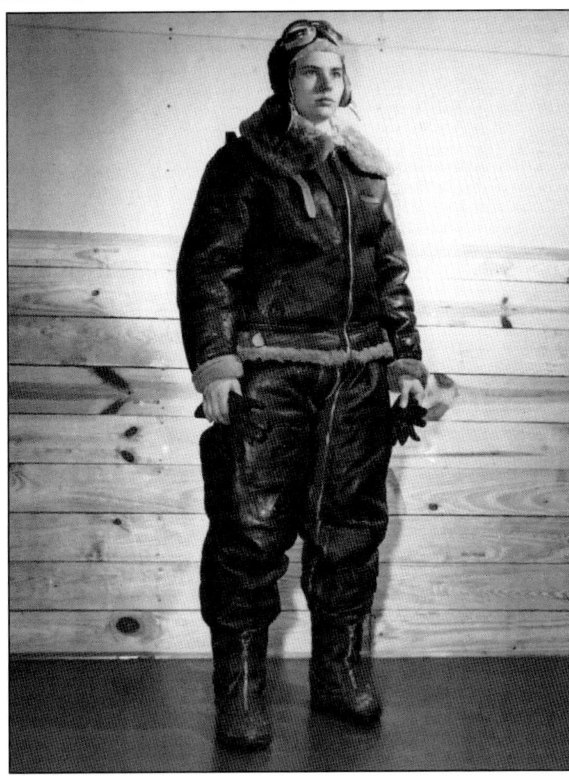

Women's Auxiliary Ferrying Squadron (WAFS) pilot Gertrude Meserve Tubbs is pictured in winter flying gear in 1942. Note the goggles for use in open-cockpit airplanes. The women flew open-cockpit airplanes in winter to places like Great Falls, Montana. The clothing was not insulated, just heavy. (JC.)

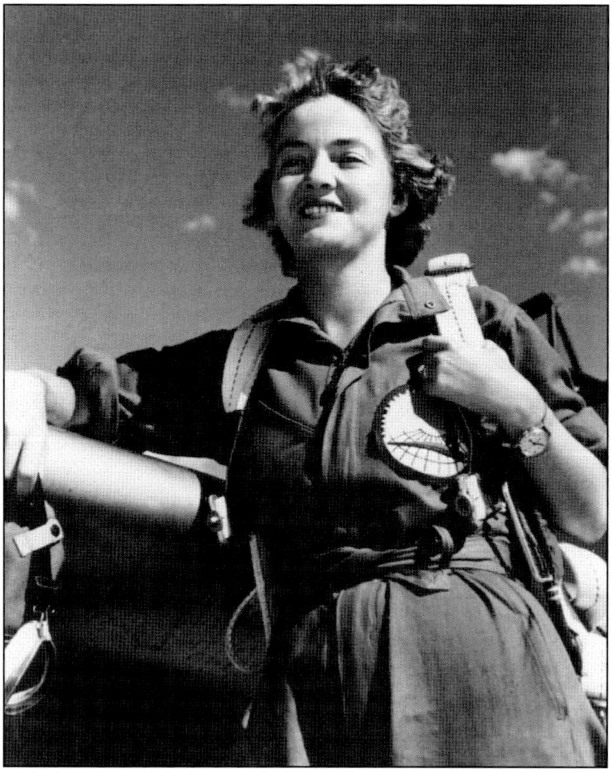

Nancy Harkness Love, WAFS squadron leader, was the first woman to fly the P-51 fighter and the B-17 four-engine bomber. Love is pictured at New Castle Army Air Base, wearing coveralls and holding her parachute. (JC.)

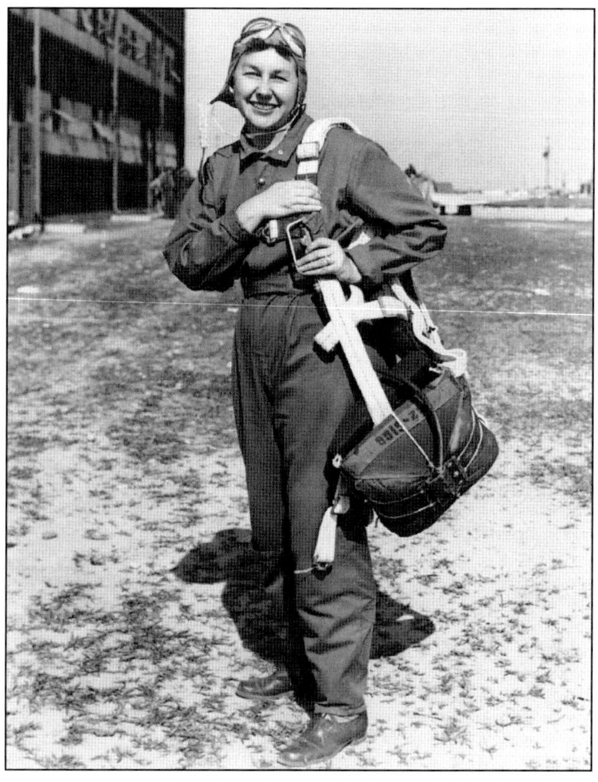

In 1942, WAFS Esther Nelson was photographed at New Castle Army Air Base with her seat-pack parachute. Nelson was an interior decorator in civilian life. One of her longest ferry flights was in a PT-19 trainer airplane from the factory in Hagerstown, Maryland, to Oklahoma. (JC.)

Adela Schaar is shown ready to get in a Bell P-39 Airacobra fighter. Her only instruction for this advanced aircraft was a short film from the Bell Company. This airplane was powered by a 1,150-horsepower Allison engine, which was situated behind the cockpit. The P-39 had a 37-mm cannon in the nose and six Browning machine guns and featured a nose wheel and car-type cockpit doors. (JC.)

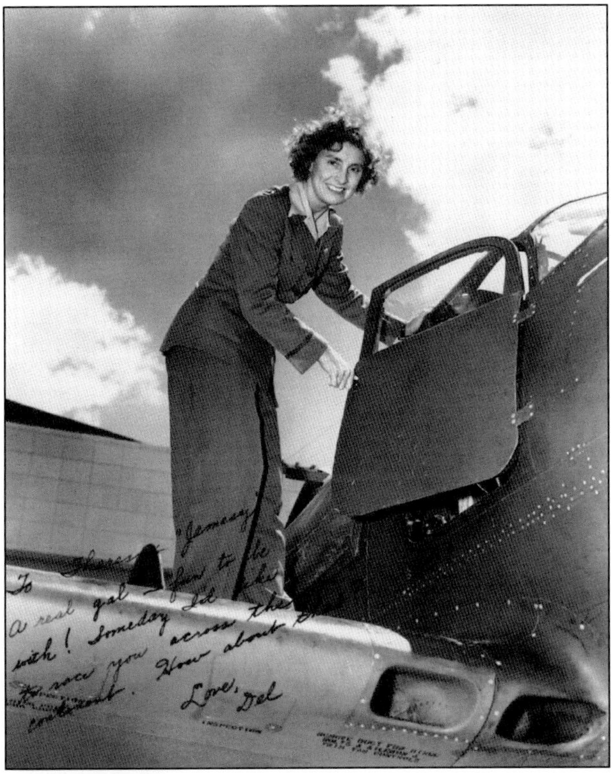

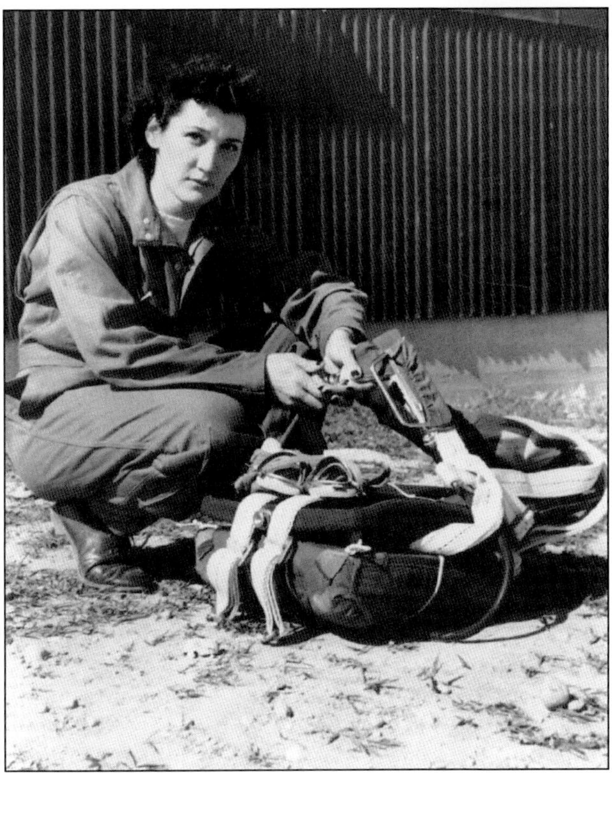

WAFS Teresa James is seen with her parachute at New Castle Army Air Base. All ferry pilots, men and women, were issued a parachute when they first arrived at New Castle Army Air Base. James joined the Air Force Reserves after World War II and retired as a major in 1976. (JC.)

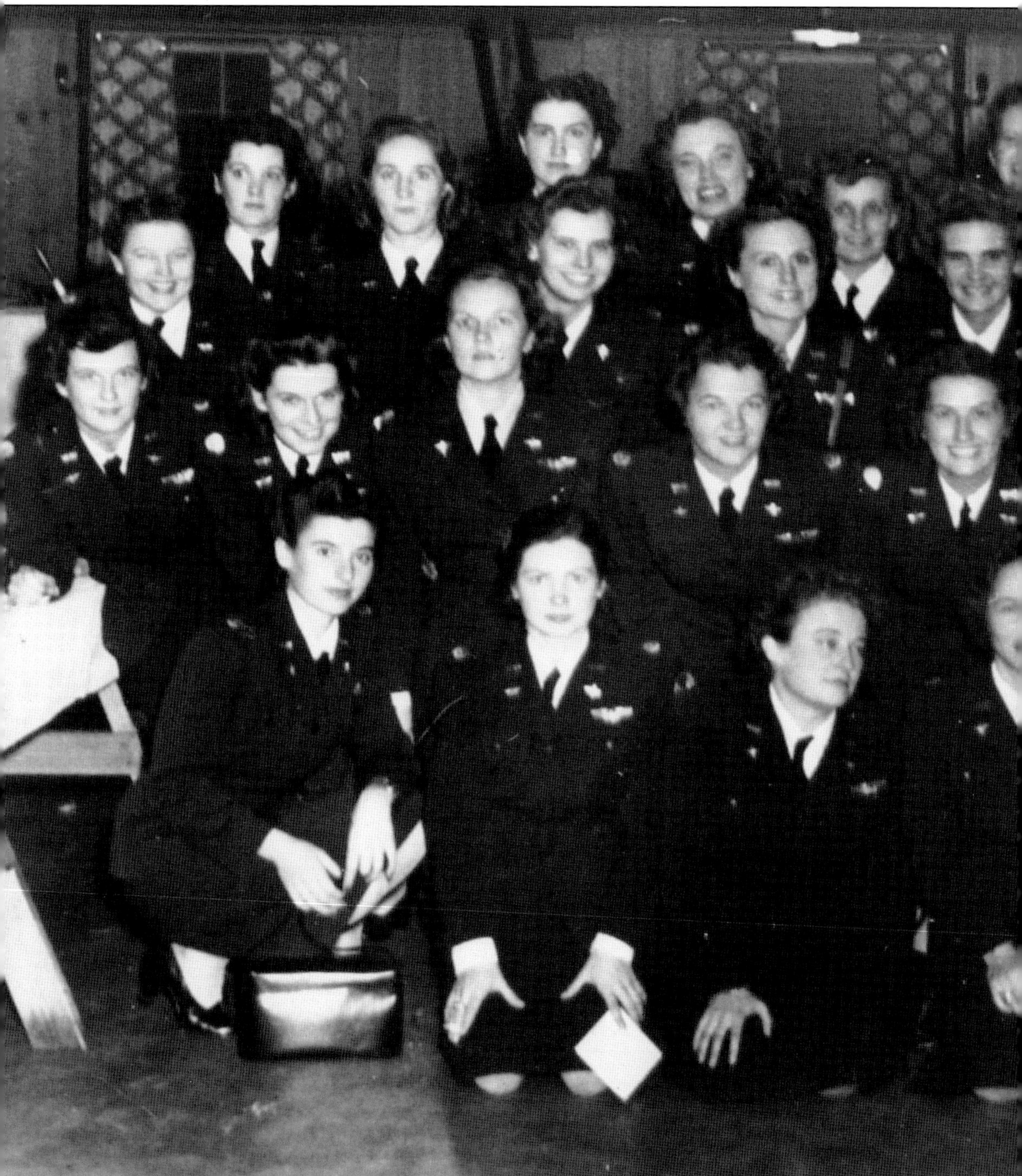

This image shows the "last supper" at New Castle Army Air Base when the Women's Air Force Service Pilots (WASP) was disbanded on December 19, 1944. Pictured are, from left to right, (first row) Mary Russo, Virginia Clair, Helen Richey, Betty Gillies, Nancy Love, Josephine Pitz, Helen McGilvery, and Nancy Baker; (second row) Florence Lawler, Anna Flynn, Betty Scantland, Jill McCormick, Janet Zuchowski, Virgie Lowell, Kathryn Bernheim, Gwendolyne Cowart, and

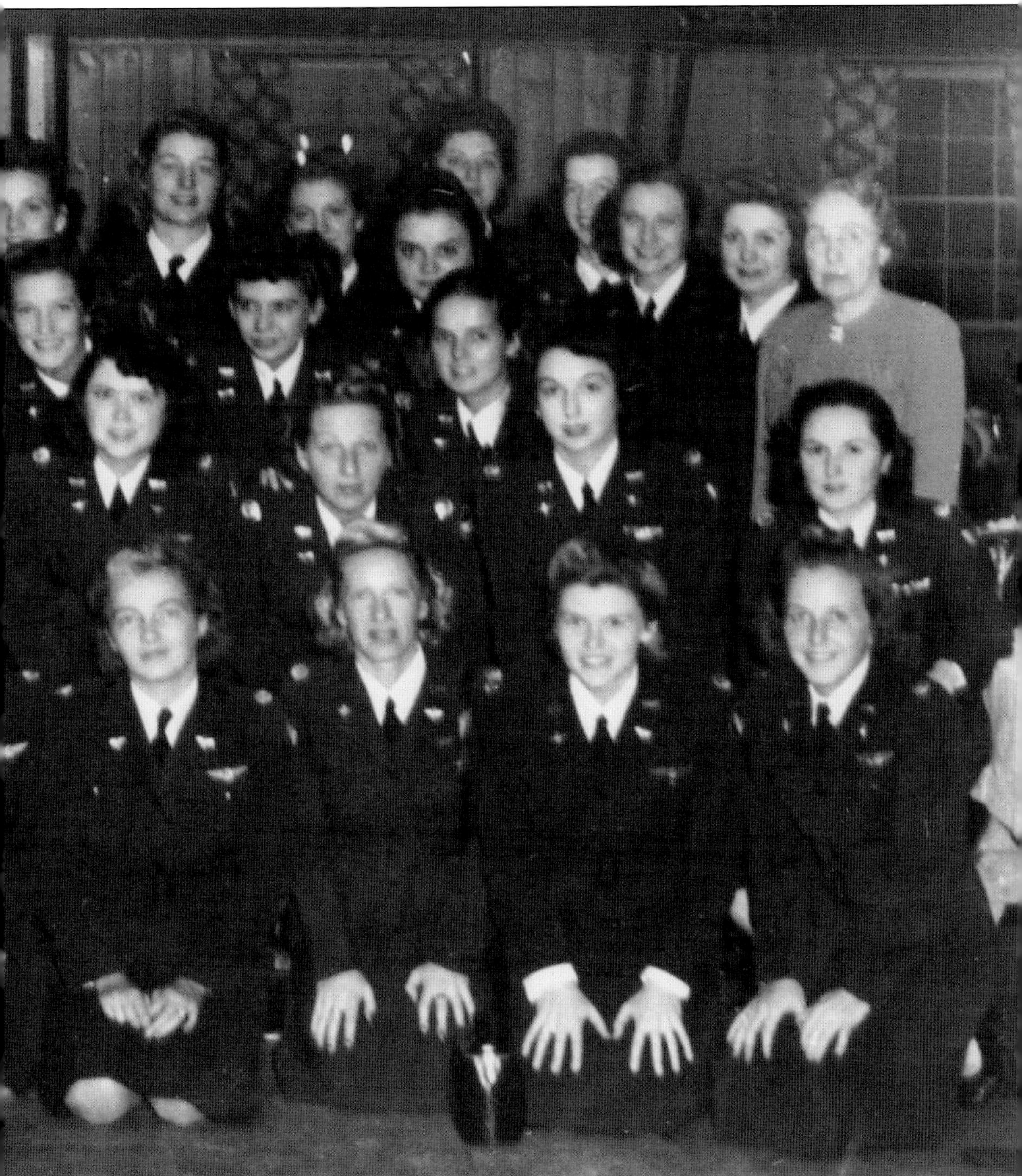

Mitchell Long; (third row) Dorothy Coburn, Gertrude Meserve Tubbs, Ruth Anderson, Celia Hunter, Helen Mary Clark, Virginia Alleman, and Ruth Adams; (fourth row) Teresa James, Grace Birge, Sarah Pearce, Marge Gray, Esther Poole, Jane Straughan, Margarite Ray, Nancy Batson, Rita Moynahan, and Marianne Beard; (fifth row) Avanell Pinkley, Emily Heisyer, Eunice Oates, Rosalie Grohman, and Margaret Anderson (house mother at the base). (JC.)

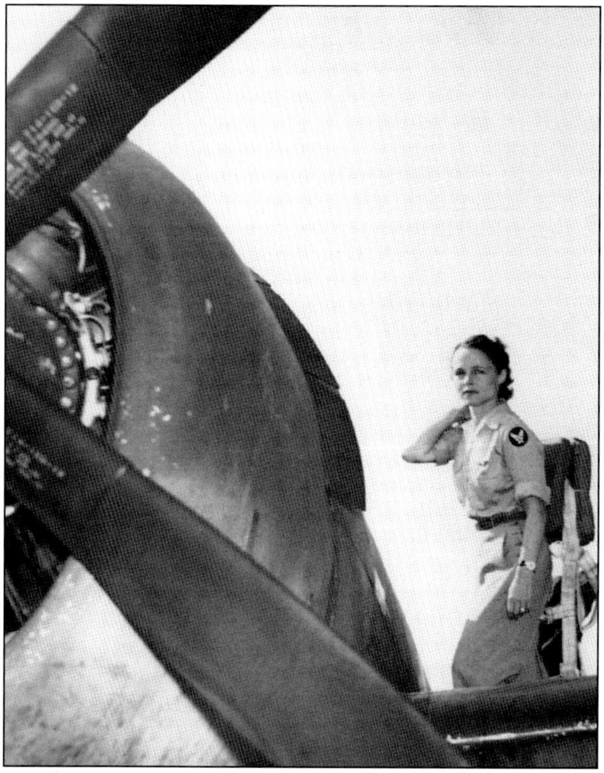

WAFS Betty Gillies was the second woman to arrive at New Castle Army Air Base in September 1942. She is pictured here getting in a P-47 Thunderbolt fighter airplane. Gillies was very short, so she used wooden blocks to help her reach the rudder pedals. Gillies and Nancy Love were the two women who began the trip to deliver a B-17 heavy bomber to England. (JC.)

The alert room is depicted at New Castle Army Air Base in 1943. The alert room, located in one of the hangars, was where the women waited for flight assignments. It was also called the ready room. This image shows Gertrude Tubbs (left) and Ruth Adams (right) at the table. (JC.)

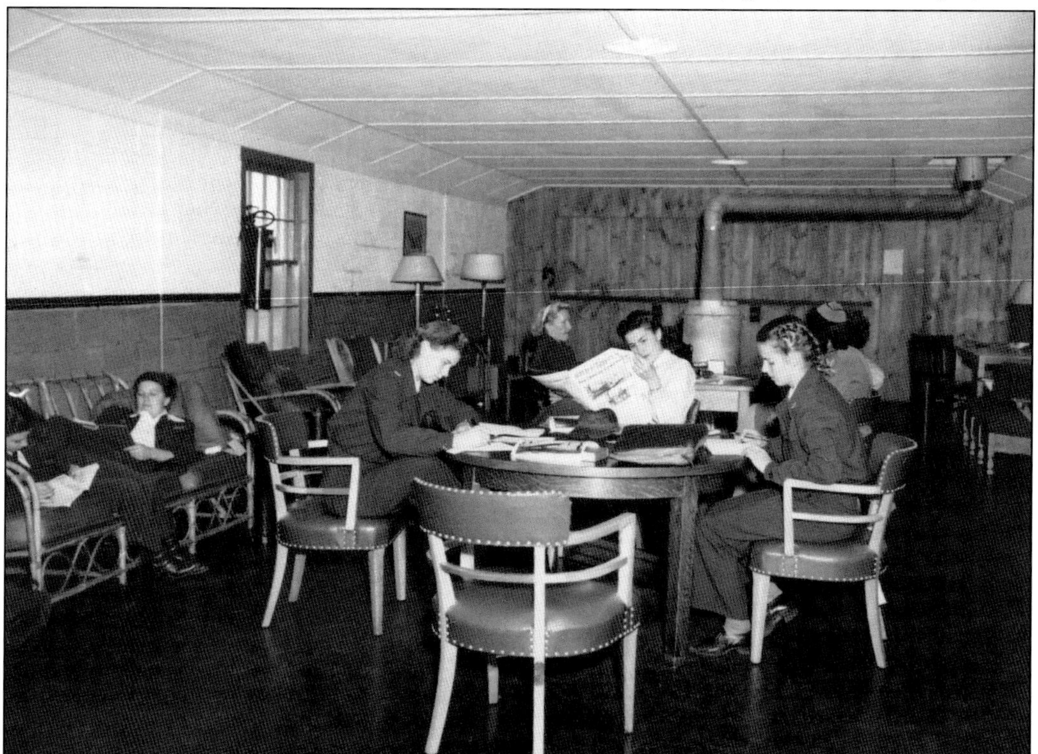

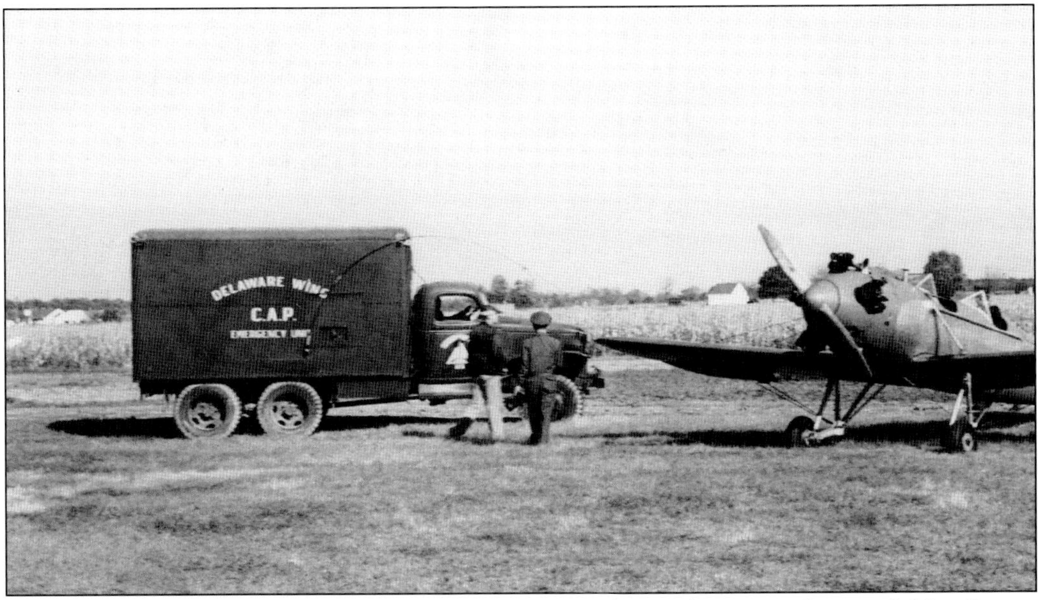

The Delaware Wing Civil Air Patrol's emergency unit is depicted at an auxiliary airfield in Sussex County during World War II. The Civil Air Patrol was able to operate its small airplanes from many fields with the help of this unit. (MM.)

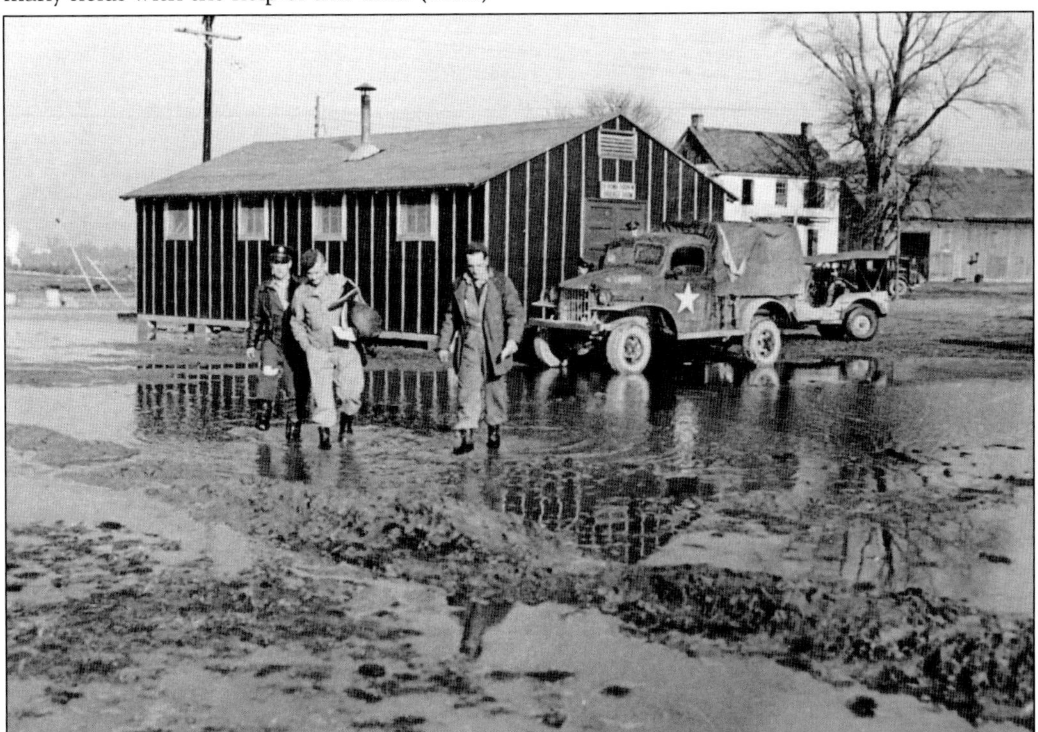

3rd Antisubmarine Squadron personnel Lunsford, Wolford, and Crowder depart the squadron orderly room in 1942. The tar paper shacks at Dover Army Air Field were little different than a hastily improvised overseas air patch in the combat zone. Heated by potbelly stoves, the buildings had no running water or electricity. (AMC.)

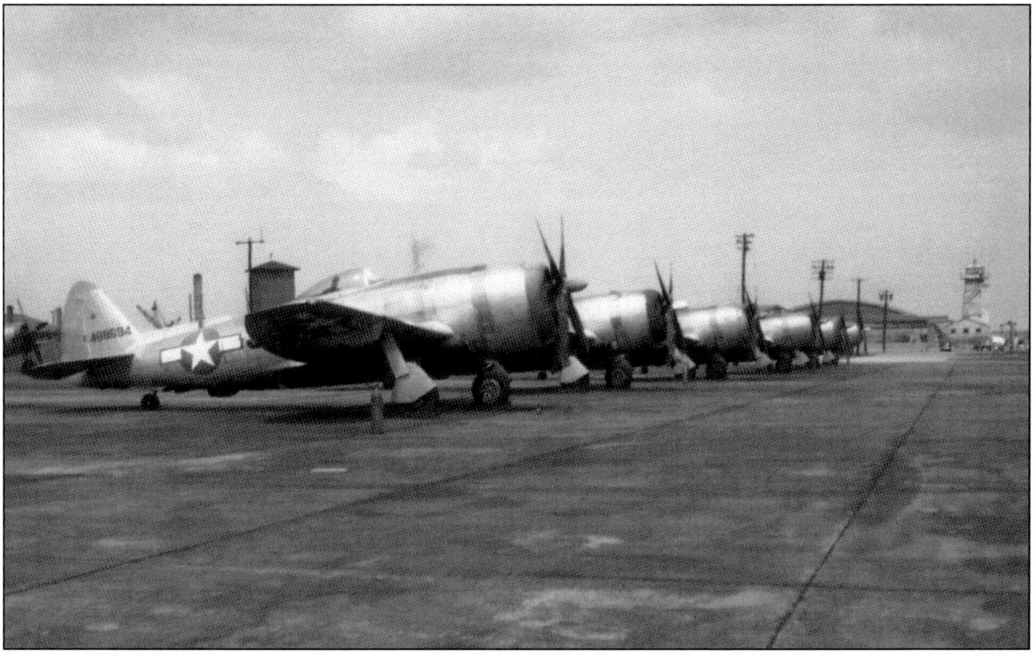

Republic P-47 Thunderbolts are on the Dover Army Air Field flight line. Built in greater quantities than any other US fighter, the P-47, also known as the "Jug," was the heaviest single-engine World War II fighter to go into production and the first piston-powered fighter to exceed 500 miles per hour. (AMC.)

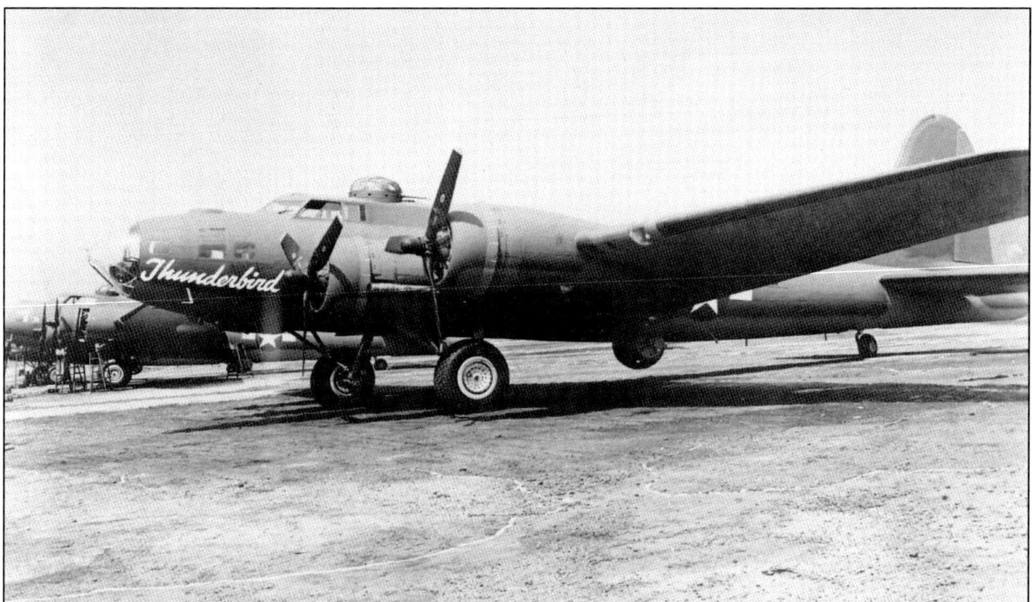

A Boeing B-17 Flying Fortress is on the ramp at New Castle Army Air Base in February 1943. Two of the WASPs who flew the B-17 were Nancy Love and Betty Gillies. The two women planned to deliver this four-engine B-17 over the North Atlantic to England, but they were stopped at Goose Bay, Labrador, by a message from Gen. Henry H. Arnold, at Army headquarters in England, before they got a chance to complete the trip. (JC.)

Three

Postwar

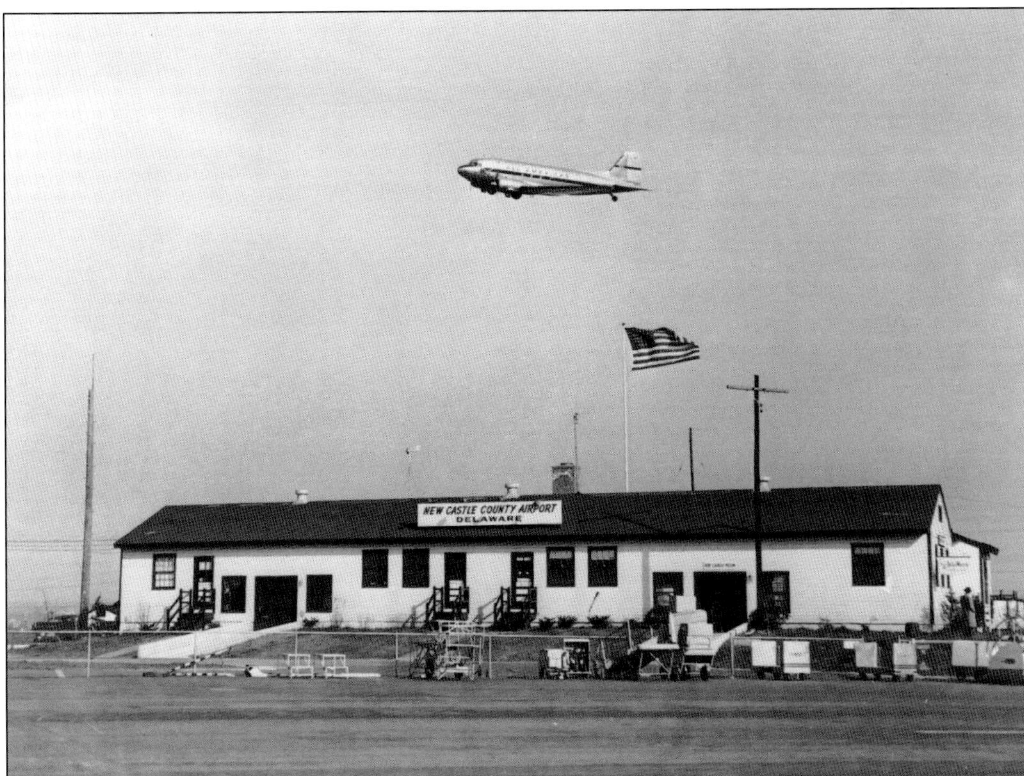

An All American Airways Douglas DC-3 is shown flying over the New Castle County Airport Terminal Building in 1947. The refurbished terminal building on the west side of the airfield was New Castle Army Building No. 44; Building No. 54, cut in half, was added to Building No. 44. Twenty-five feet were filled in between the legs of the "U" to make a larger lobby. (JC.)

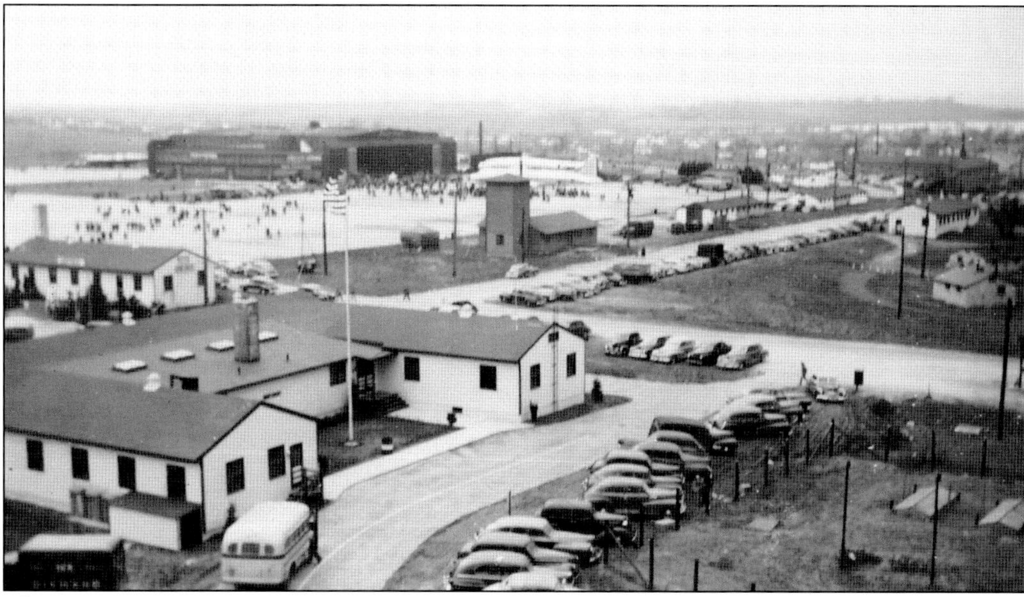

The New Castle County Airport Terminal Building, seen from the back side, included parking for automobiles. Facilities for passengers of the airlines, beginning service after World War II, were important. The Transcontinental Division of TWA landed its first passenger plane, a Douglas DC-3, at New Castle on November 29, 1947. Capt. Benjamin Southworth was its pilot. (JC.)

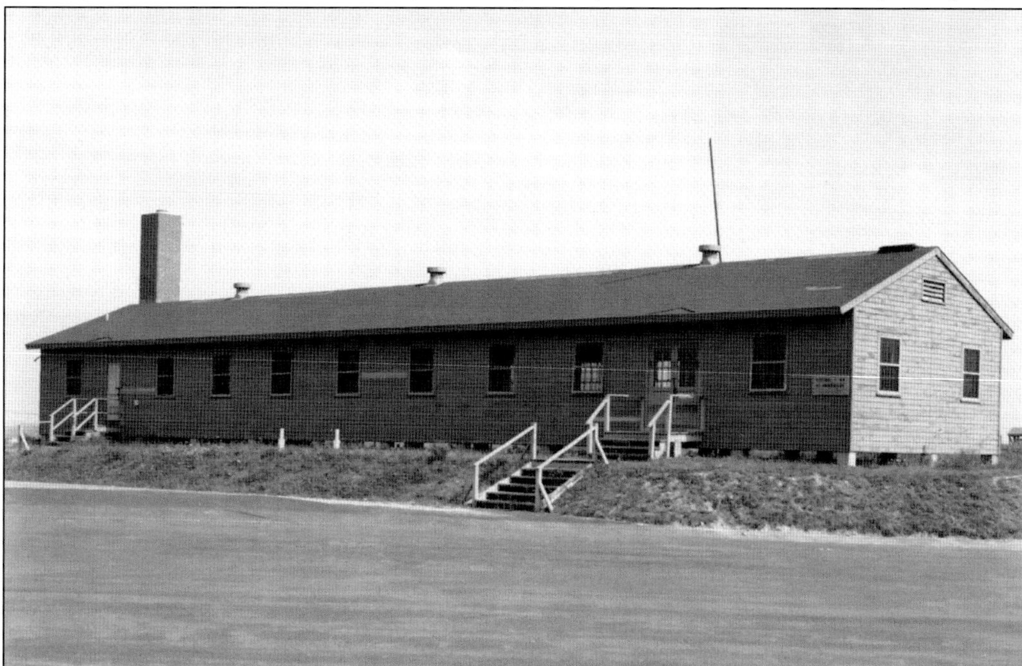

This building served as a terminal for passengers on the west side of New Castle County Airport until 1956, when a terminal was constructed on the other side of the airport. On November 29, 1947, American Airlines arrived in a four-engine Douglas DC-4, the *Flagship Buffalo*, from New York and bound for Chicago. American Airlines christened another airplane *Flagship Delaware*. (JC.)

This image shows the construction of a new terminal building on the east side of New Castle County Airport in 1956. Access to the west side of the airport was not large enough for parking cars, and National Guard traffic was considerable. Also, the airlines operating from the west terminal had a longer taxi distance to the runways. (JC.)

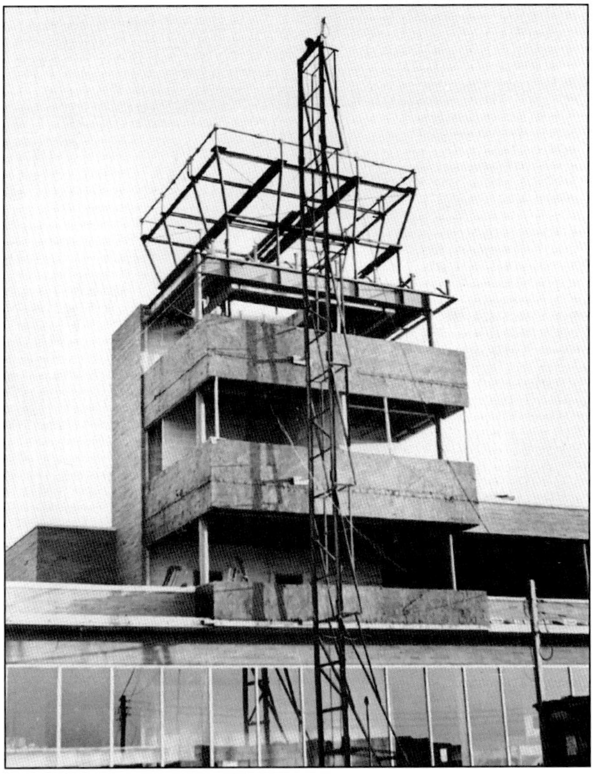

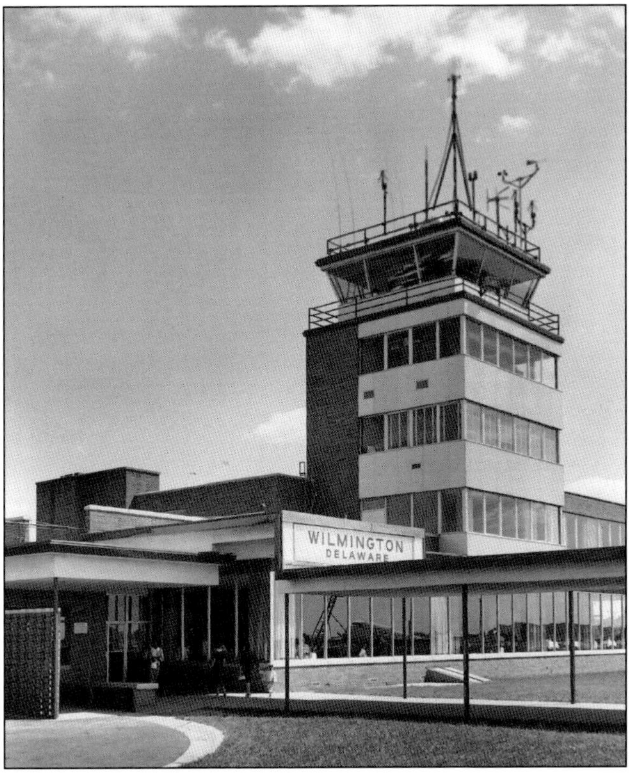

This photograph shows the new control tower and terminal building on the east side of New Castle County Airport. Just below the window area, allowing air traffic controllers to see in all directions, was a floor with an observation deck open to the public at all times. The terminal, which opened July 16, 1956, included a restaurant. (JC.)

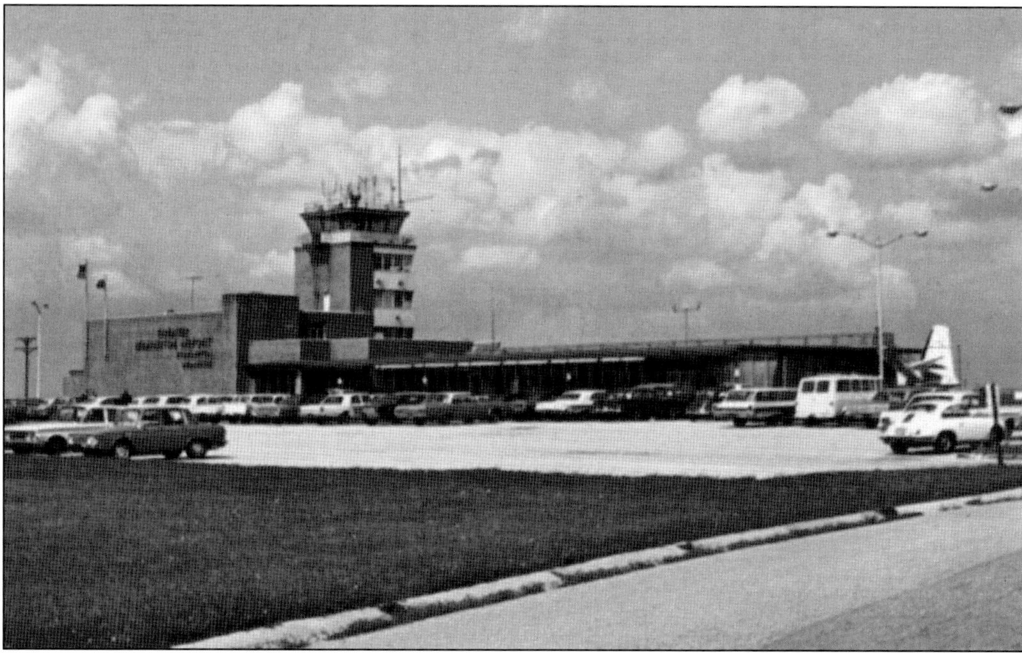

This image shows the Greater Wilmington Airport's control tower, terminal building, and parking lot. On June 1, 1961, the name of the New Castle County Airport was officially changed to Greater Wilmington Airport (Resolution No. 61-233). On November 23, 1982, New Castle County Resolution No. 81-181 changed the name of the airport back to New Castle County Airport. (JC.)

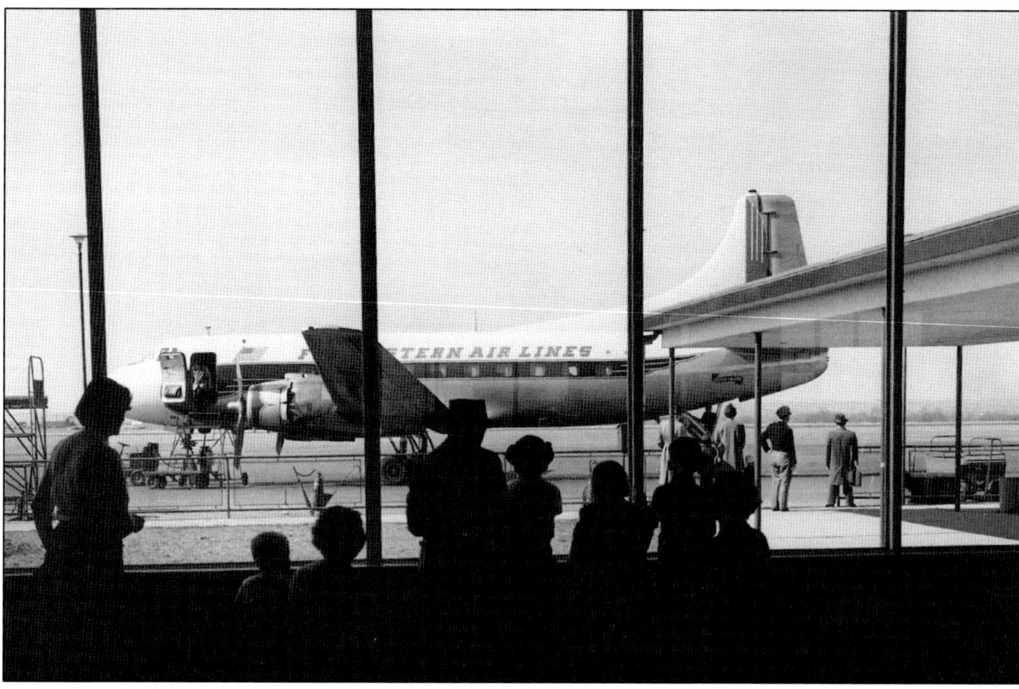

A view from the waiting room in the new terminal building shows an Eastern Airlines plane. Eastern began *Silver Falcon* flights in 1947 with service to Georgia, North Carolina, West Virginia, Kentucky, New York, and Boston. (JC.)

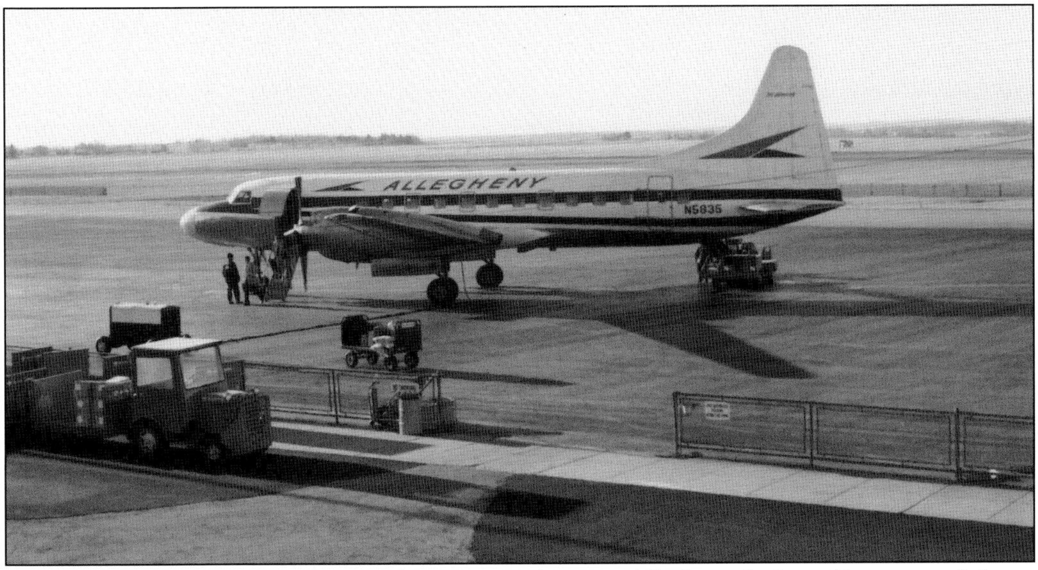

This photograph, taken from the new dining room, shows an Allegheny Airlines 40-passenger Martin plane on the terminal ramp. There was also a snack bar and cocktail lounge just off the main dining room. For cooling during the summer, there was an 80-ton capacity air-conditioning unit. (JC.)

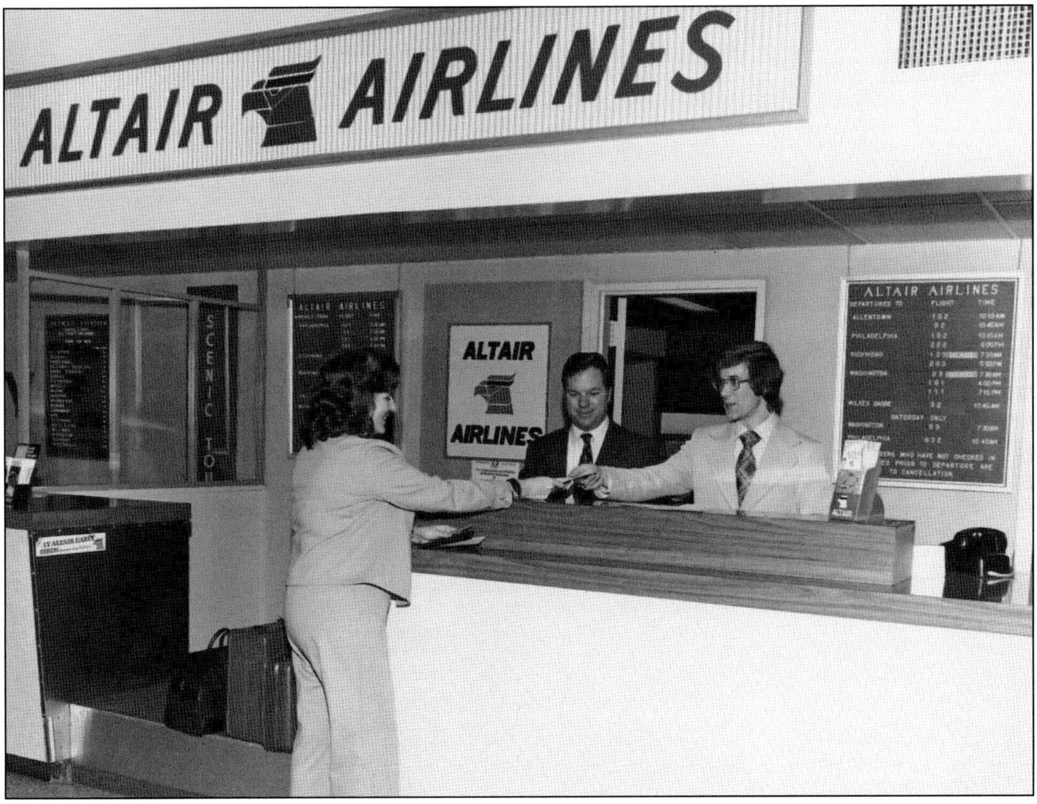

Altair Airlines had a ticket counter in the terminal building. At various times, ticket counters served TWA, American, Capitol, Crown, Wheeler, United, Summit, Saturn, Delta, Atlantic Southeast, Dover Air Transport, and Zantop International Airlines. (JC.)

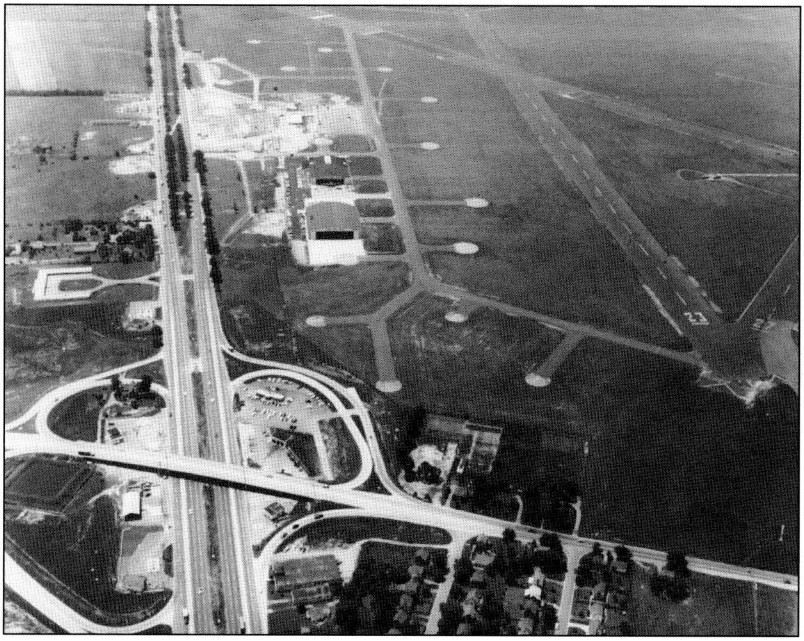

This 1968 aerial view, looking southwest, shows the fourth runway, No. 23, before it was changed to a taxiway. In the foreground, just north of Highway 13, was the Peter Pan Restaurant, a popular place for pilots. Today, the restaurant is known as Arner's. (JC.)

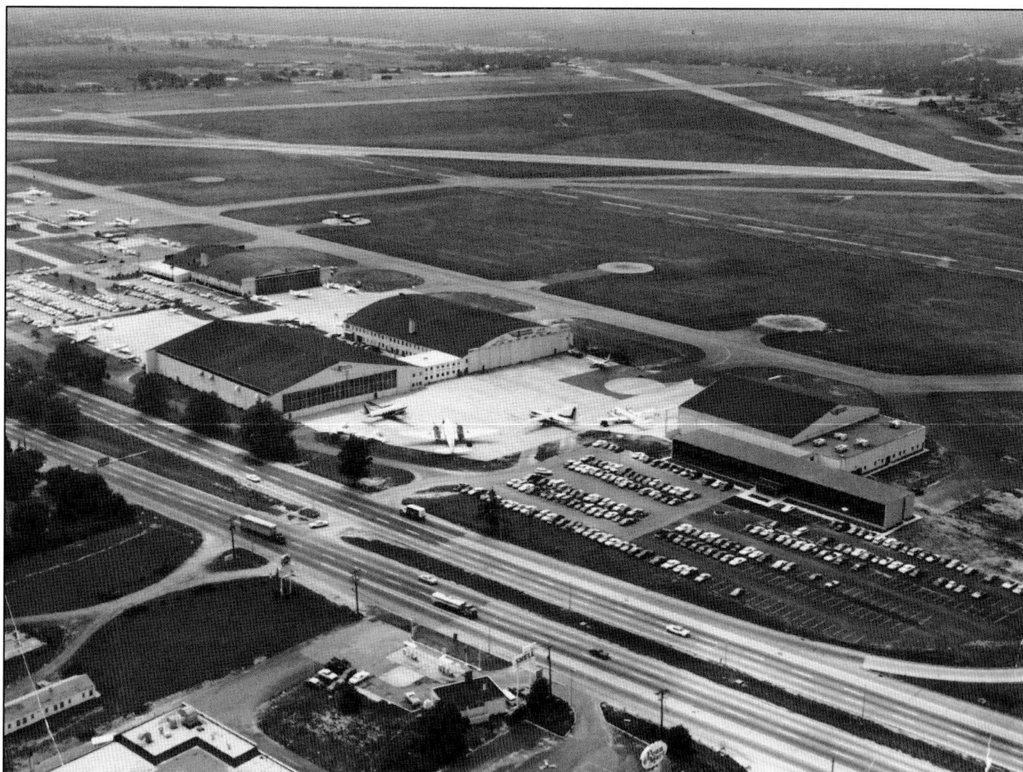

This aerial view of the Greater Wilmington Airport, alongside Highway 13, shows Atlantic Aviation's hangars. Atlantic Aviation, Inc., was formed by Henry Belin duPont Jr. from his business at DuPont Airfield prior to World War II. Atlantic Aviation Service, Atlantic Aviation Supply, and Atlantic Aviation Sales were merged into the new company. (JC.)

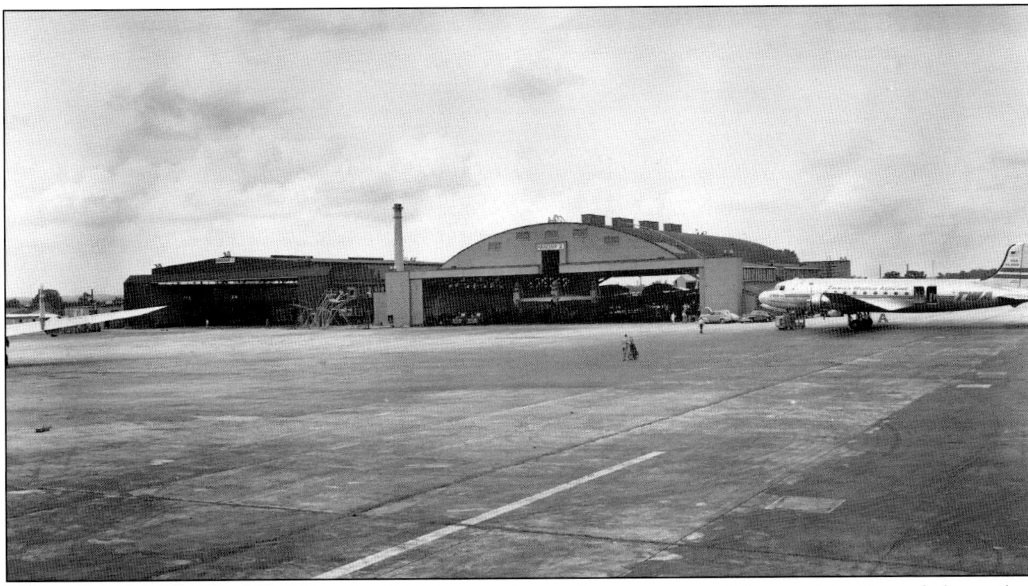

This image shows a TWA Douglas DC-4 aircraft on the ramp near Hangar No. 2, and the tail of a TWA Constellation airplane is sticking out from the hangar. TWA operations at New Castle County Airport were suspended on June 9, 1953, after the Civil Aeronautics Board decided that both TWA and Allegheny Airlines could not serve the airport. Allegheny continued to serve the airport until November 1974. (JC.)

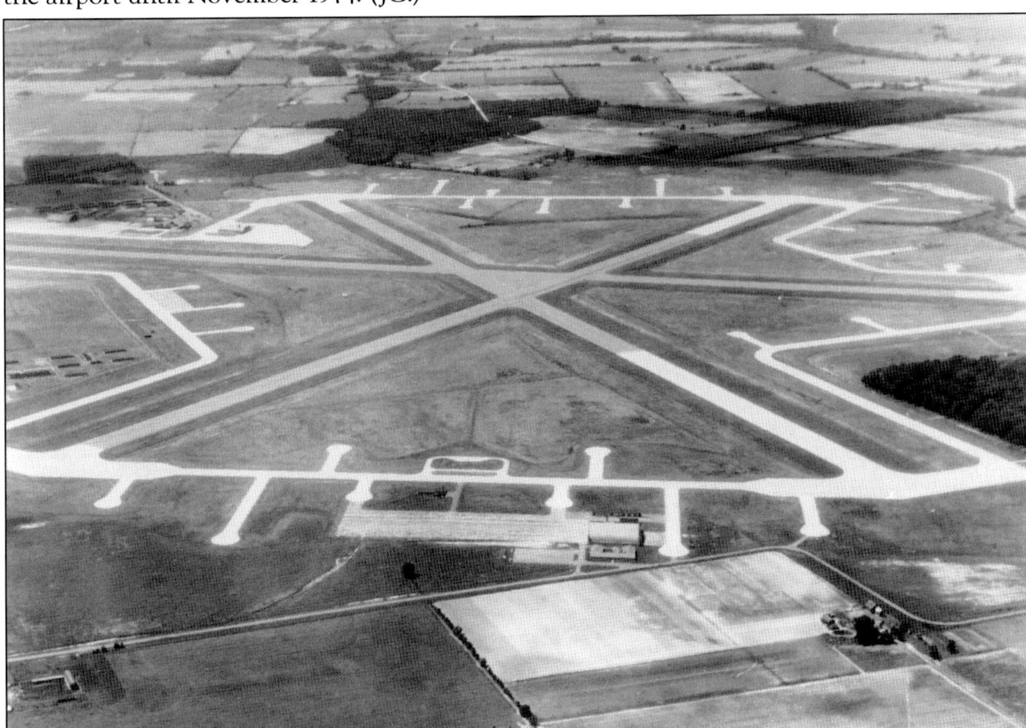

The original star pattern of three intersecting runways is evident in this 1948 photograph of Dover Air Force Base. (AMC.)

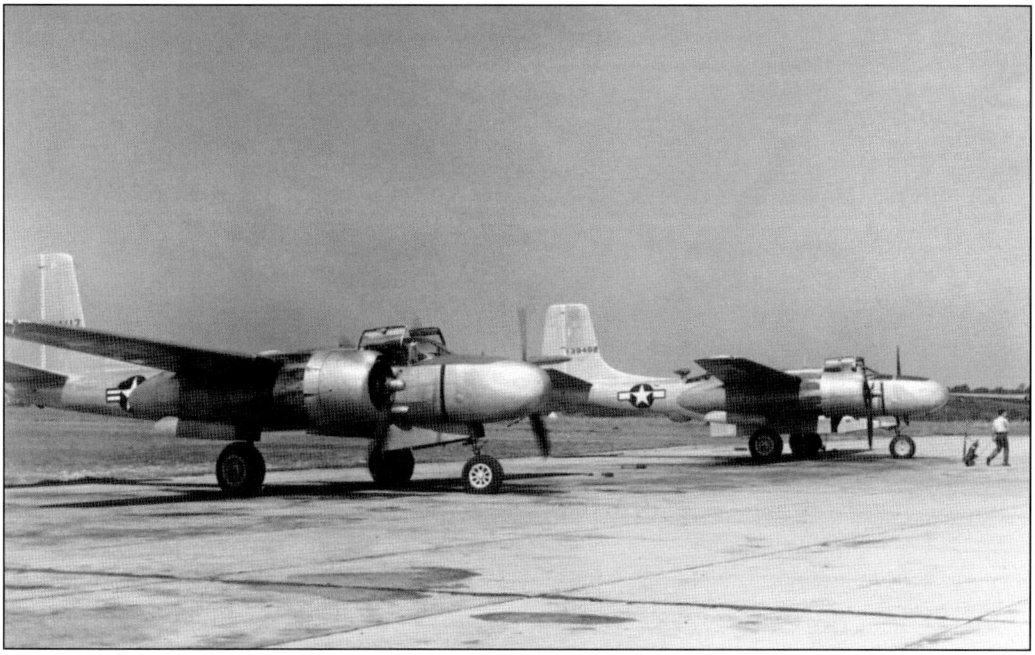

The Douglas B-26 Invader was used by the Delaware Air National Guard as a tow plane for aerial targets to hone the fighter pilot's gunnery skills. (DMHEF.)

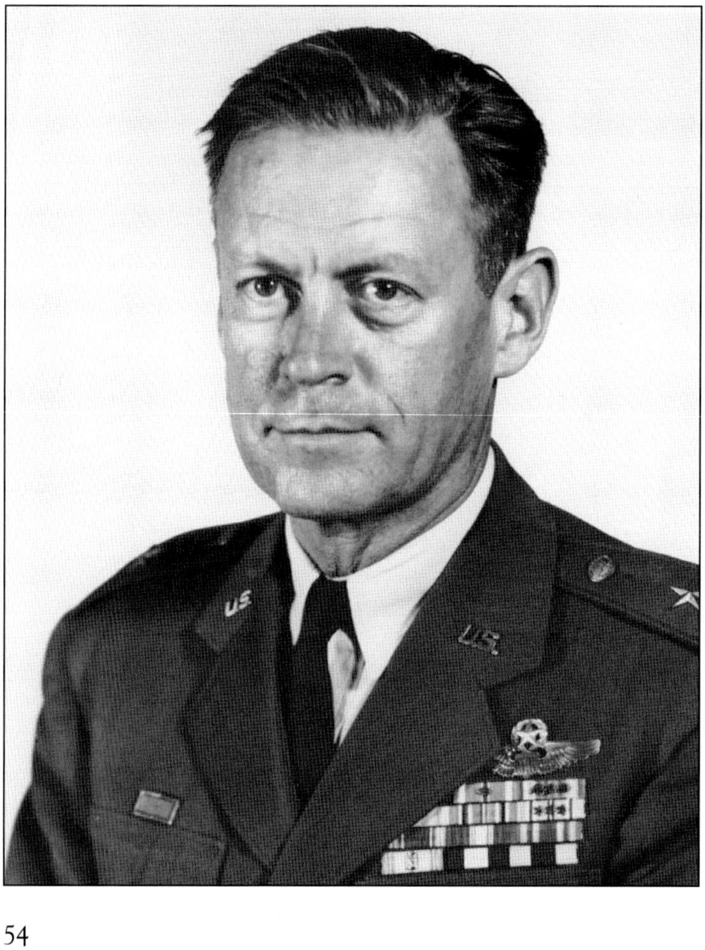

William W. Spruance was a charter member of the Delaware Air National Guard. He was a veteran of the China-Burma-India theater, flying over the hump during World War II. He rose to the rank of brigadier general, leading the organization for many years. General Spruance was inducted into the Delaware Aviation Hall of Fame in 2002. (DMHEF.)

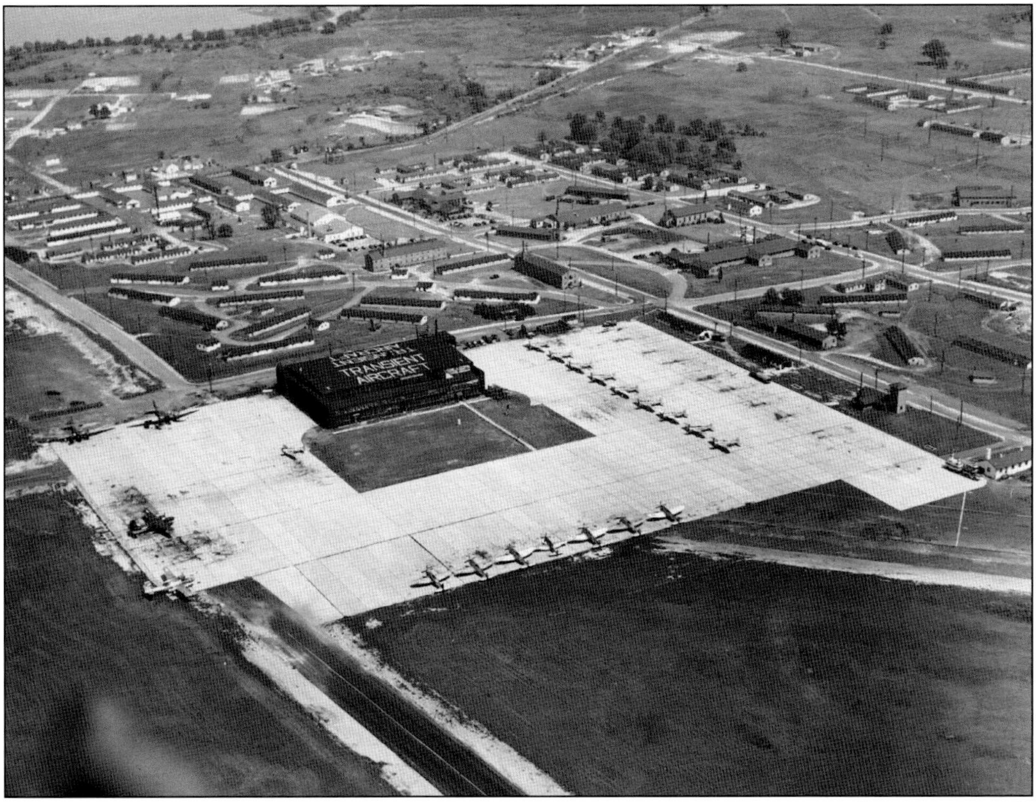

This late-1940s aerial view shows the Delaware Air National Guard hangar and ramp area with parked F-47s, two C-47s, and two A-26s. The four twin-engine Douglas A-26 Invaders arrived at New Castle in March 1947; the Delaware Air National Guard used them for target towing. (JC.)

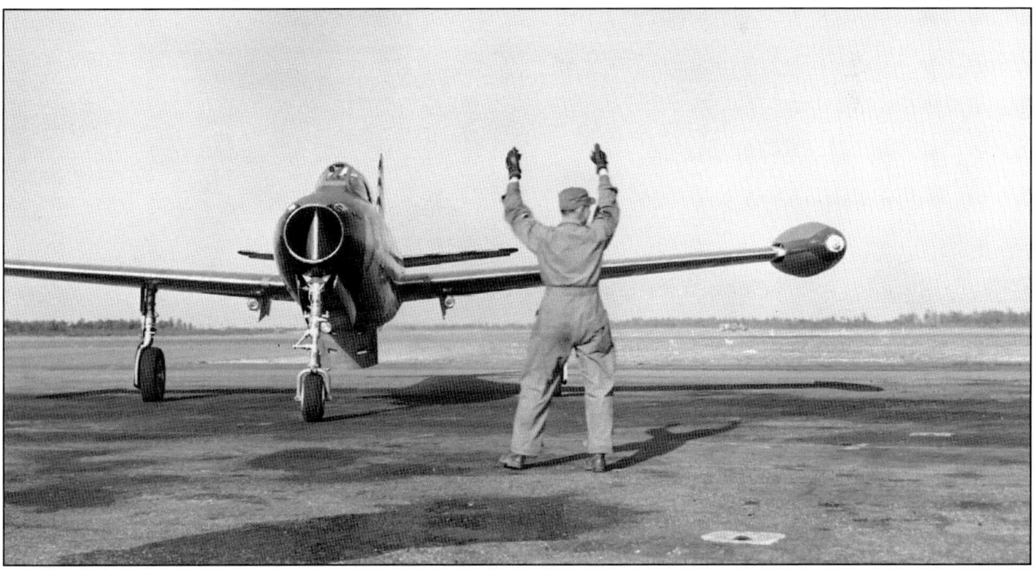

The Delaware Air National Guard was among the very first units to receive its first jets in February 1950. They were F-84C Thunderjets, which would go to war in Korea when the unit was mobilized just 21 months later. (JC)

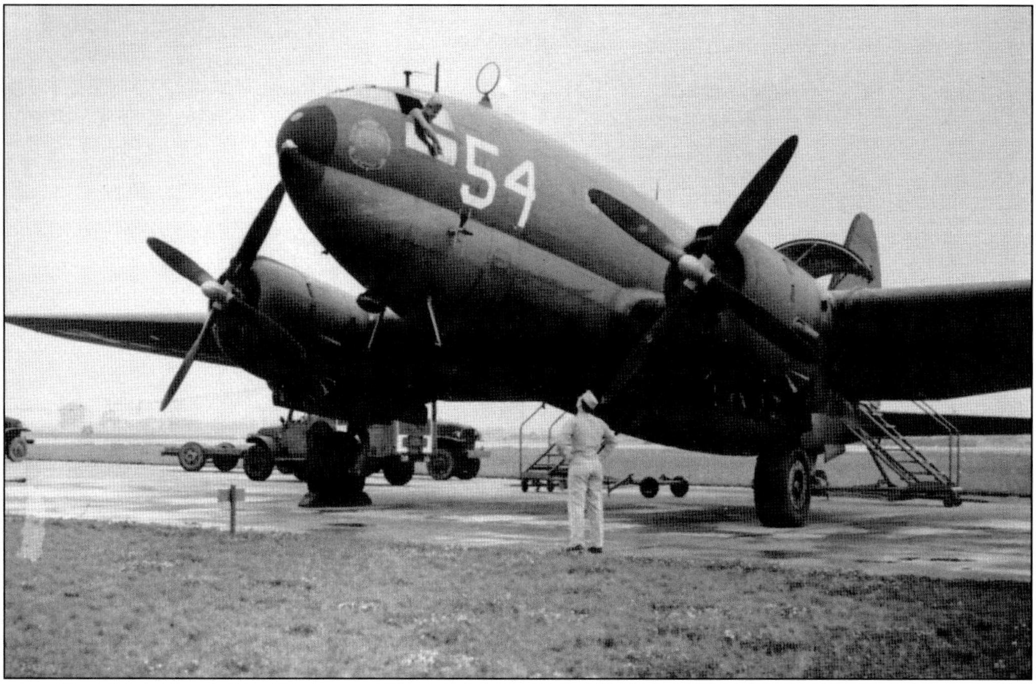

A Curtiss C-46 Commando, flown by the Air Force Reserve and the 512th Troop Carrier Group, is seen at a Dover Air Force Base open house just after World War II. The 512th Troop Carrier Group was based at New Castle Airport at the time. (AMC.)

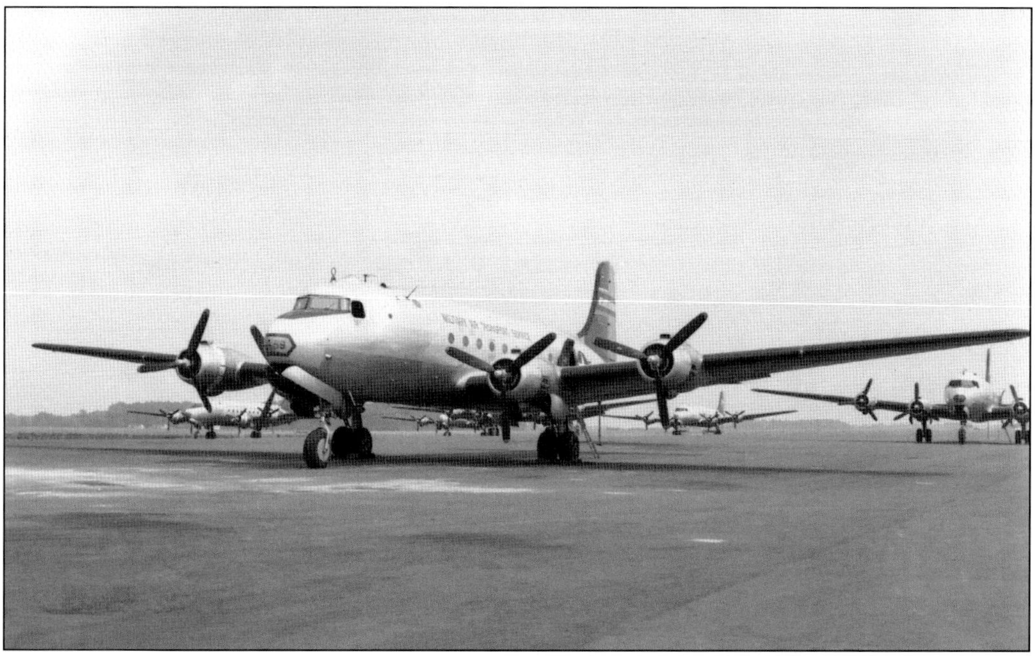

In March 1953, the F-94C Lockheed Starfighter 332nd Fighter-Interceptor Squadron (FIS) joined the 334th FIS at New Castle. In 1955, the fighter units at New Castle were upgraded to a group level with the activation of the 82nd Fighter-Interceptor Group. The squadrons were redesignated the 97th and 96th Fighter-Interceptor Squadrons. (AMC.)

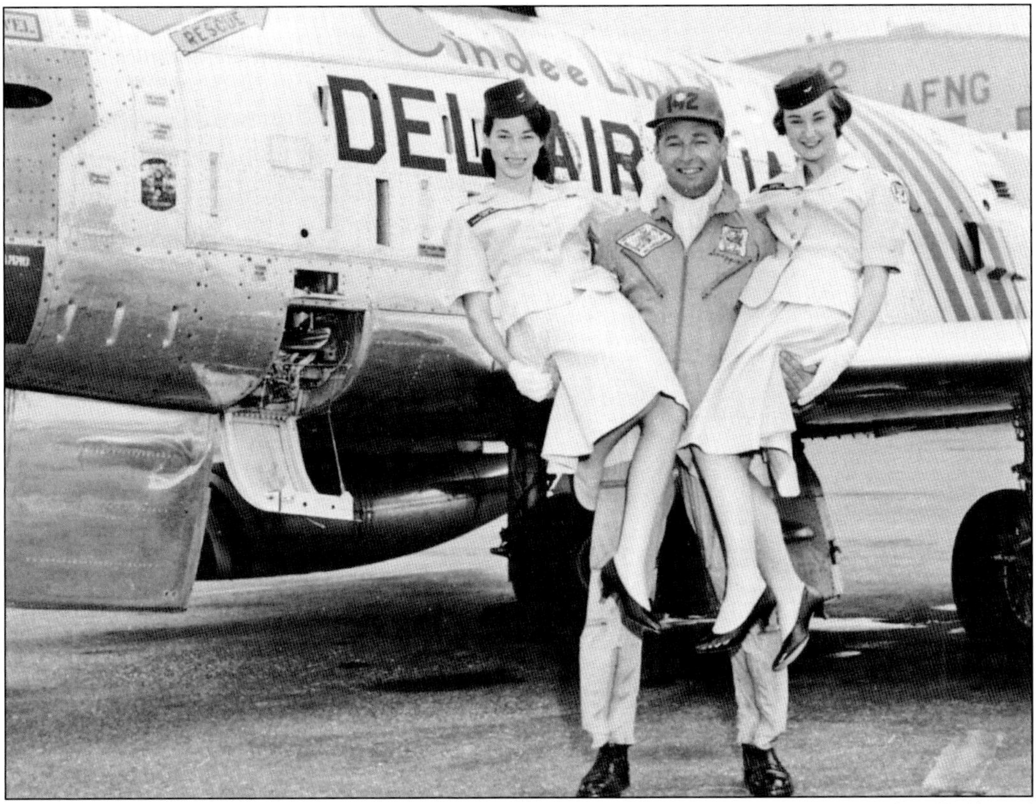

Lt. Col. David F. "Snapper" McCallister, shown here with his two daughters, Cindee (left) and Linda, both CAP cadets, assumed leadership of the 142nd Fighter Squadron after the Korean War, when the unit converted to North American F-86 Sabre jets. (DMHEF.)

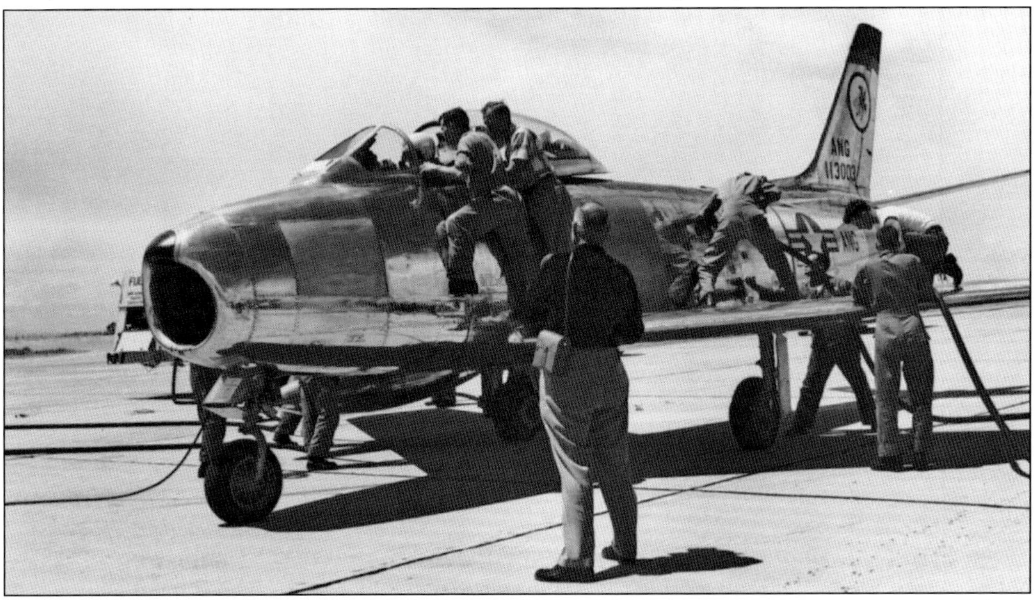

Lt. Col. David F. McCallister won the 1956 Ricks Memorial Trophy Race, setting a record from California to New Orleans in this F-86 with only one drop tank. (DMHEF.)

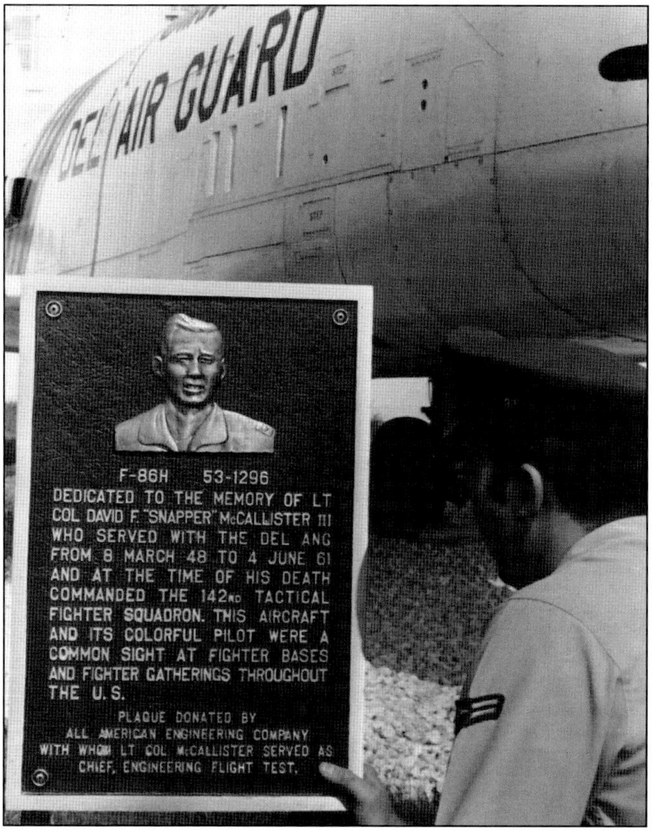

This plaque dedicated to the memory of Lt. Col. David F. McCallister stands at the entrance to the Delaware Air National Guard in front of McCallister's F-86, named *Cindy Lind* after his daughters. All American Engineering Company donated the plaque. (JC.)

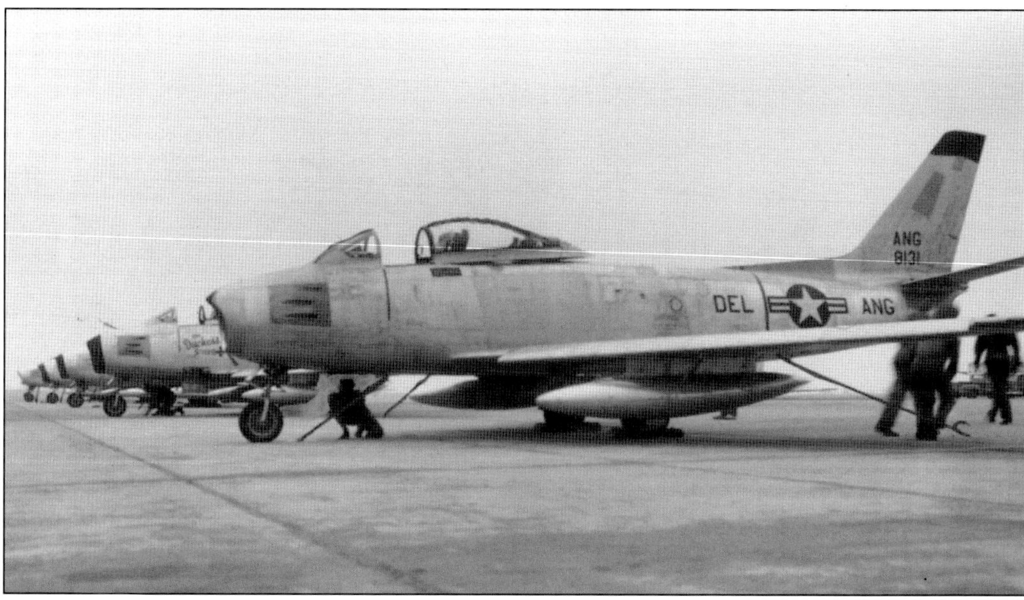

The 142nd Fighter Squadron flew a succession of F-86s from 1953 to 1962, including the F-86 A, E, F, and H models in the interceptor, fighter-bomber mission. The 4th Fighter-Interceptor Wing, flying new F-86 Sabre jets, was based at New Castle where its pilots trained from August 14, 1950, to December 12, 1950, prior to going to Korea. (JC.)

A 1950 open house demonstrated the flying capabilities of the Delaware Air National Guard F-84s, shown here taxiing before a crowd. The Republic F-84 Thunderjet was flown as a fighter-bomber in Korea by Delaware Air National Guard pilots, activated for the Korean War. (JC.)

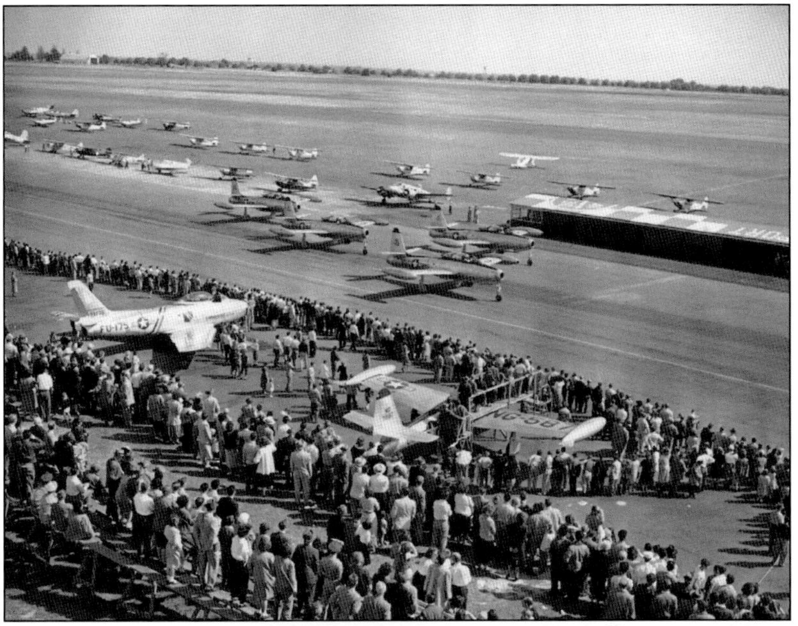

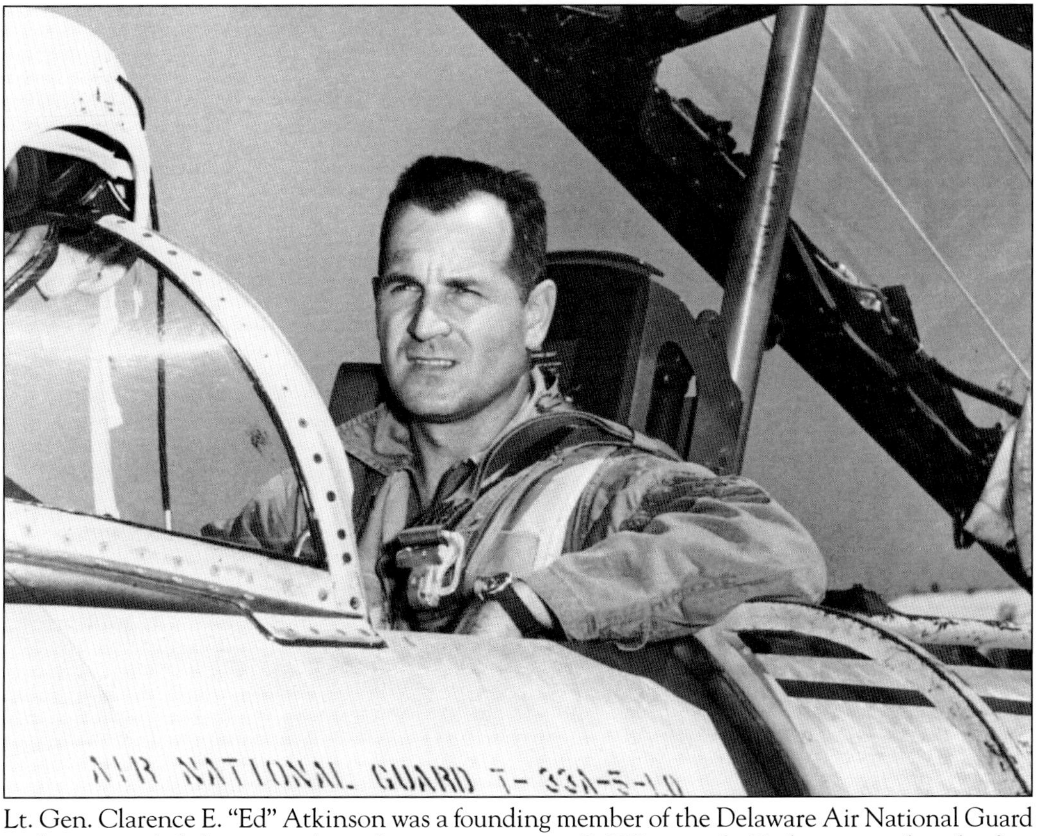

Lt. Gen. Clarence E. "Ed" Atkinson was a founding member of the Delaware Air National Guard and commanded the group through its transition to C-97G aircraft. He later served as the first Air National Guard adjutant general. He is depicted here in the cockpit of a T-33 trainer. General Atkinson was inducted into the Delaware Aviation Hall of Fame in 2004. (DMHEF.)

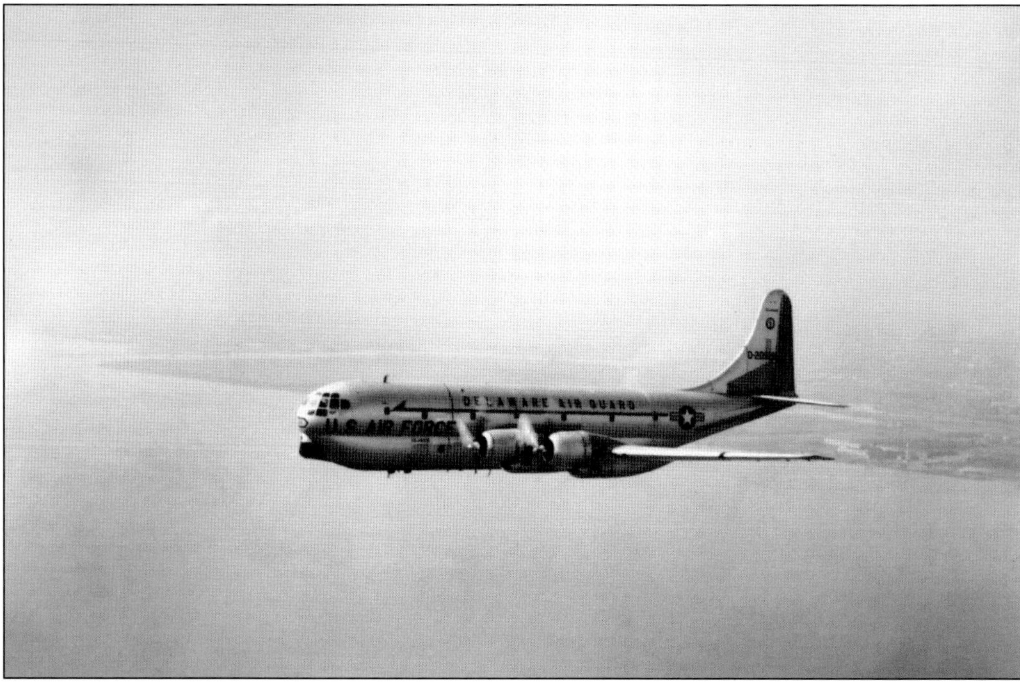

The Boeing C-97G Stratocruiser was the primary mission aircraft of the Delaware Air National Guard from 1962 to 1971. It was a strategic airlifter in use all over the globe. Delaware aircrews flew airlift support missions to Vietnam during the Vietnam War. (JC.)

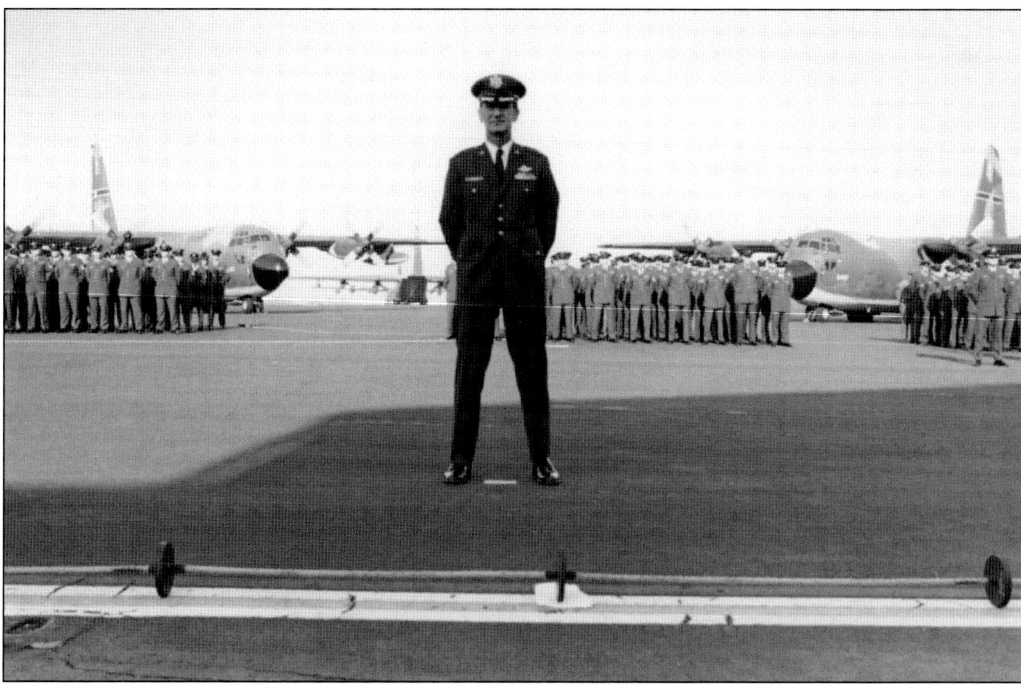

Brig. Gen. William F. Hutchinson Jr. was the air commander for the Delaware Air National Guard for over 11 years, leading the 166th Airlift Group when it flew the C-130. A Korean War veteran, Hutchinson was inducted into the Delaware Aviation Hall of Fame in 2007. (DMHEF.)

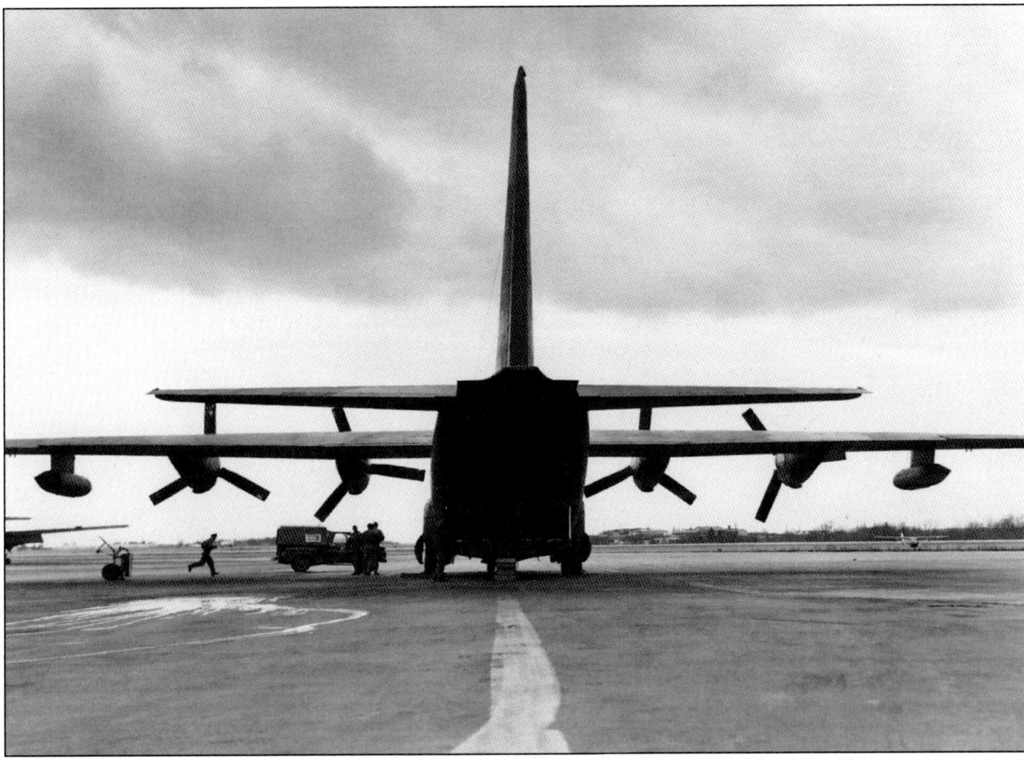

The DE ANG received its first C-130A models in 1971. Note the early three-bladed propellers. Delaware Air National Guard converted to new C-130H aircraft in 1985 and has flown them as its primary mission aircraft ever since. (DMHEF.)

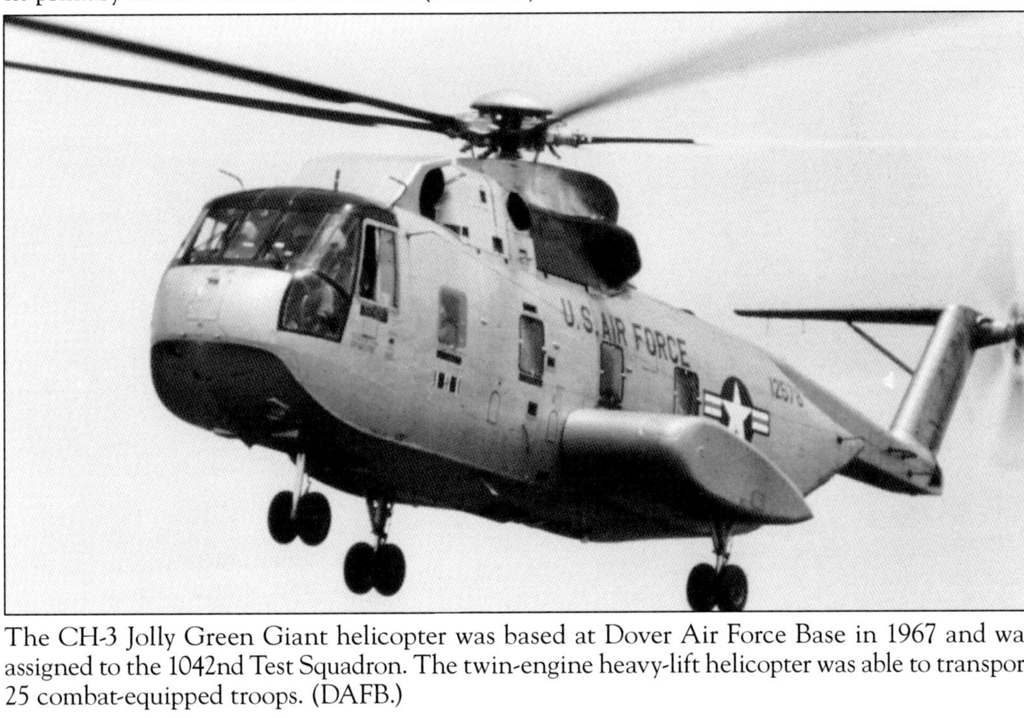

The CH-3 Jolly Green Giant helicopter was based at Dover Air Force Base in 1967 and was assigned to the 1042nd Test Squadron. The twin-engine heavy-lift helicopter was able to transport 25 combat-equipped troops. (DAFB.)

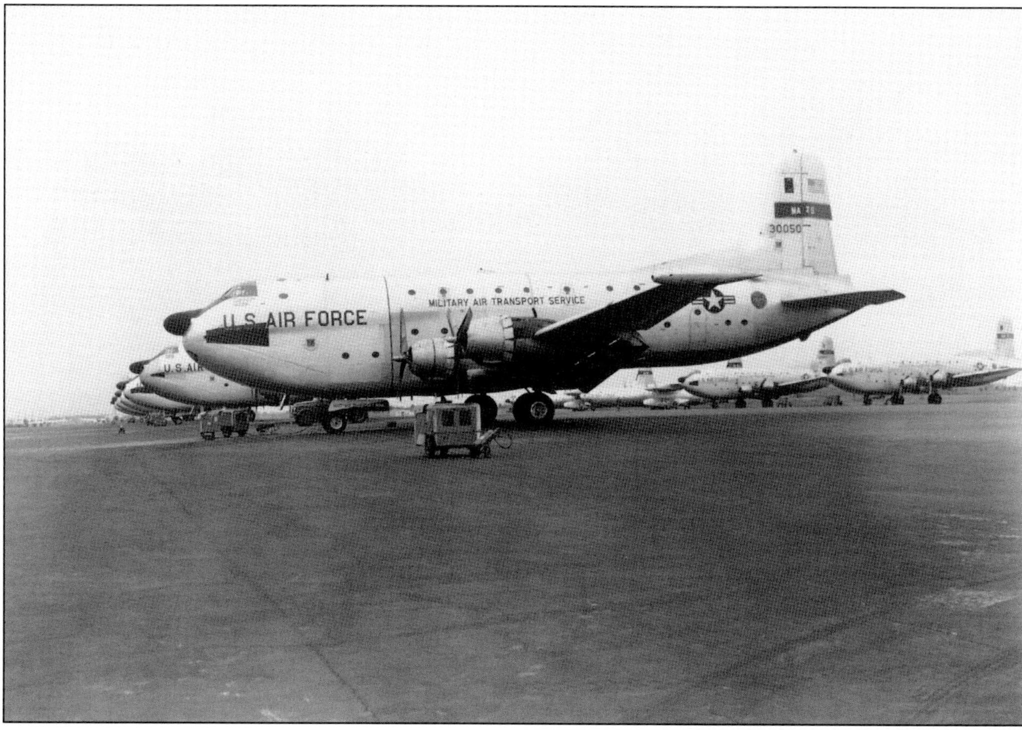

The Douglas C-124 Globemaster II was the principle mission airlifter based at Dover Air Force Base in the 1950s and early 1960s. (DAFB.)

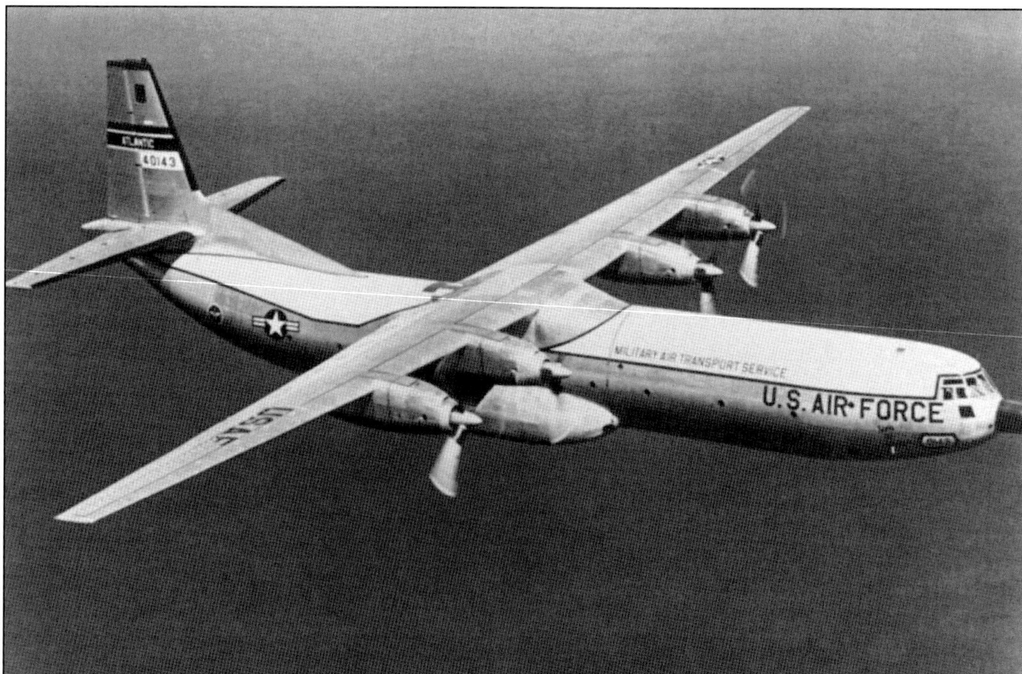

The Douglas C-133 Cargomaster was based at Dover Air Force Base. It was the largest airlifter in the world at the time, able to transport intercontinental missiles. (AMC.)

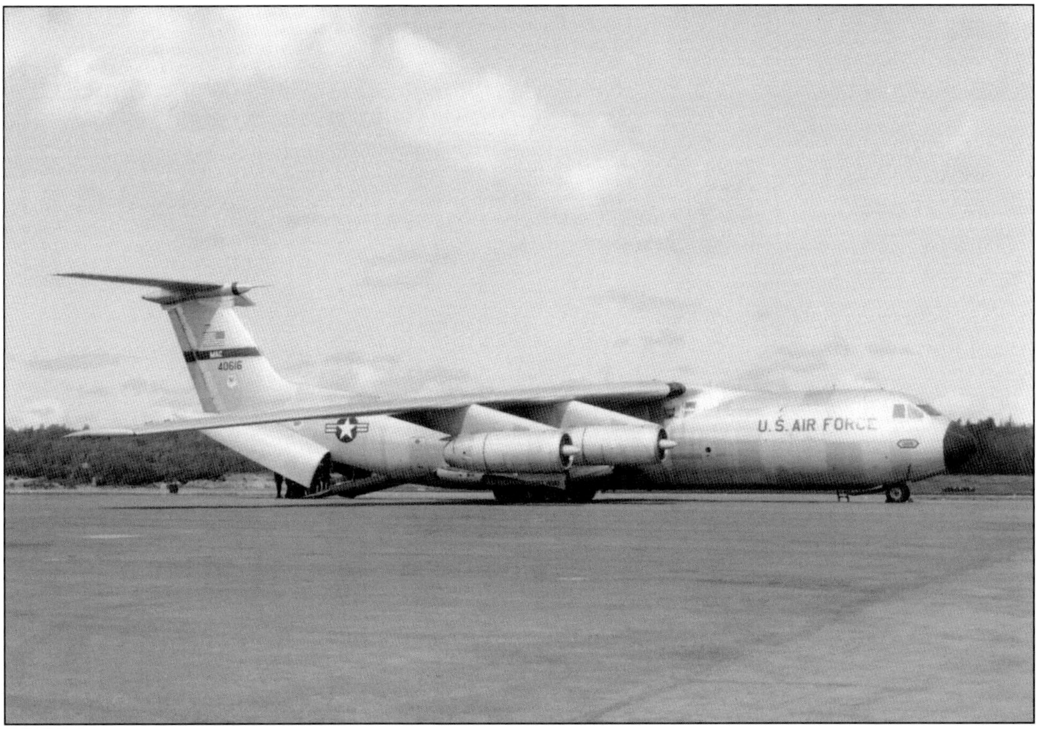

Dover Air Force Base entered the jet age with the Lockheed C-141 Starlifter, replacing the aging Globemaster IIs in 1965. (AMC.)

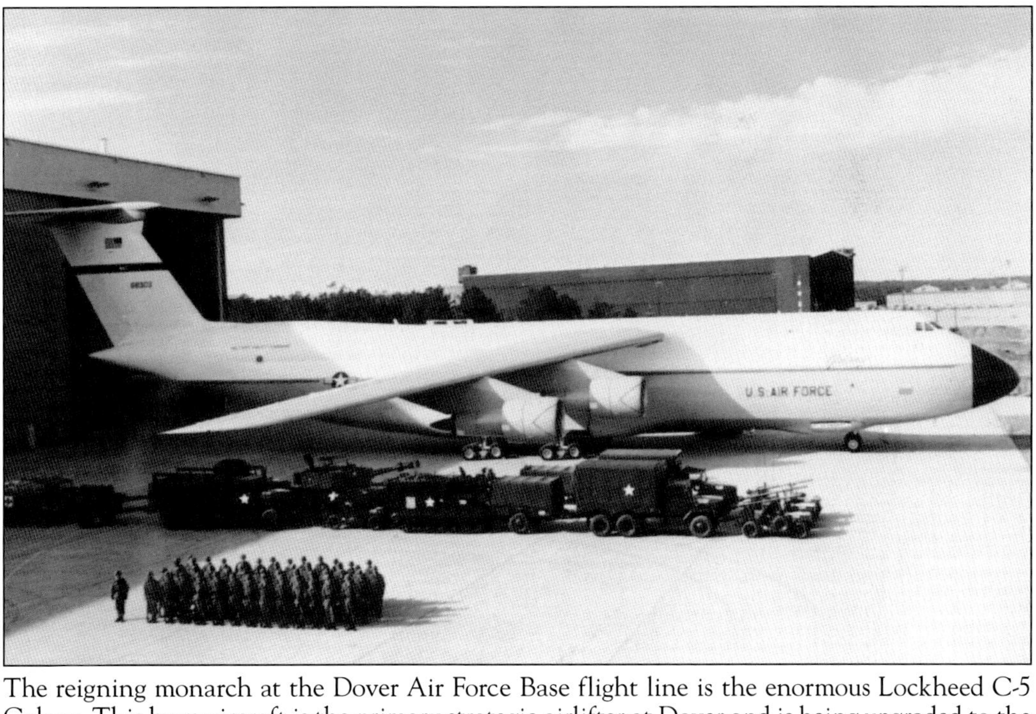

The reigning monarch at the Dover Air Force Base flight line is the enormous Lockheed C-5 Galaxy. This huge aircraft is the primary strategic airlifter at Dover and is being upgraded to the C-5M standard for the fleet. (AMC.)

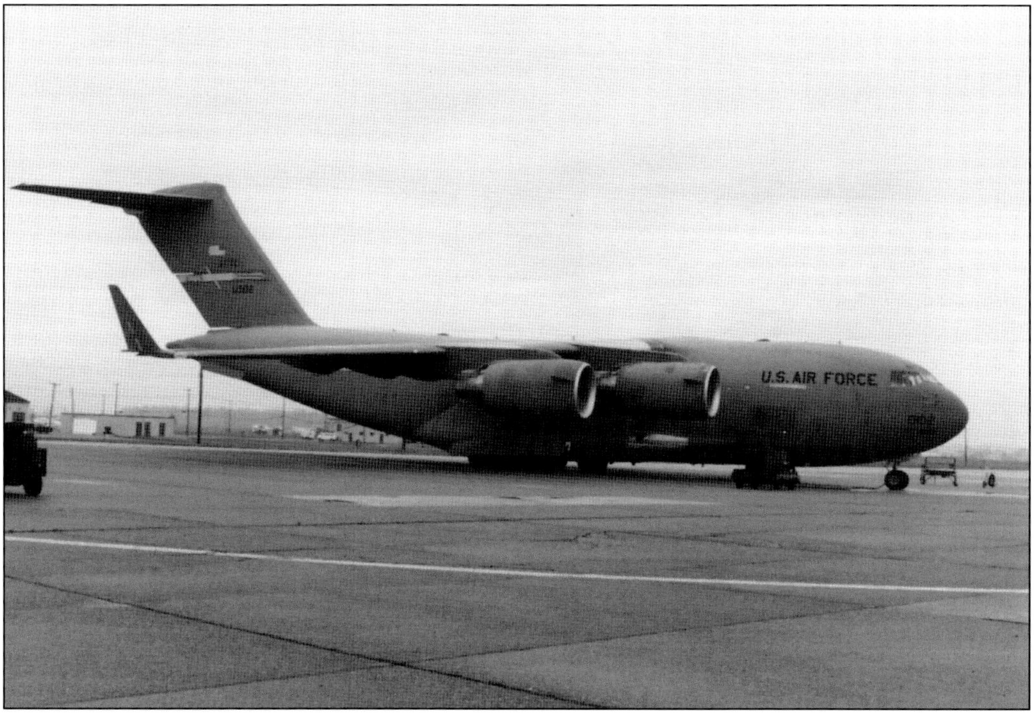

Not as large as the C-5, but more flexible and capable in other ways, the C-17 is the Air Force's newest airlifter based at Dover Air Force Base. (AMC.)

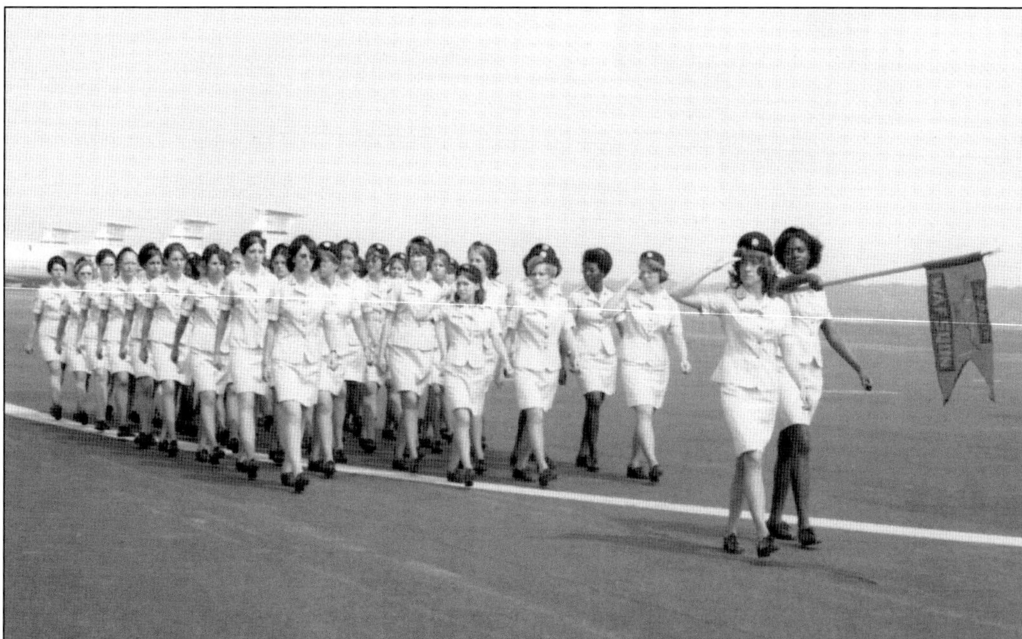

Dover Air Force Base's first Women in the Air Force (WAF) squadron was activated as part of the 436th Air Base Group on September 1, 1970. 2nd Lt. Virginia Alden was appointed officer in charge of the 436th WAF Squadron. The squadron was deactivated in 1975, and assigned personnel were integrated with almost every organization on Dover Air Force Base. (AMC.)

The wing's first female C-5 pilot, 1st Lt. Gayle I. Westbrook, became the first female pilot in the 21st Air Force to be certified as an aircraft commander. (AMC.)

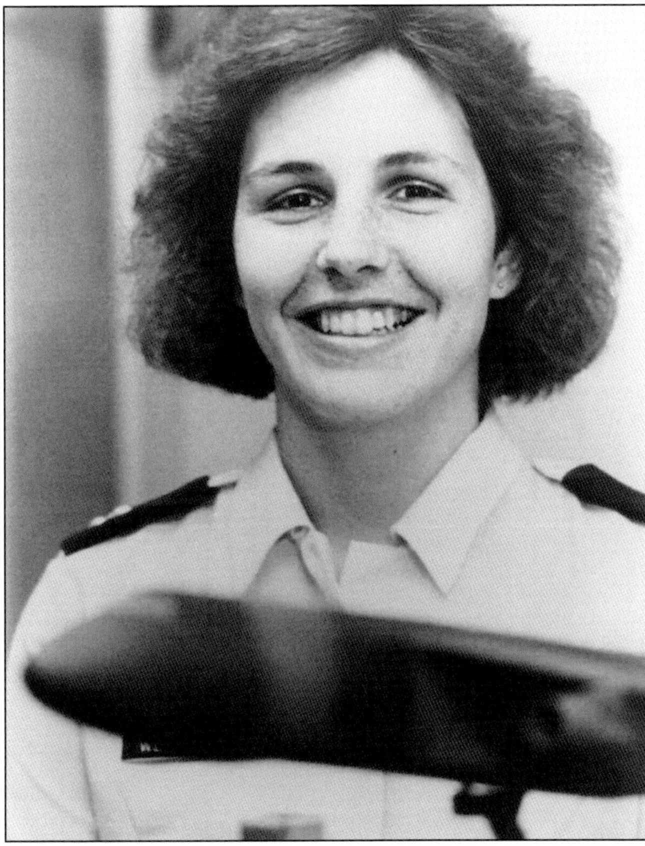

At Dover Air Force Base, this all-female C-5 crew flew a seven-day European mission as part of the US Air Force Women's history month celebration on March 28, 1988. The crew of 17 included members of the 436th Military Airlift Wing and the 512th Military Airlift Wing, plus two artists and a photographer from the Pentagon. (AMC.)

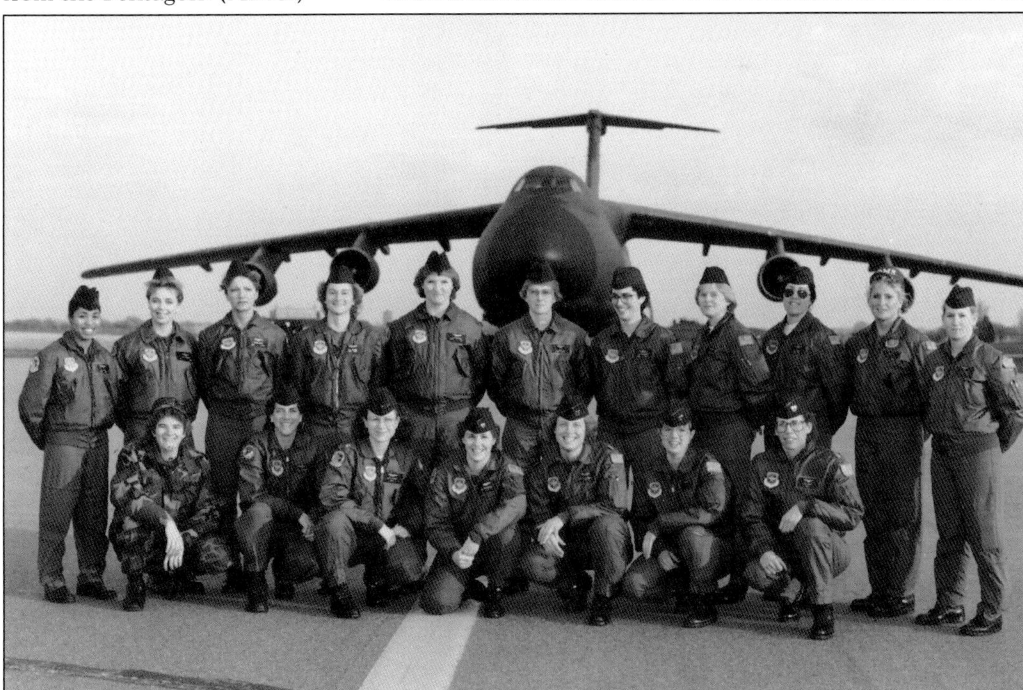

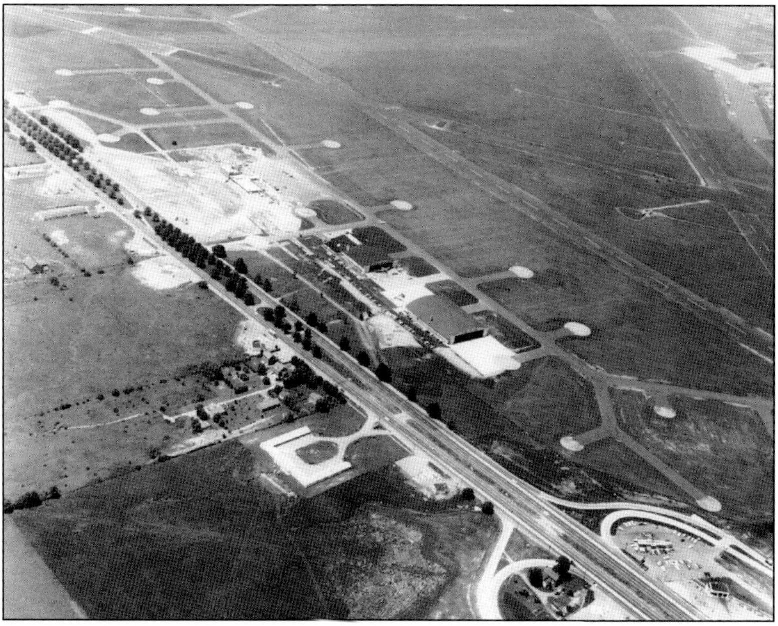

New Castle County Airport is pictured in the late 1950s. (JC.)

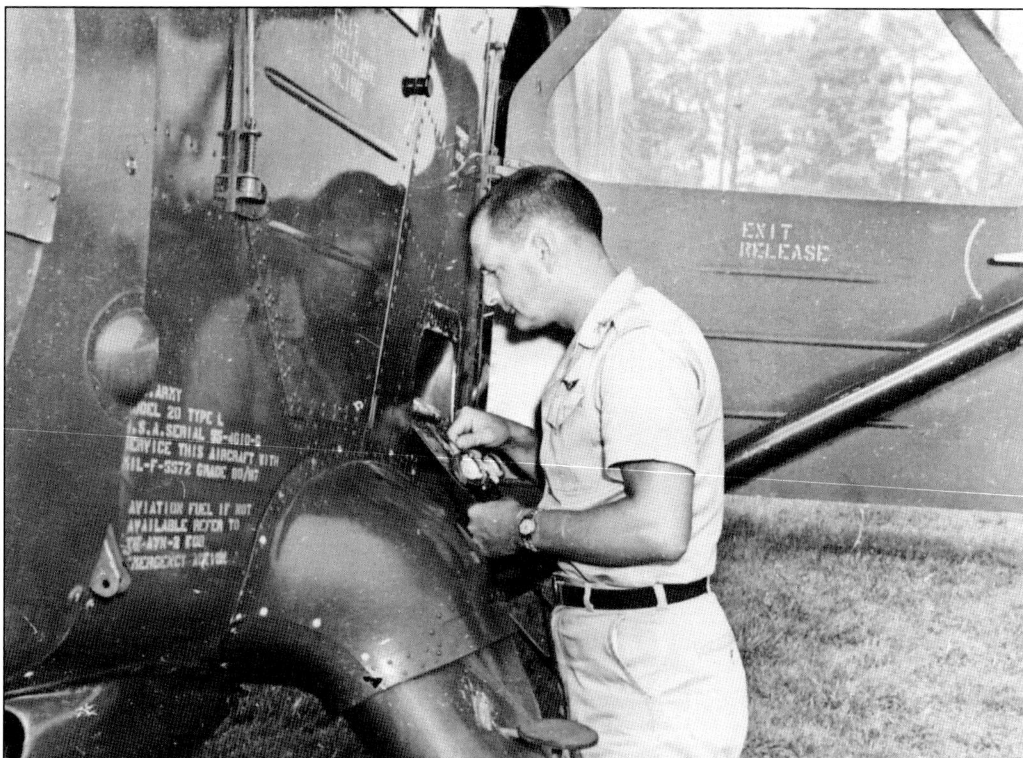

Capt. James R. Sulpizi is inspecting a U-6A Beaver in August 1960. Sulpizi was known as "the Father of Aviation" in the Delaware Army National Guard. In 1962, he received the Distinguished Flying Cross for rescuing 10 Guardsmen from heavy Atlantic seas in a gale. Sulpizi retired as a colonel in 1984 with more than 5,000 helicopter and fixed-wing hours. He was inducted into the Delaware Aviation Hall of Fame in 2000. (DMHEF.)

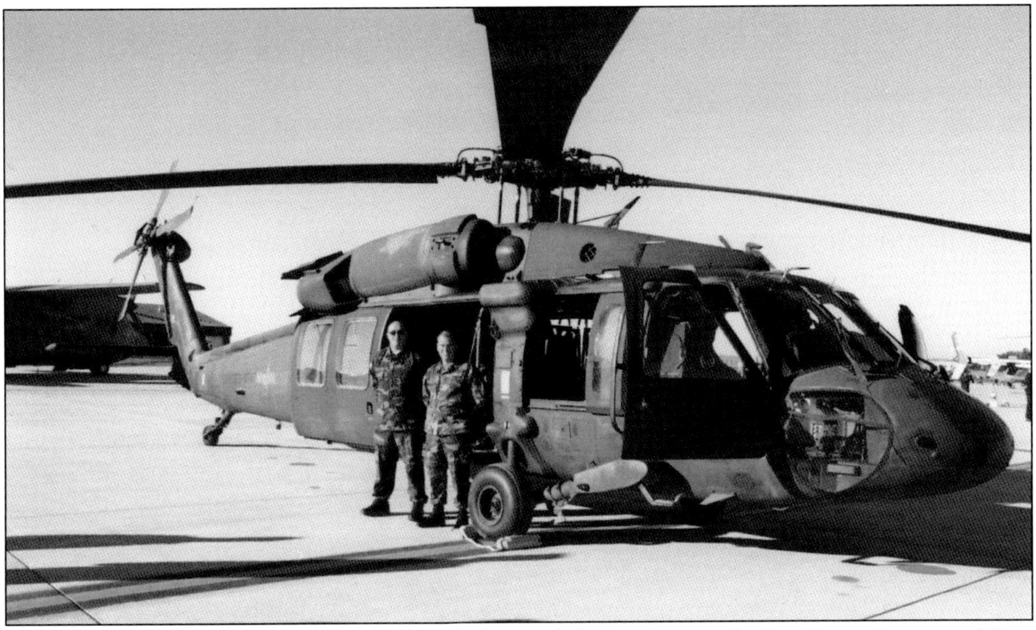

The Delaware Army National Guard's Black Hawk helicopter, with Sgt. Brett James and Sgt. Matthew Booz, put on a demonstration at an open house at the Air National Guard Base in New Castle in 2006. (JC.)

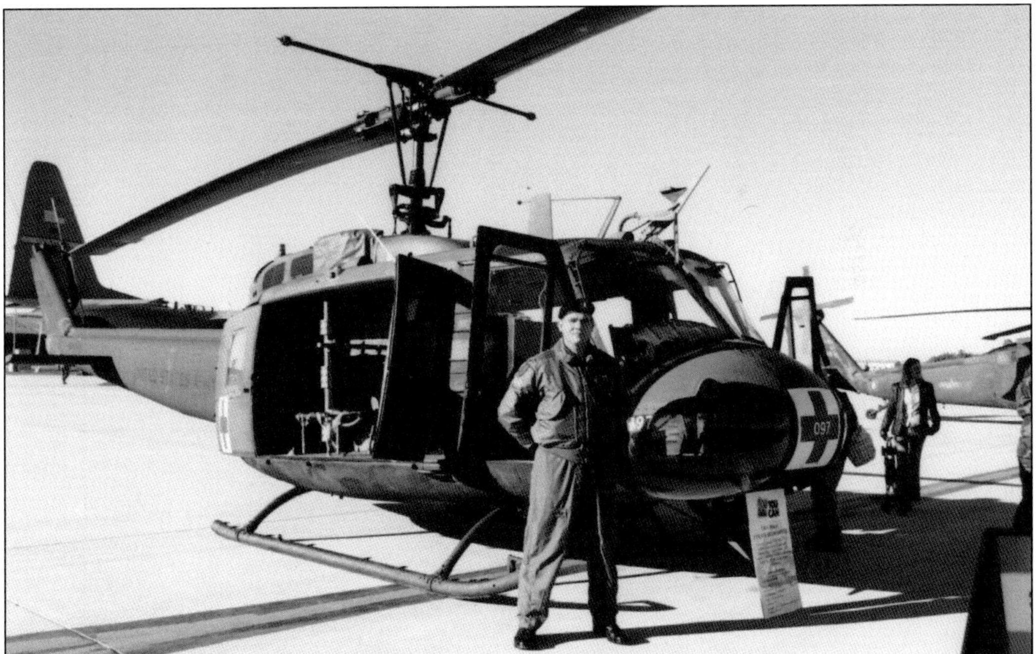

The Delaware Army National Guard's UH-1 Huey is pictured with 1st Lt. Joseph J. Maccari at the 2006 open house at the Delaware Air National Guard Base in New Castle. The Delaware Army Guard operated the popular Huey for pilot training. At the open house, Guardsmen demonstrated a hoist/extraction, lowering a man to the ground, then extracting him, and hoisting him into a hovering Huey. (JC.)

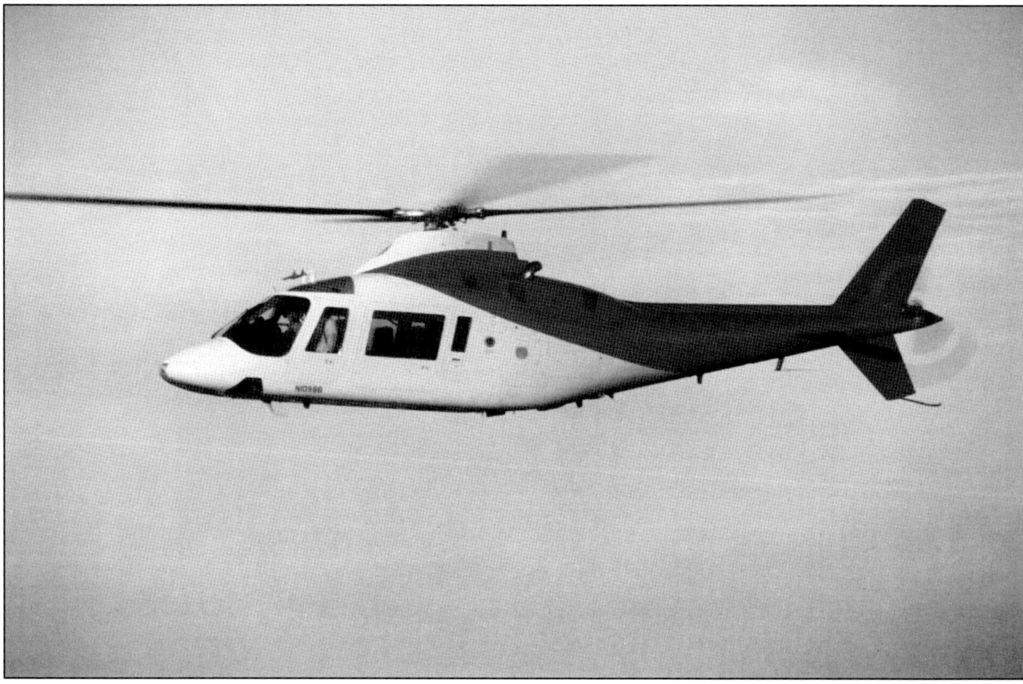

The first helicopter used by the DuPont Company was based at the Greater Wilmington Airport. Licensed N109W, it began operations on October 20, 1978. The helicopter was used for executive transport between Wilmington, Delaware; New York City; and Washington, DC. (CW.)

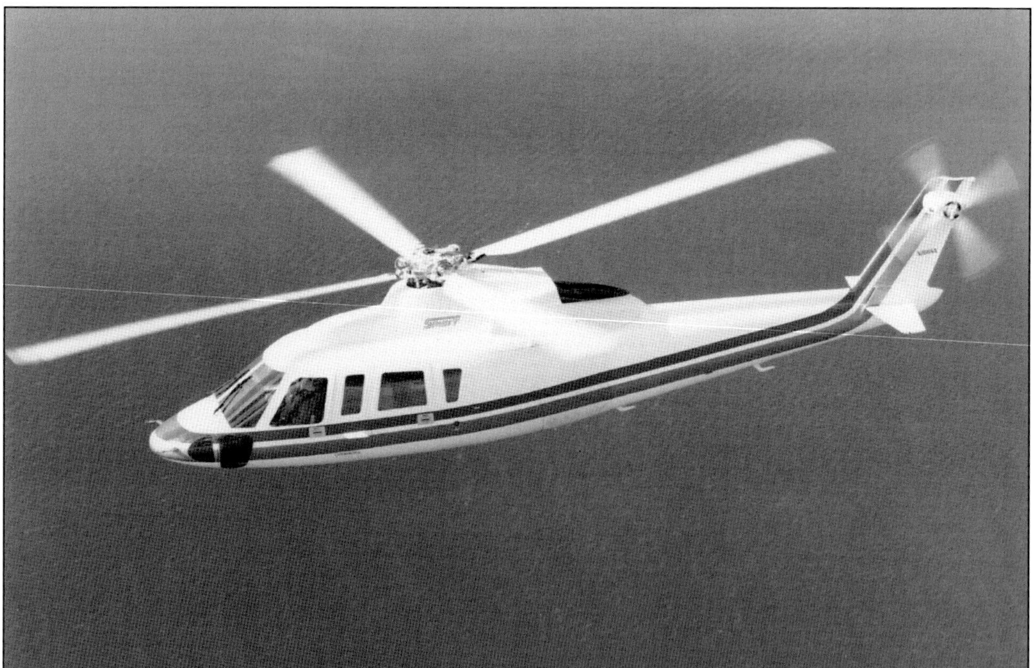

The second DuPont Company helicopter, N766SA, later changed to N1547F, began service in February 1981. This Sikorsky S-76 was also used for executive transport to close-in locations in New York City and Washington, DC. (CW.)

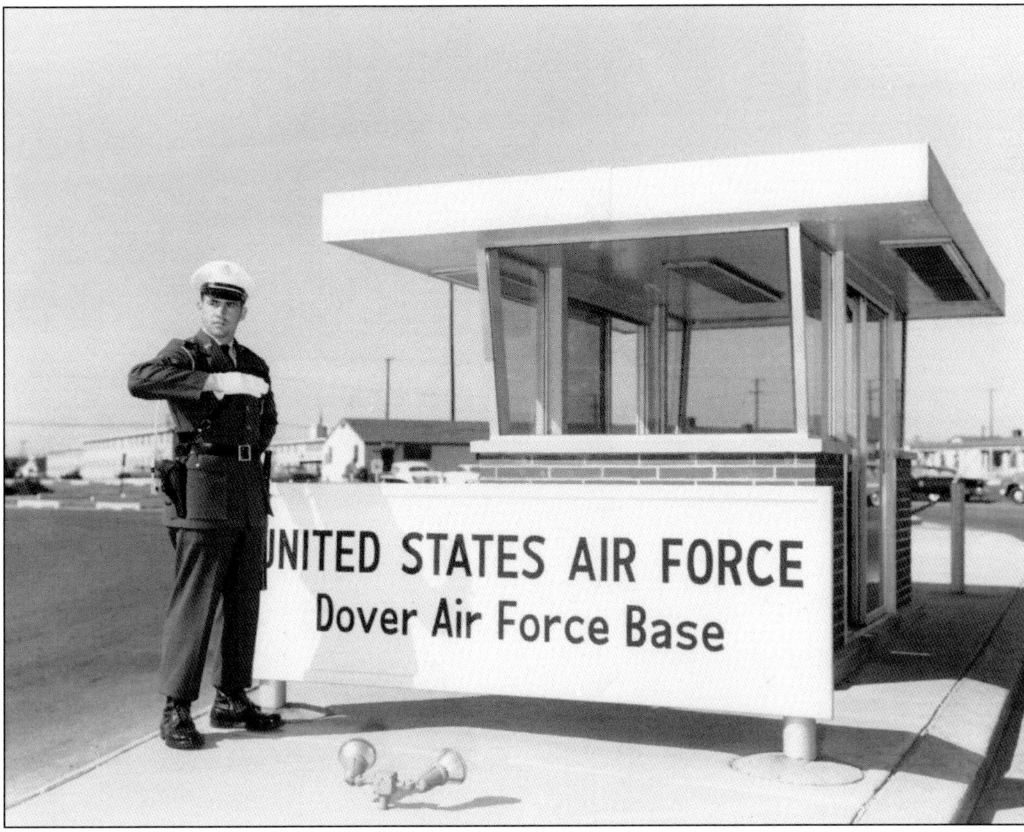

The main gate at Dover Air Force Base is depicted here in the late 1950s. Put into mothballs after World War II, Dover Air Force Base was reopened during the Korean War and flourished during the 1950s, as a new airlift mission became its primary mission. (AMC.)

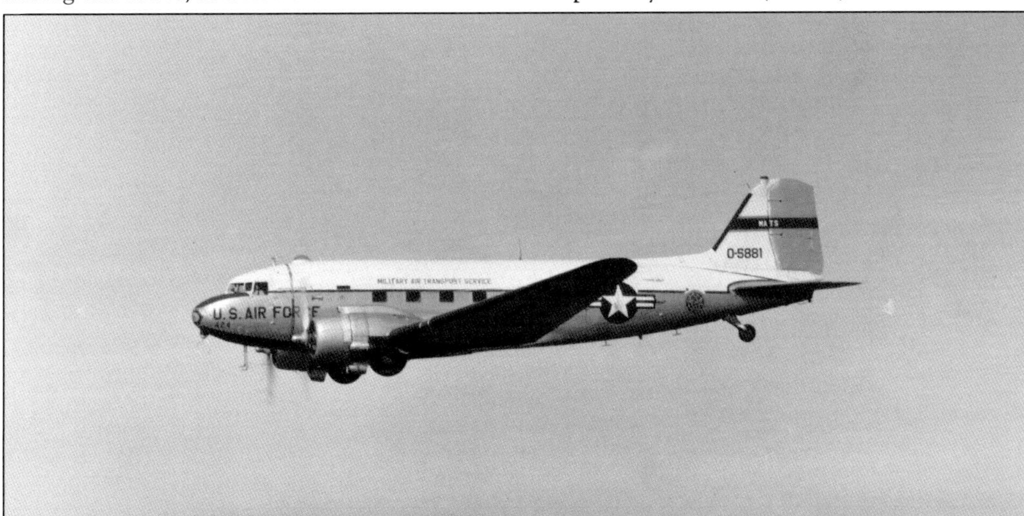

The 1607th Air Base Group used the Douglas C-47 "Gooney Bird" at Dover Air Force Base as a utility aircraft from 1949 to 1961. General Eisenhower credited the C-47, the jeep, the bulldozer, and the 2.5-ton truck "as the most vital to our success in Europe." (AMC.)

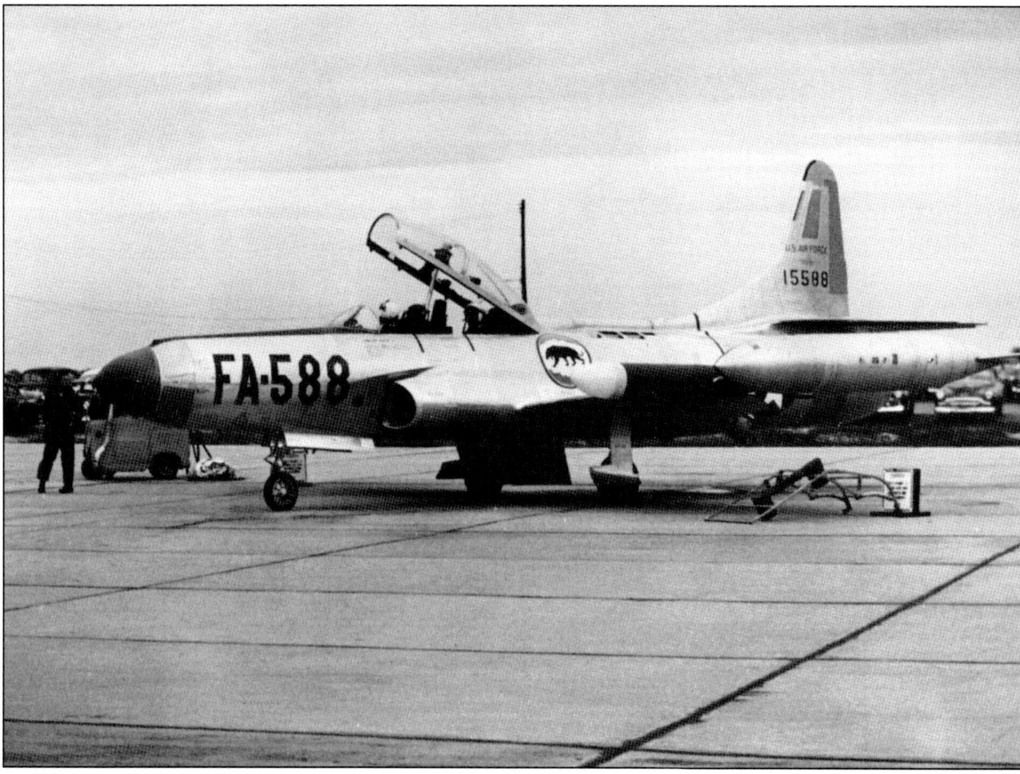

An F-94 of the 46th Fighter-Interceptor Squadron is seen at Dover Air Force Base. Note the black saber-toothed tiger emblem on the fuselage. The Lockheed F-94 Starfire was the US Air Force's first operational jet-powered, all-weather interceptor aircraft. (AMC.)

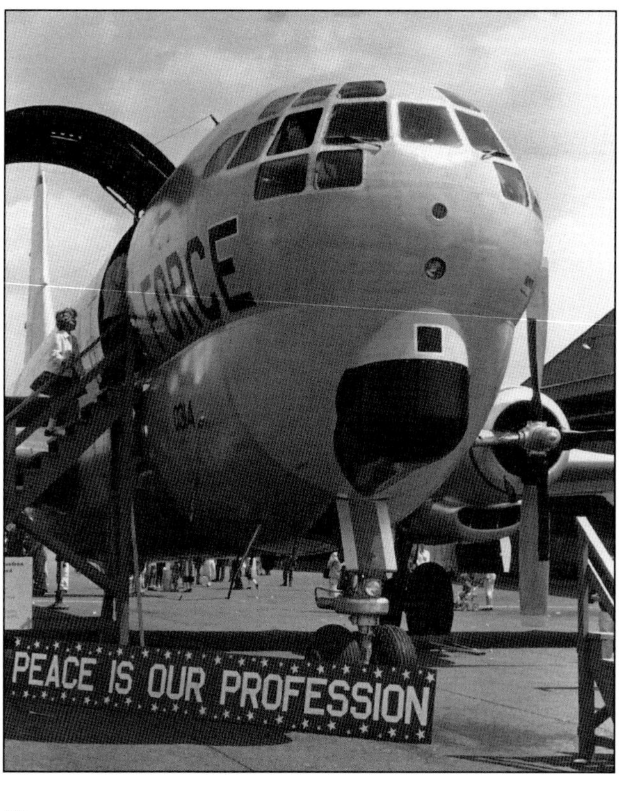

The first of 21 KC-97 Air Refueling aircraft arrived at Dover Air Force Base on May 31, 1960. Col. Gilmer E. Walker Jr. led the 11th Air Refueling Squadron; the unit consisted of approximately 630 personnel. (AMC.)

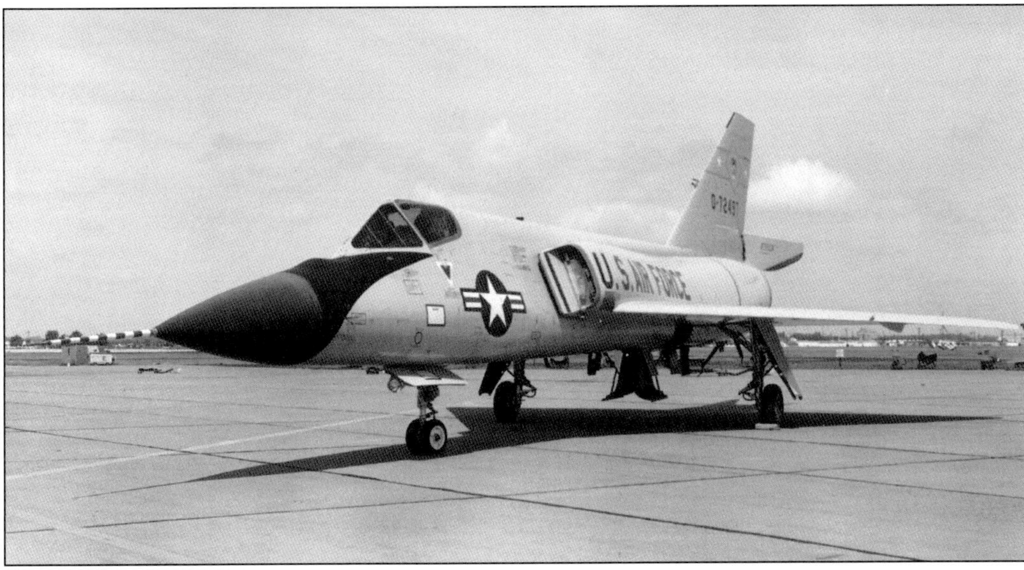

The first Convair F-106 Delta Dart arrived at Dover Air Force Base as part of the fleet of the newly assigned 95th Fighter-Interceptor Squadron, or "Boneheads." The all-weather F-106 interceptor first flew in 1956. The Delta Dart carried four Falcon missiles and a Genie nuclear rocket. (AMC.)

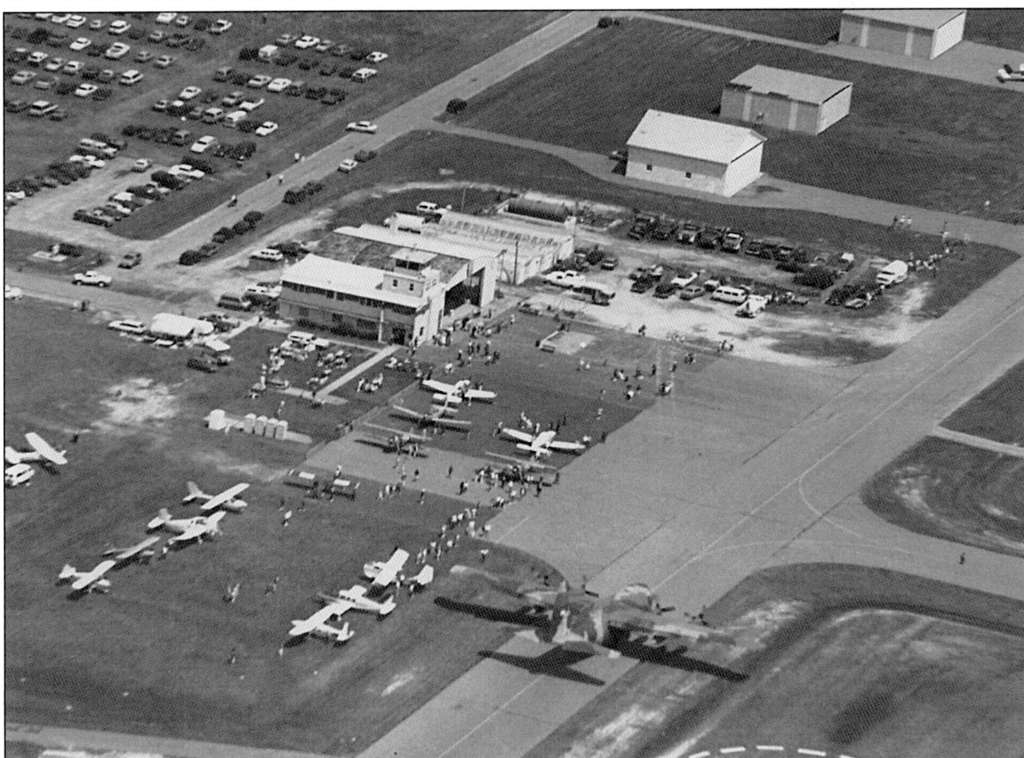

The Delmarva Aircraft FBO (Fixed Base Operation) office and maintenance hangar at the Georgetown Airport was dedicated on May 6, 1995. The dedication celebrated the resurfaced and extended runway and updated facilities for the airport whose roots went back to its World War II origins. (GF.)

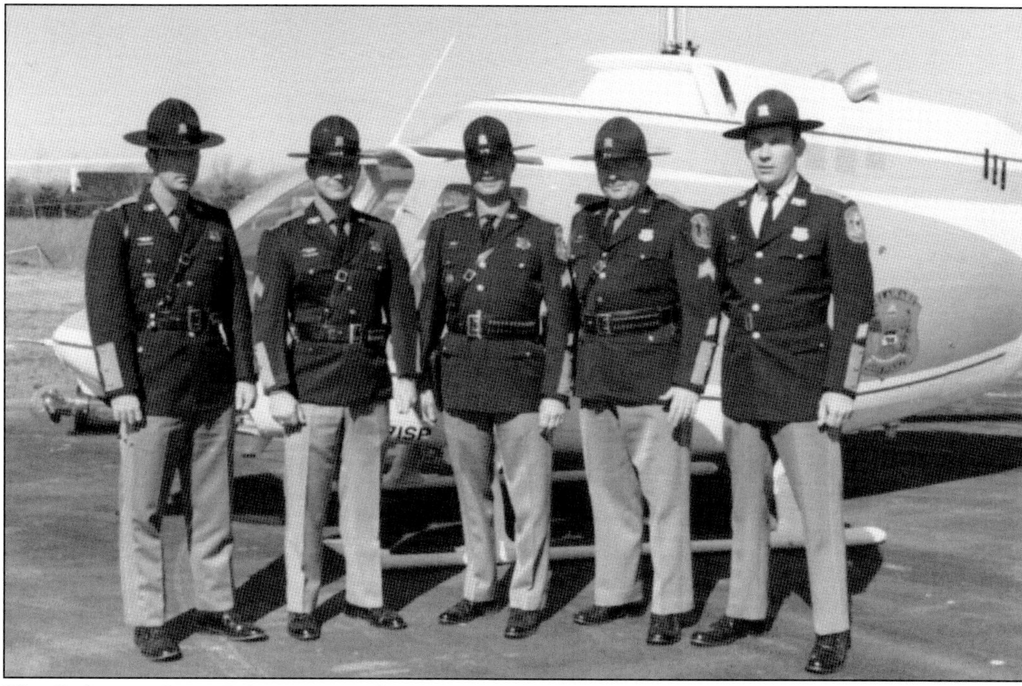

The Delaware State Police acquired an aviation unit in 1971 that would eventually include both rotary- and fixed-wing assets. The pioneer Delaware State Police aviators are posed here before their first Bell Jet Ranger. From left to right are Trooper William Boyle, Cpl. William Wiley, Cpl. Frank Clair, Sgt. Charles Nabb (officer in charge), and Sgt. William Willin. (CN.)

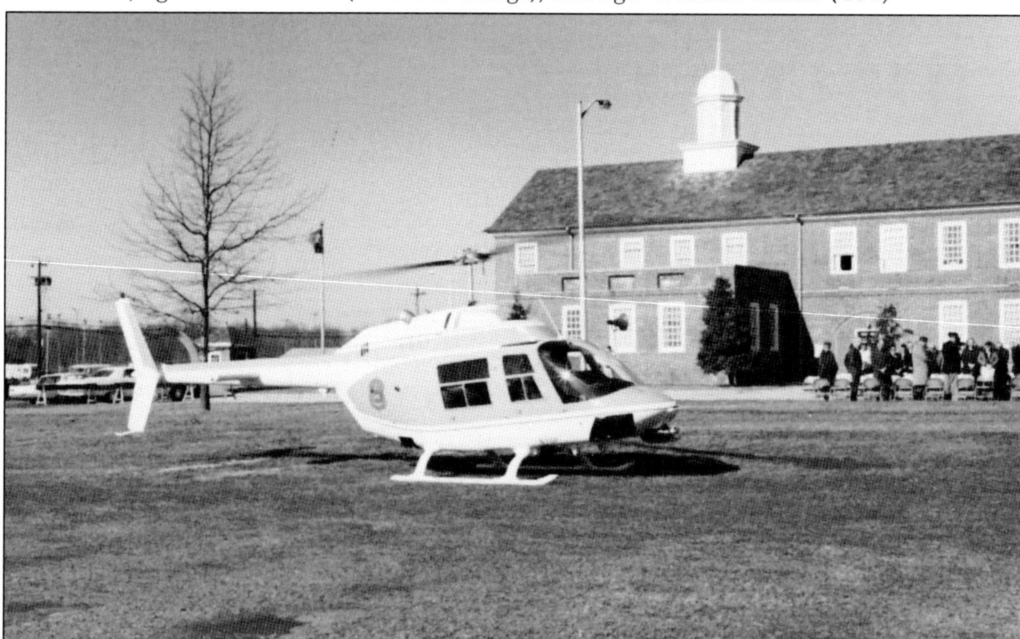

A new Bell Jet Ranger in its Delaware State Police livery is seen perched before the state police headquarters building in Dover in 1971. It carried a two-person crew, a pilot, and a trooper-medic. (CN.)

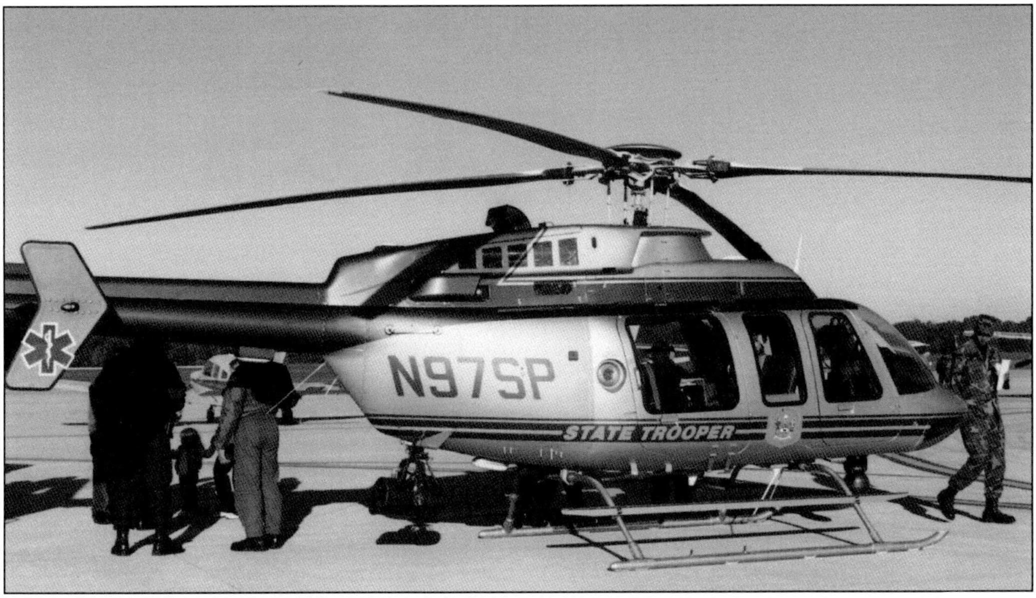

Today, the Delaware State Police Aviation Unit flies four helicopters and one fixed-wing aircraft from two locations in Georgetown and at Summit Airfield in Middletown. Annually, this section averages approximately 2,000 missions, transports approximately 300 trauma patients, and flies almost 1,500 hours. (JC.)

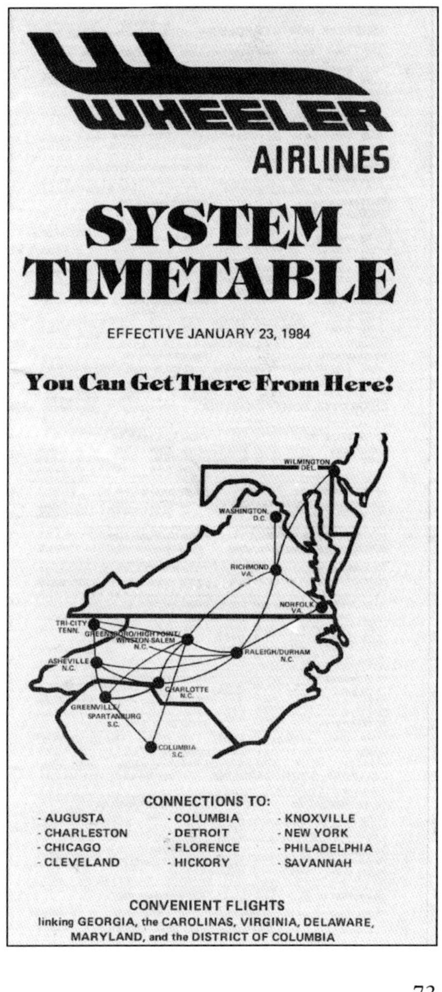

Wheeler Airlines operated in five states and had flights to the Civil Air Terminal at Dover Air Force Base, from which passengers could fly to Baltimore to make connections on other flights. This map shows Wheeler Airlines' routes in 1984. (JC.)

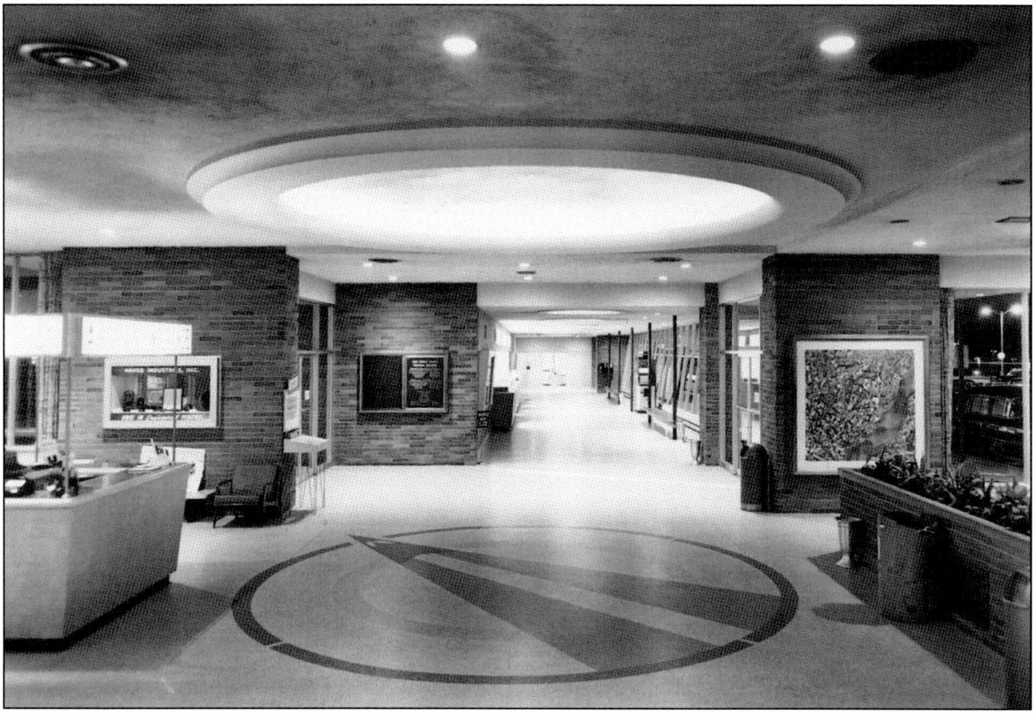

This is the interior of the new terminal building erected in 1956. A portion of the first-floor ceiling is recessed, approximately 15 feet in diameter, and painted black with small lights for stars. On the floor below the ornamental ceiling is a directional arrow pointing north. Dedication plaques note that the airport was activated for public use on November 29, 1947, and that this terminal building was dedicated August 5, 1956. (JC.)

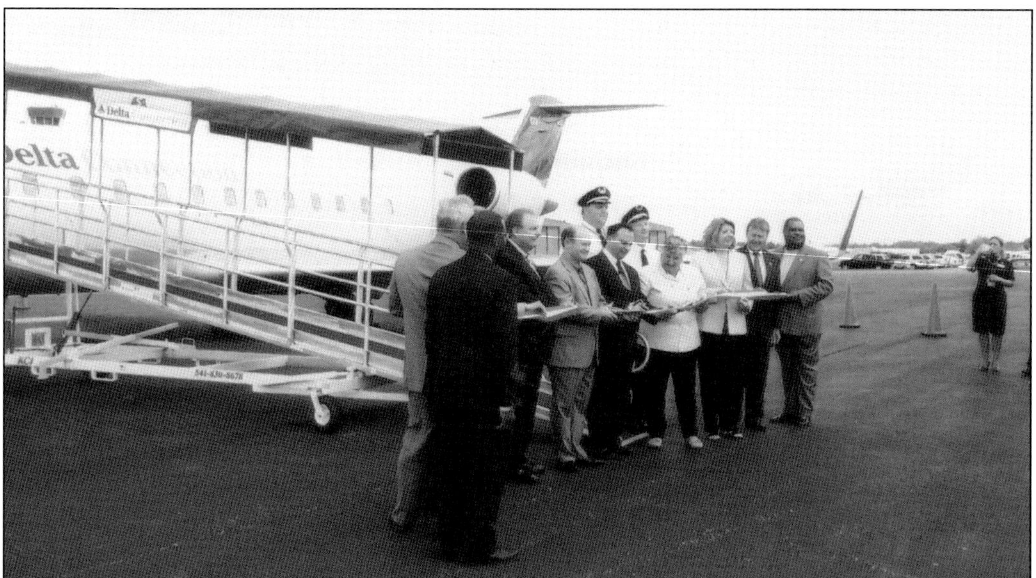

A ribbon-cutting ceremony was held June 2006 by Delaware governor Ruth Ann Minner and county executive Chris Coons for Atlantic Southeast Airlines, a Delta regional carrier. Two daily flights were flown to Hartsfield-Jackson International Airport in Atlanta, Georgia. (JC.)

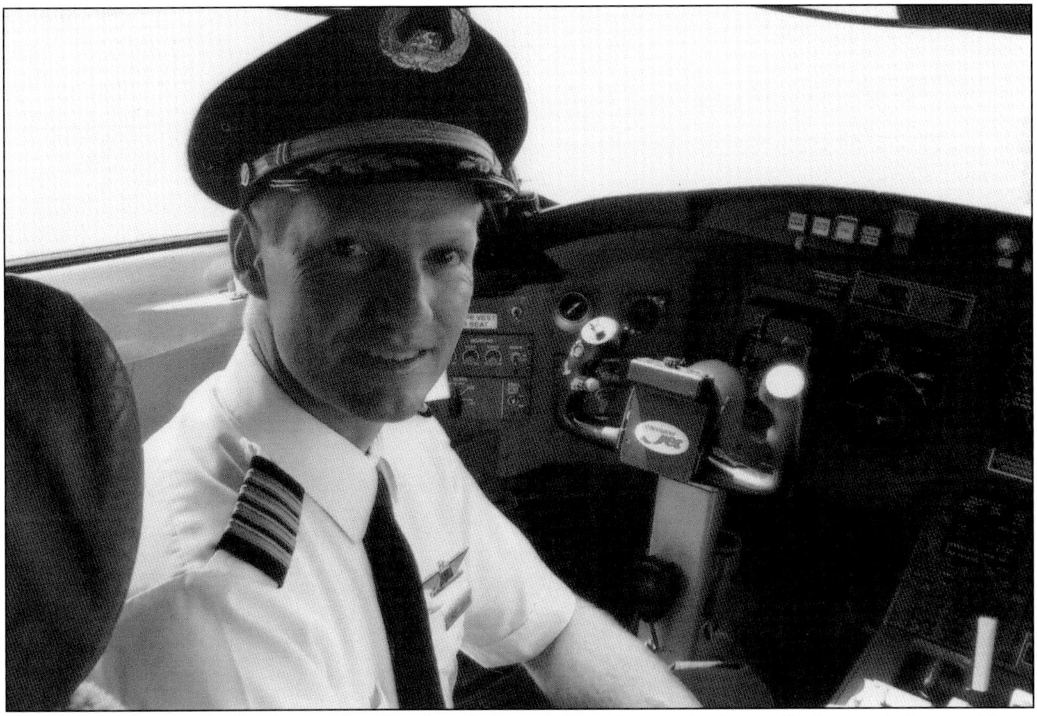

Chris Ludwick was the first pilot for the Atlantic Southeast Airlines flight to Atlanta. He is shown here in a 40-passenger Bombardier CRJ200 jet preparing for the airline's first flight from Wilmington. (JC.)

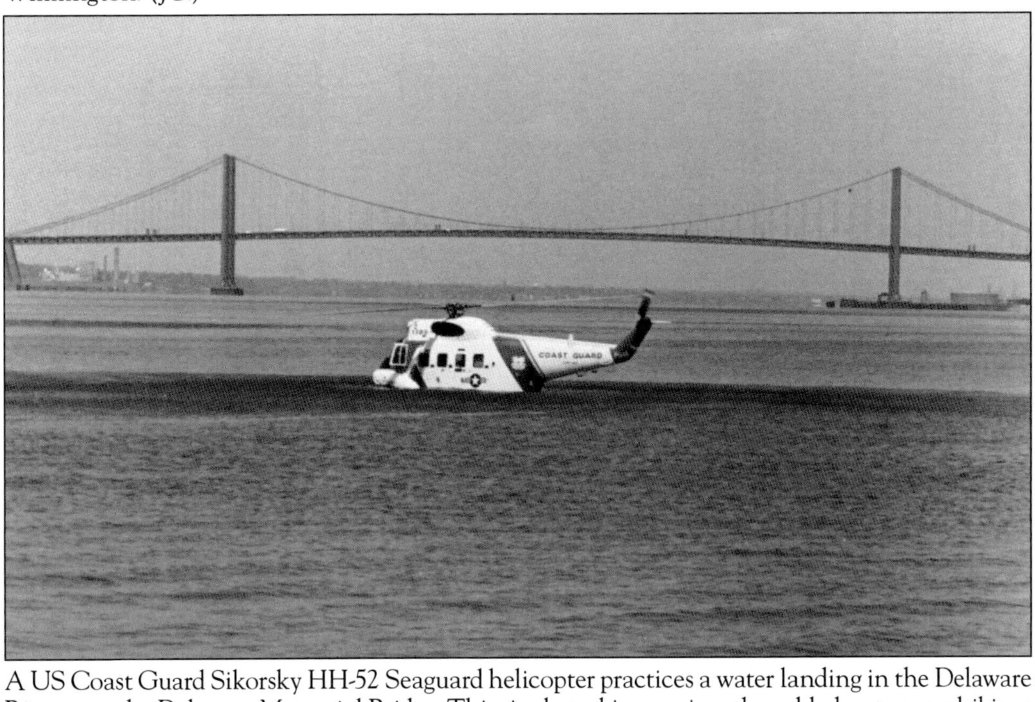

A US Coast Guard Sikorsky HH-52 Seaguard helicopter practices a water landing in the Delaware River near the Delaware Memorial Bridge. This single-turbine engine, three-blade rotor amphibious helicopter was used primarily for air-sea rescue. (DMHEF.)

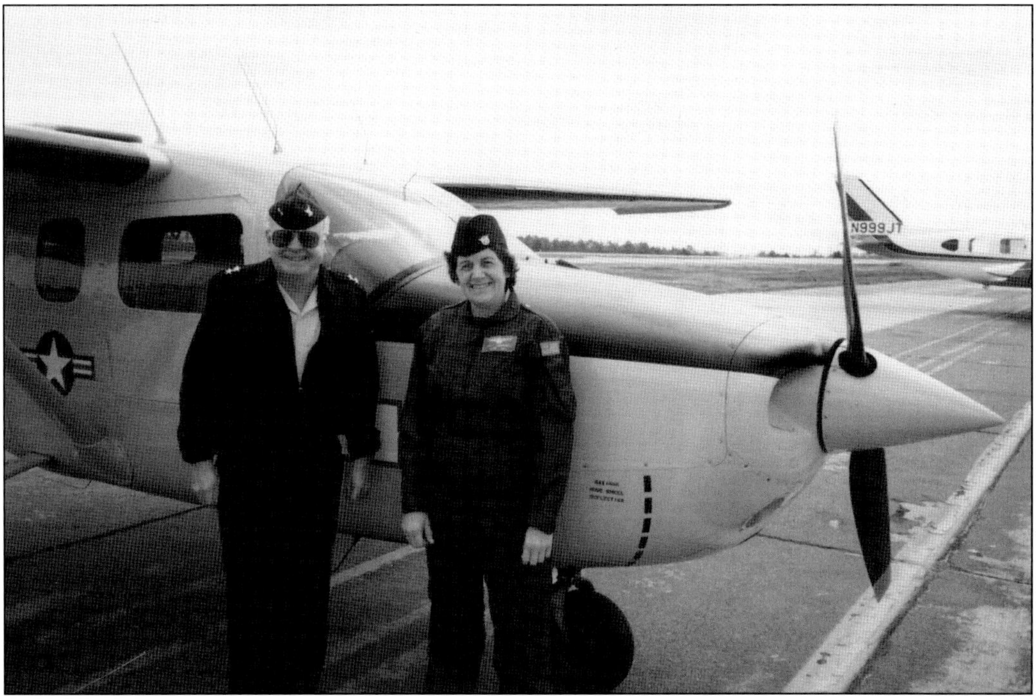

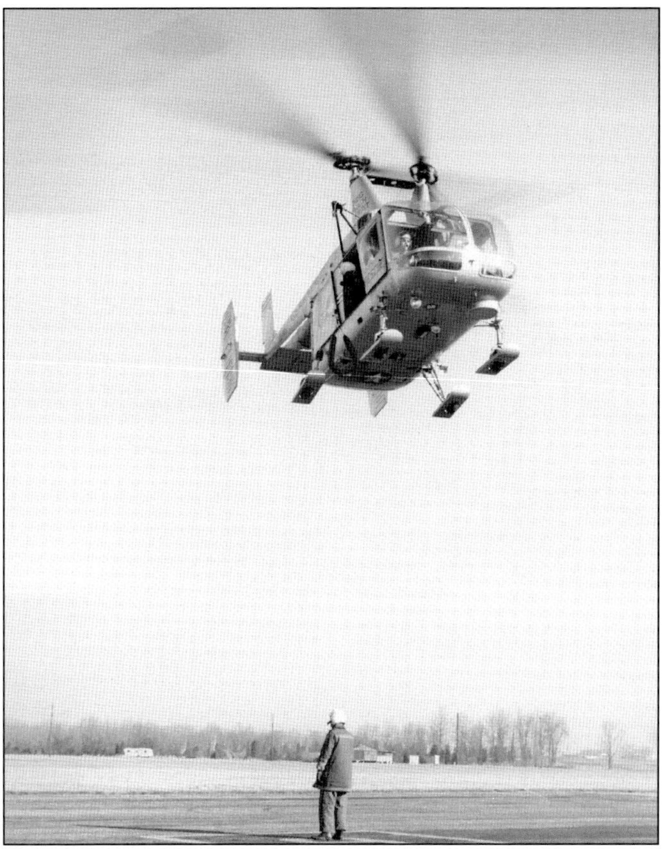

Adm. Ted Leland, US Coast Guard, is seen with US Coast Guard Auxiliary aircraft commander and pilot Jan Churchill after a flight in Churchill's O-2 from New Castle County Airport to Wallops Island, Virginia, which is a licensed US Coast Guard facility. (JC.)

A single HH-43 Huskie was assigned to Dover Air Force Base from 1959 to 1962. The Huskie was used primarily for crash rescue and aircraft firefighting. The Huskie not only set high-altitude records, but it held the best safety record of any US military aircraft. (DAFB.)

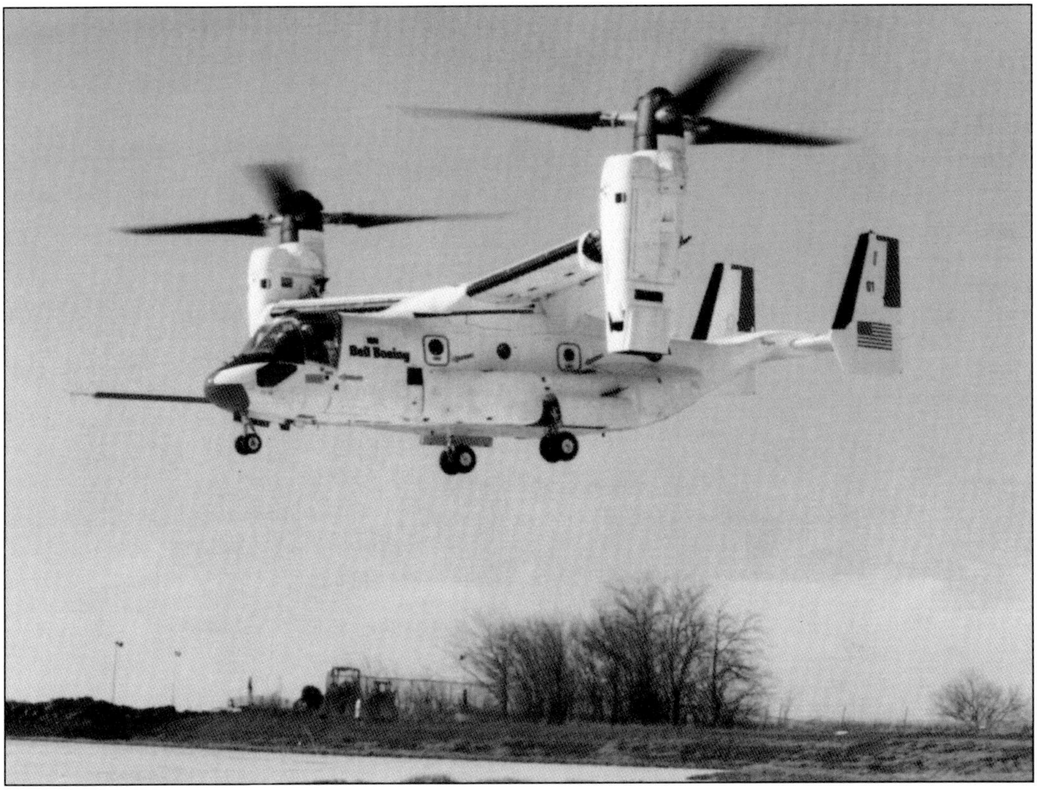

Boeing Vertol began an operation at New Castle County Airport on July 1, 1974, as a modern test facility near its main location in Ridley Park, Pennsylvania. The Bell-Boeing Osprey tilt-rotor aircraft, pictured here, flew many of its early test flights at New Castle County Airport. (JC.)

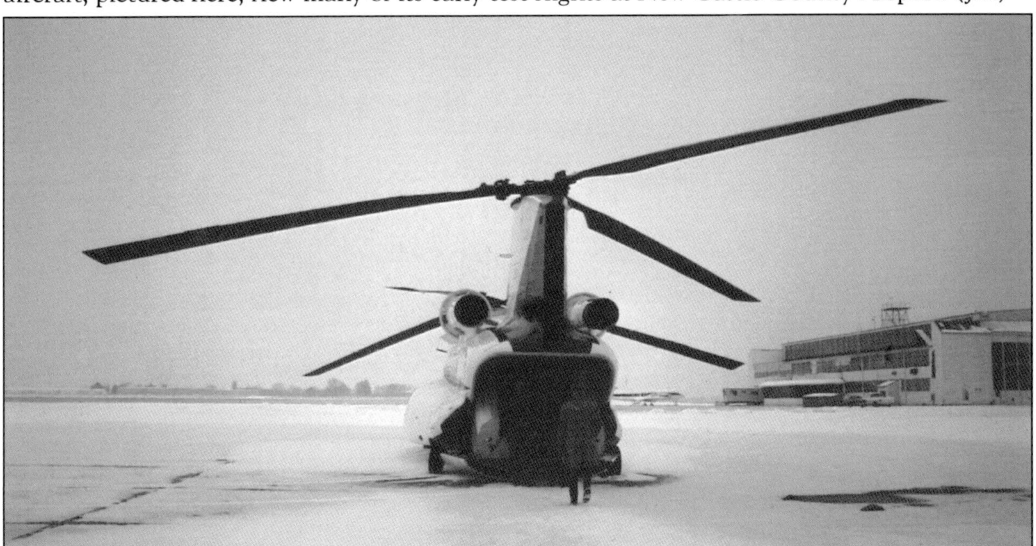

This image shows a 44-passenger Boeing 234 giant helicopter preparing for departure from New Castle County Airport for a flight to Lakefront Airport, New Orleans, Louisiana, on January 11, 1985, in a snowstorm. The takeoff gross weight was 42,500 pounds in this civilian version of the CH-47 Chinook. The pilots were Richard Balzer and Frank Duke. (JC.)

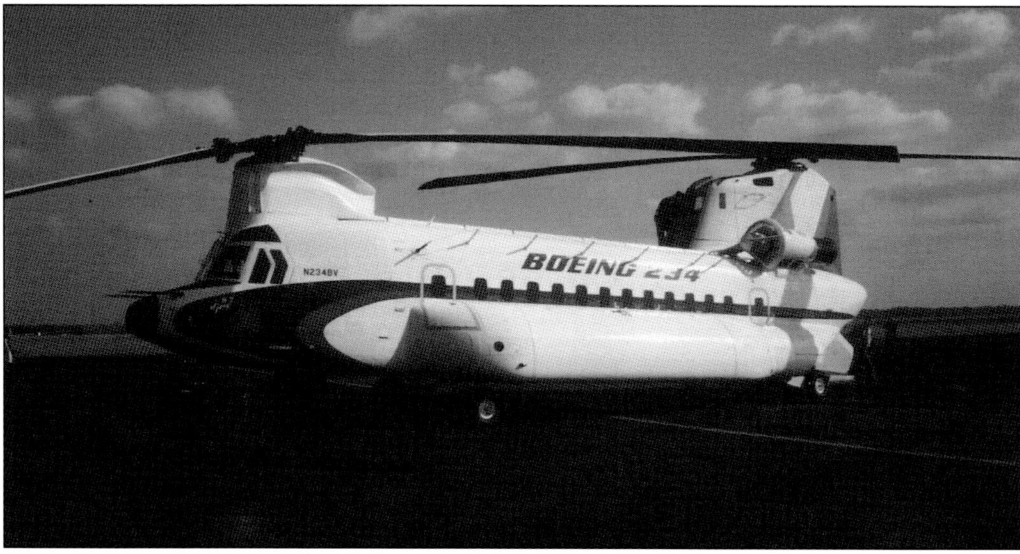

Accompanying the press on this flight were Frank Jensen, president of the International Helicopter Convention; retired general Alfred Wolf, noted aviation lawyer; and his wife, Leda. One fuel stop was made in Augusta, Georgia. (JC.)

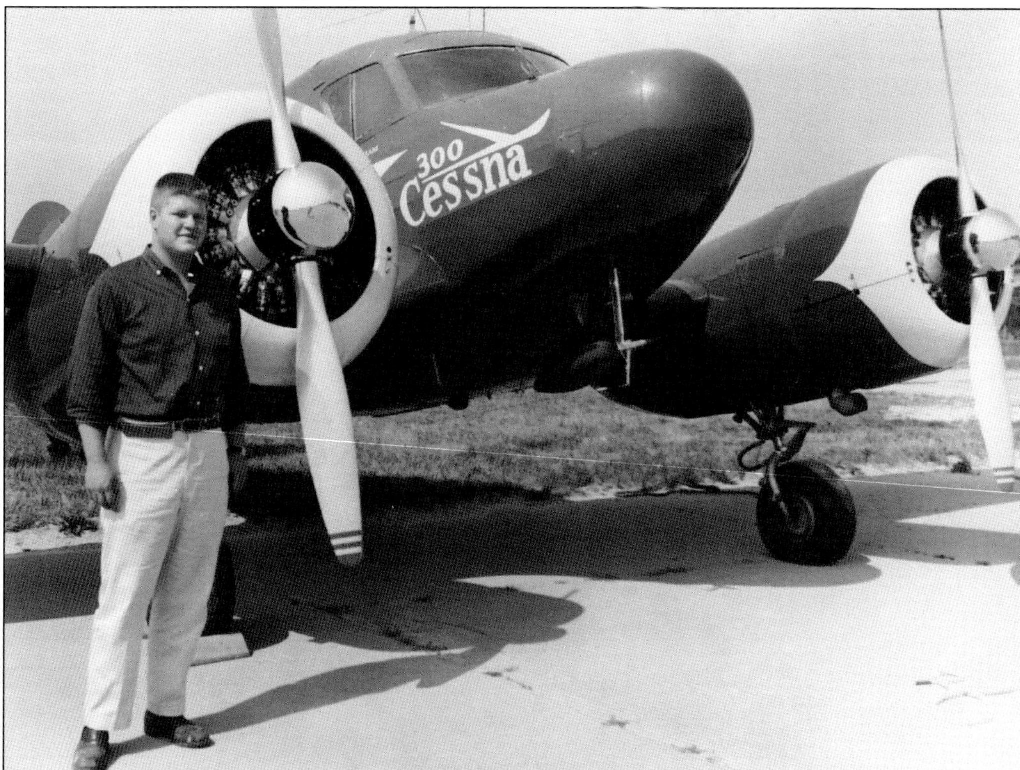

A youthful Richard C. "Kip" duPont Jr. poses before a Cessna 300. He was the son of Richard C. duPont. Kip soloed at age 16 in 1953. He served in the Delaware Air National Guard and flew for Mohawk Airlines. His first venture was operating Rehoboth Airport for a brief time with his wife, Caroline. (CduP.)

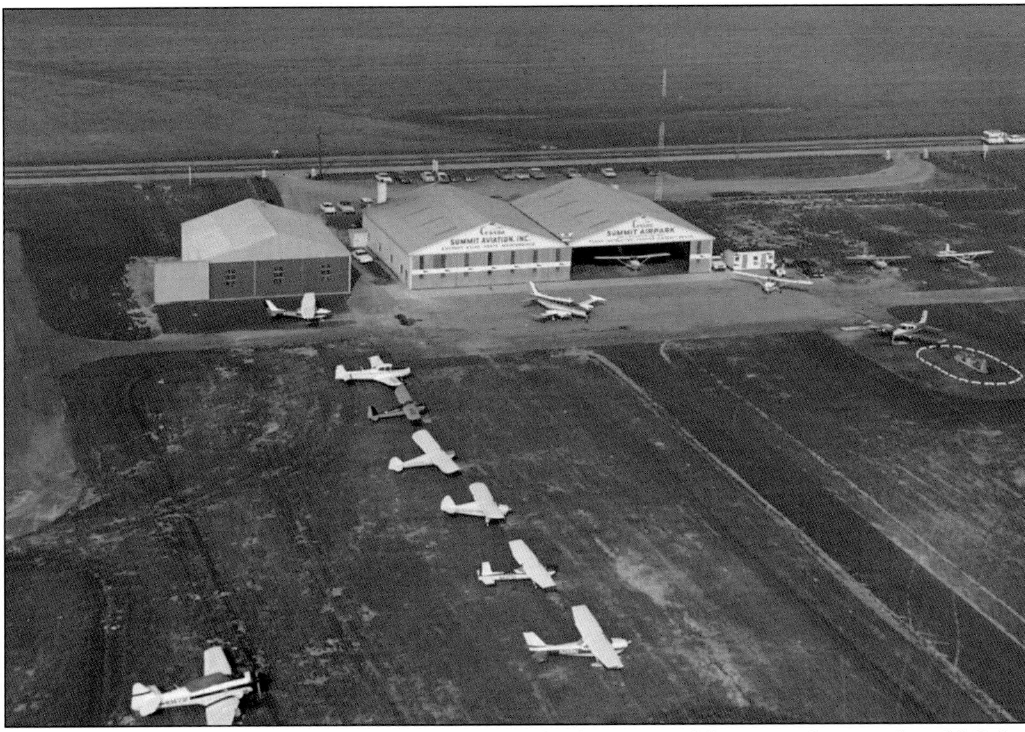

Richard C. duPont Jr. founded Summit Aviation by leasing and later purchasing the old Baker Field north of Middletown in 1960 and developing it into a fixed-base operation. The original facility was located at New Castle County Airport, known as Manor Aviation, flying charters in a twin-engine Beechcraft 18. In 1960, the organization moved to Middletown as Summit Aviation. In addition to flight instruction, aircraft maintenance, and charter flights, Summit offered Cessna and Enstrom helicopters and was one of the first Learjet dealerships. (CduP.)

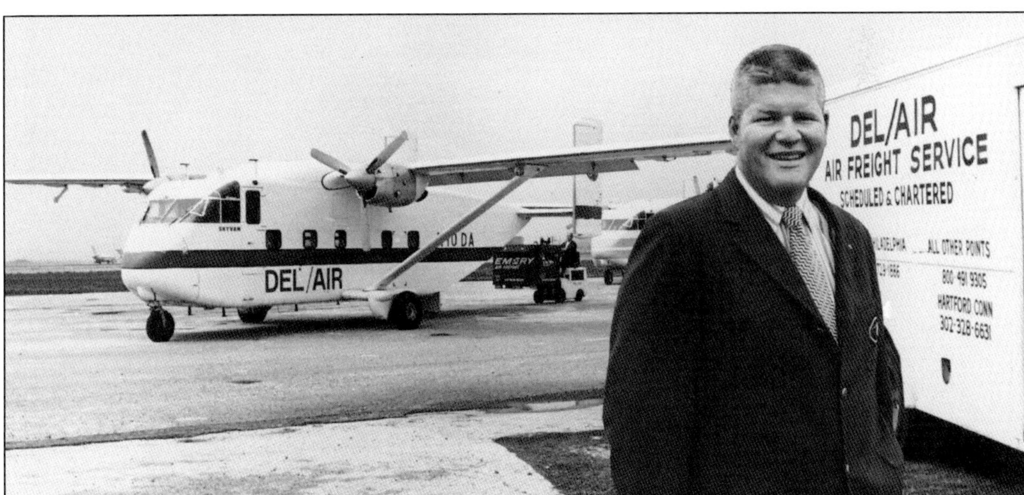

Summit Aviation operated a charter freight airline called DelAir, later renamed Summit Airlines. The fleet included the Short Skyvan, depicted here with Kip duPont, as well as a turboprop Convair 240. Summit Airlines flew passengers from the Greater Wilmington Airport in its Convair 240. The company moved to the Philadelphia International Airport in 1972. (CduP.)

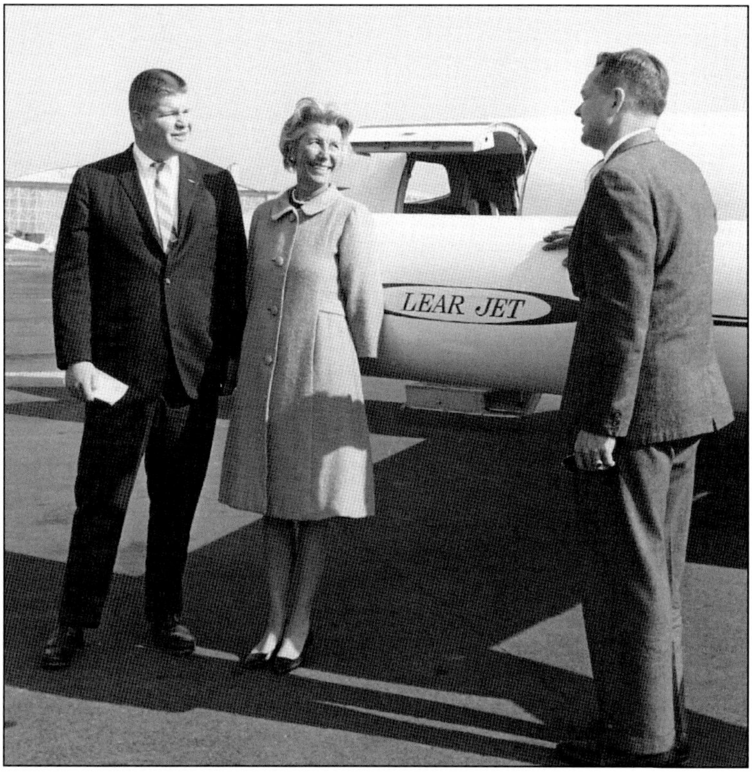

Pictured are Richard C. Kip duPont and his mother, Helena Allaire duPont, listening to a salesman after a demo ride in a Learjet on November 4, 1964. When Richard duPont obtained a Learjet dealership, he built Hangar No. 6 and called his operation Summit North at the Greater Wilmington Airport. After two years, the Learjet dealership was transferred to Atlantic Aviation at the same airport. (CduP.)

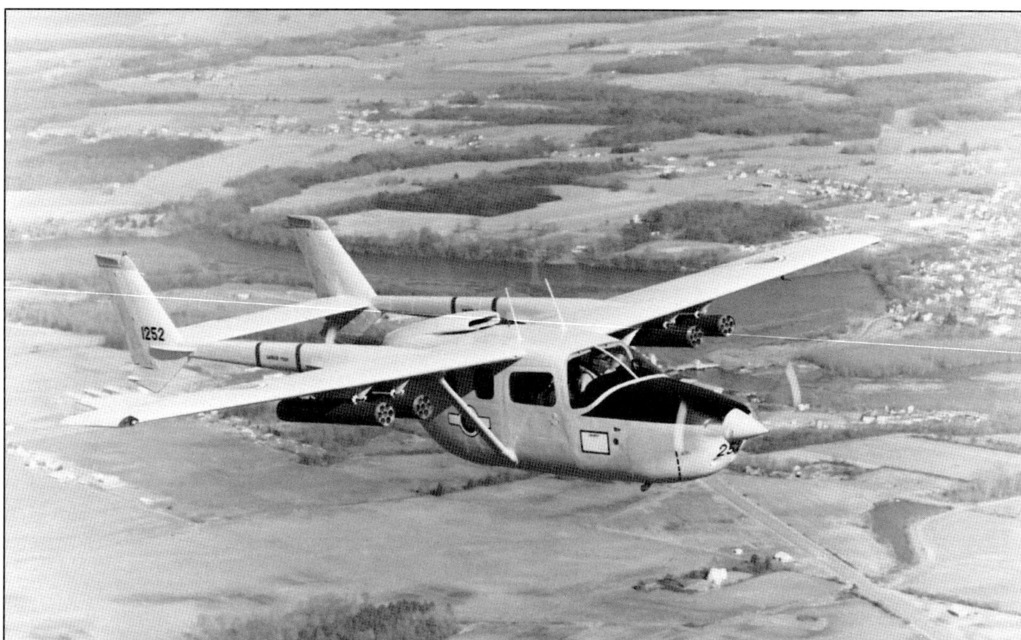

Summit Aviation won a contract to modify Cessna O-2s and began an export program to train and equip Central American air forces with this airplane, dubbed the "Sentry." Some of the noncombat O-2s were transferred to Nicaragua in 1984. Six of these modified airplanes, the Summit Sentry aircraft, were sold to the Royal Thai Navy in 1980. (CduP.)

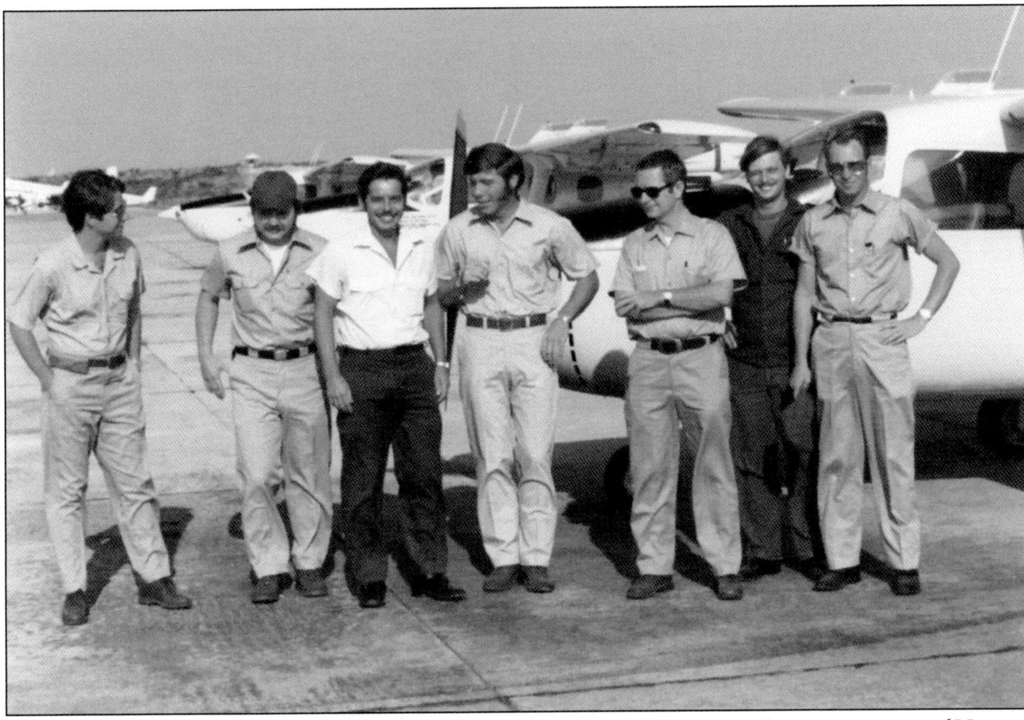

Pictured in front of several Cessna O-2 Summit Sentry twin-engine airplanes is a group of Haitian pilots, with Summit Aviation flight instructor Steven Wojdylak at center. The Haitian pilots were trained in flight skills, from basic flying to gunnery, in 1976 and 1977. (CduP.)

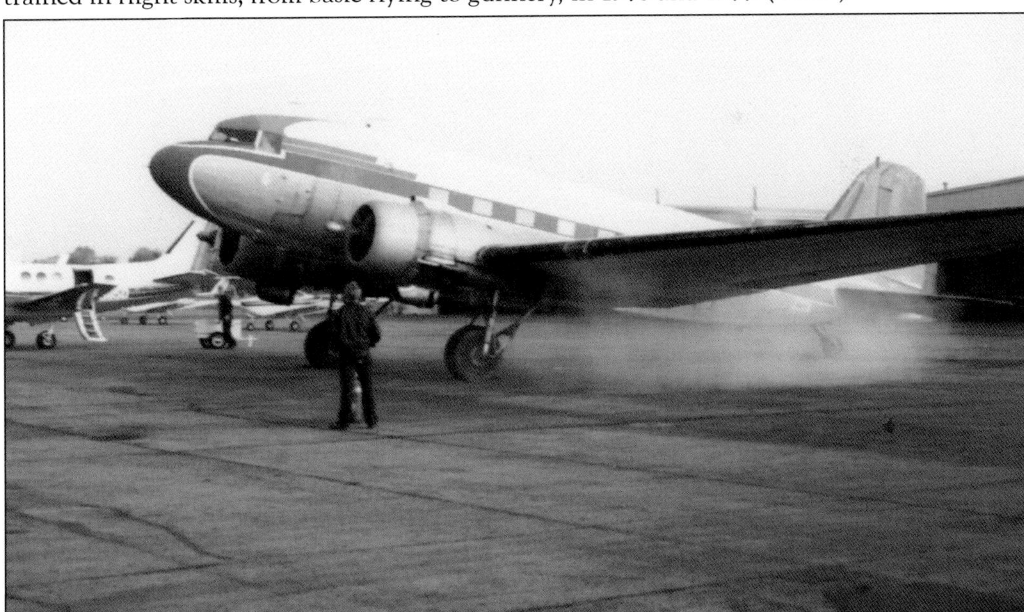

Kip duPont maintained a stable of personal aircraft, including this Douglas DC-3, which he used as a VIP aircraft. Destinations for the N711 Yankee included the Turks and Caicos Islands, Cap Haitien, the Bahamas, Disney World, and the National Soaring Museum in New York. After DuPont owned N711Y, it was destroyed in a fire in DeKalb, Texas, in 1986. (CduP.)

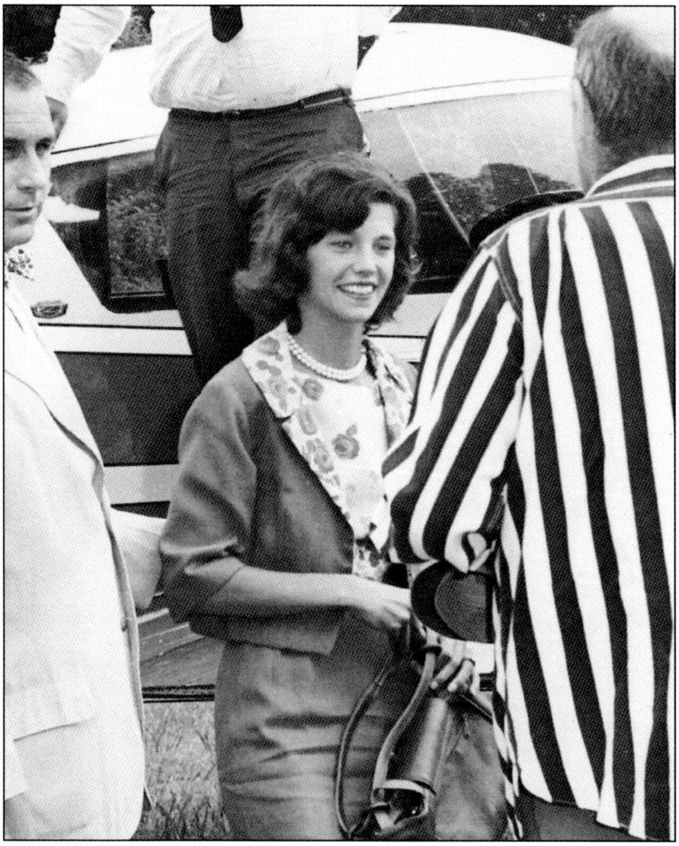

Caroline duPont took over Summit Aviation after her husband, Kip duPont, died in 1986 at the age of 49. In the face of some difficult challenges, she successfully ran and improved the venture until her retirement in 2010. An aviator in her own right, she teamed with author Jan Churchill to enter the last Powder Puff Derby Transcontinental Air Race in 1977. (CduP.)

Banking on the final approach to Summit Airfield, this plane spots the runway's number, 35, which indicates a heading of 350 degrees for the paved runway. Across from the hangars and aircraft tie-down area, there is a grass runway in an east-west direction. Note the paved taxiway parallel to the paved runway. (JC.)

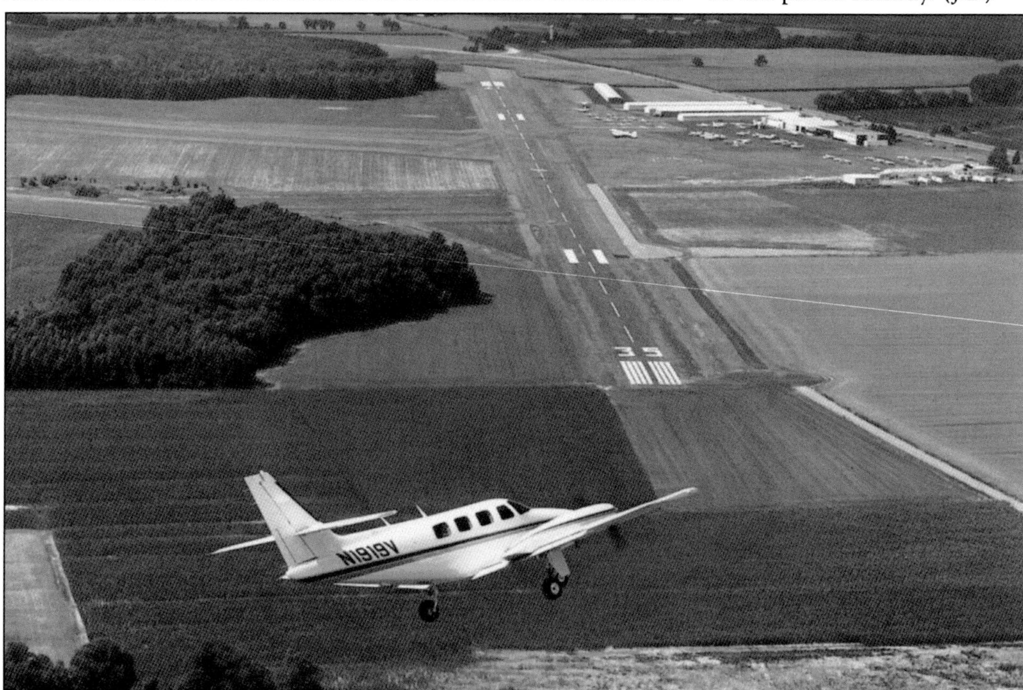

Four

Air Shows and Events

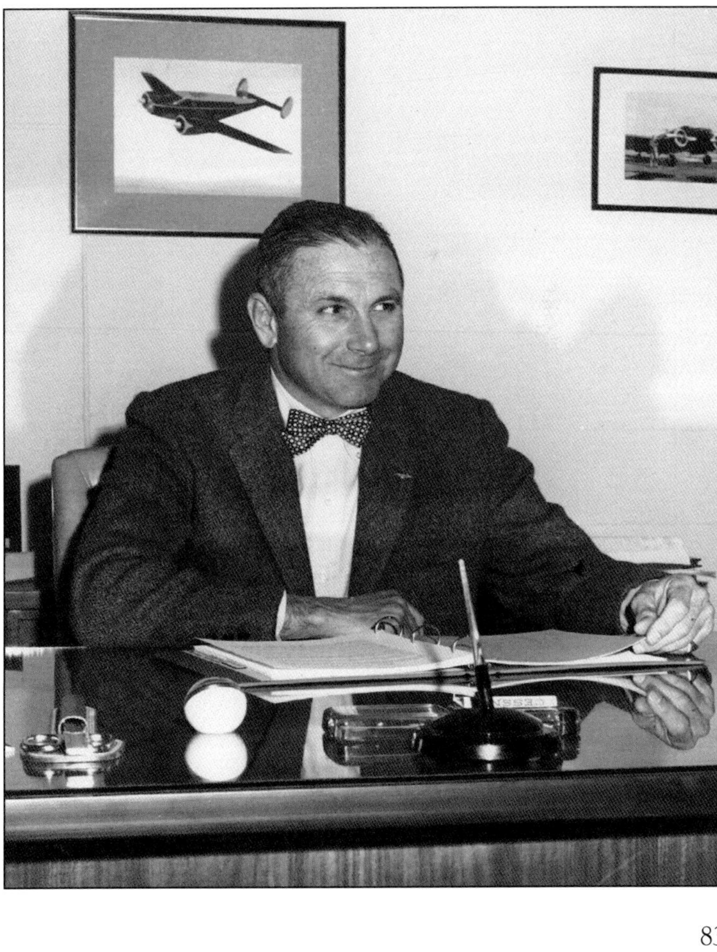

Aviation pioneer John McChesney "Johnnie Mac" Morgan was America's youngest pilot in 1931 at the age of 16. Morgan was chief pilot for the Air Transport Command, 3rd Foreign Transport Group in the Pacific during World War II. Prior to World War II, he operated the Air Service hangar at Bellanca Airfield. After the war, he was chief pilot at Air Service, Bellanca Airfield. In 1965, he became general manager at Summit Aviation in Middletown. In 1973, the National Business Aircraft Association cited him for 1.5 million miles of safe flying. Morgan was inducted into the Delaware Aviation Hall of Fame in 2001. (JC.)

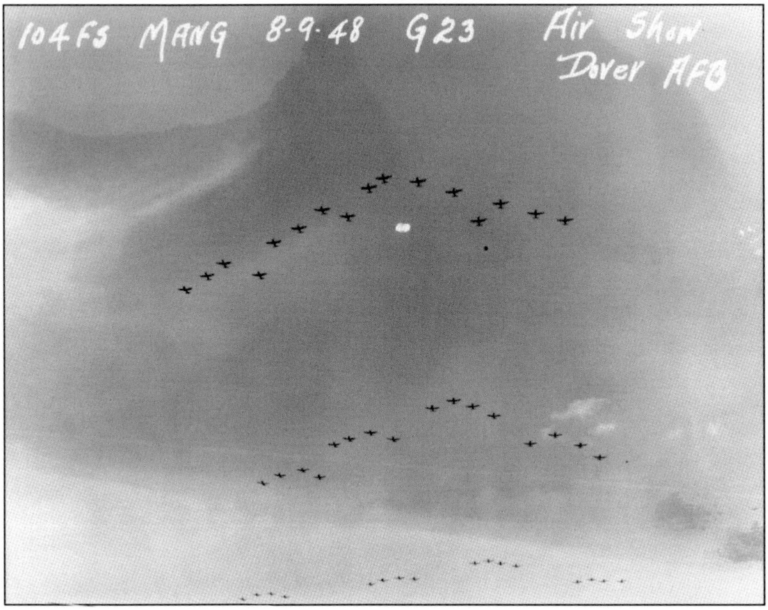

An impressive group formation of 48 Maryland Air National Guard F-47s demonstrates airpower over Dover Air Force Base at an air show in 1948. (AMC.)

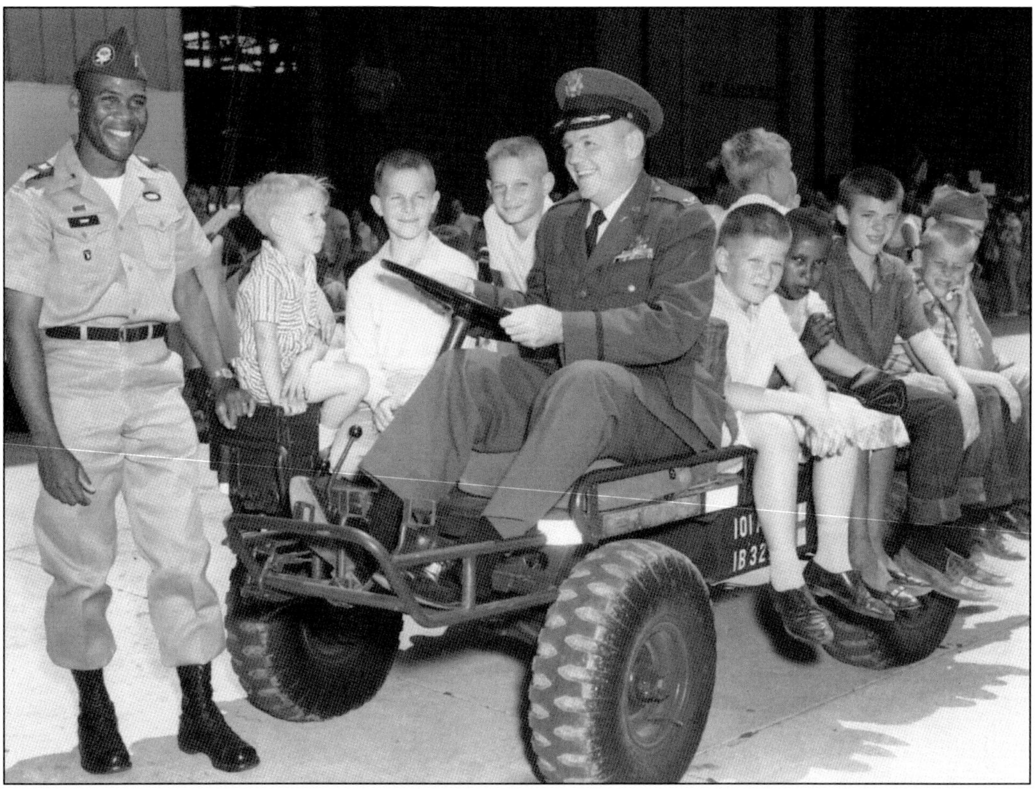

An unnamed Air Force colonel chauffeurs visiting children in a powered ground cart at Dover Air Force Base during an open house in 1948. In December 1948, the Army transferred the base to the Continental Air Command (CONAC). This command utilized the Douglas C-47 until February 18, 1949, when it transferred to the Ninth Air Force. The base was host to National Guard units for summer training during this period of relative inactivity. (AMC)

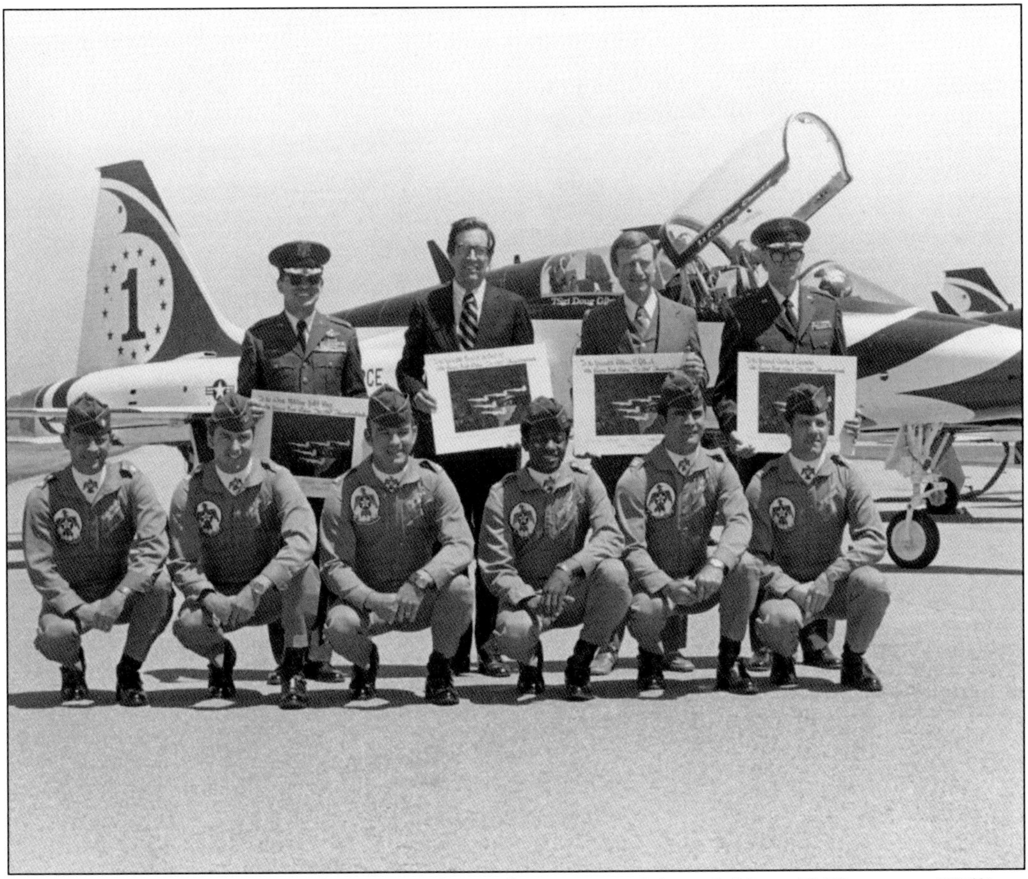

Delaware governor Pierre S. duPont IV (second row, second from left) and US senator William Roth (second row, third from left) pose with the uniformed pilots of the legendary Thunderbirds aerial demonstration team during an open house at Dover Air Force Base. (AMC.)

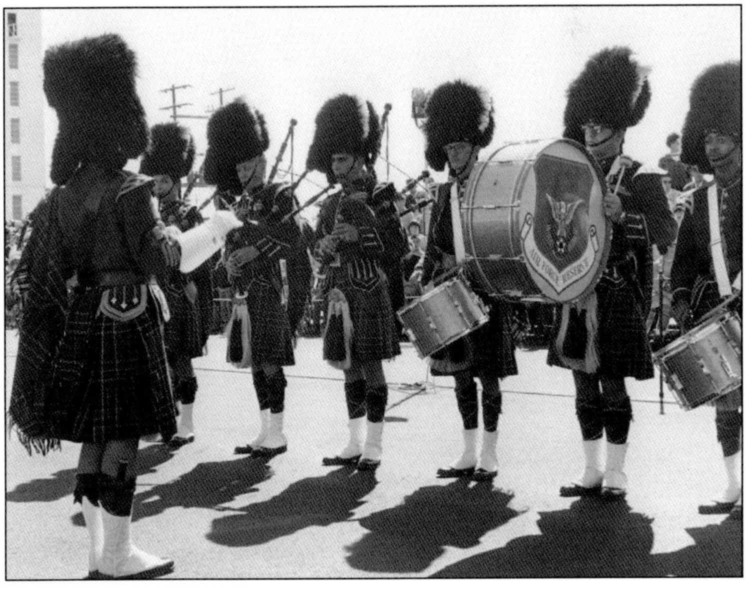

A highlander pipe band of the Air Force Reserve performs at a Dover Air Force Base open house. The annual open house event drew huge crowds and was often headlined by the Air Force's precision flying team, the Thunderbirds. (AMC.)

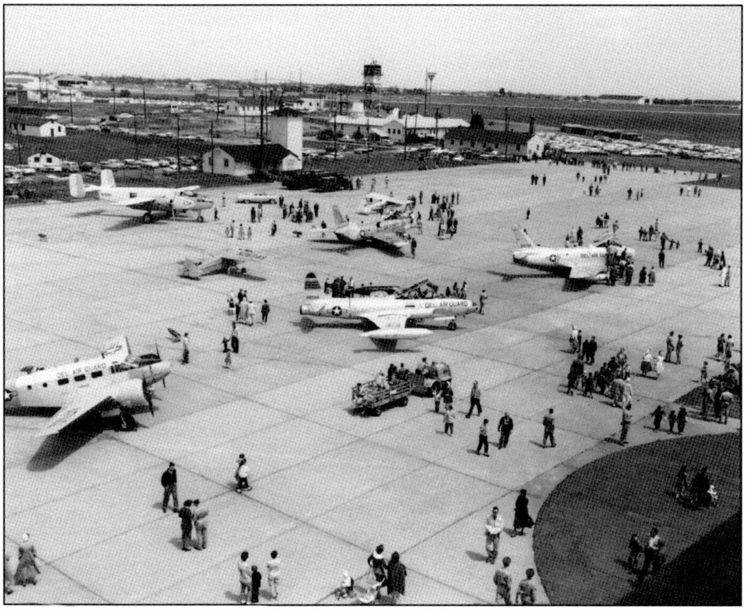

Aircraft on static display at New Castle County Airport during Operation Firecracker, celebrating Independence Day in 1957, include, from left to right, a C-45 transport, T-33 trainer, F-86 fighter, and a B-25 bomber in the background. (DMHEF.)

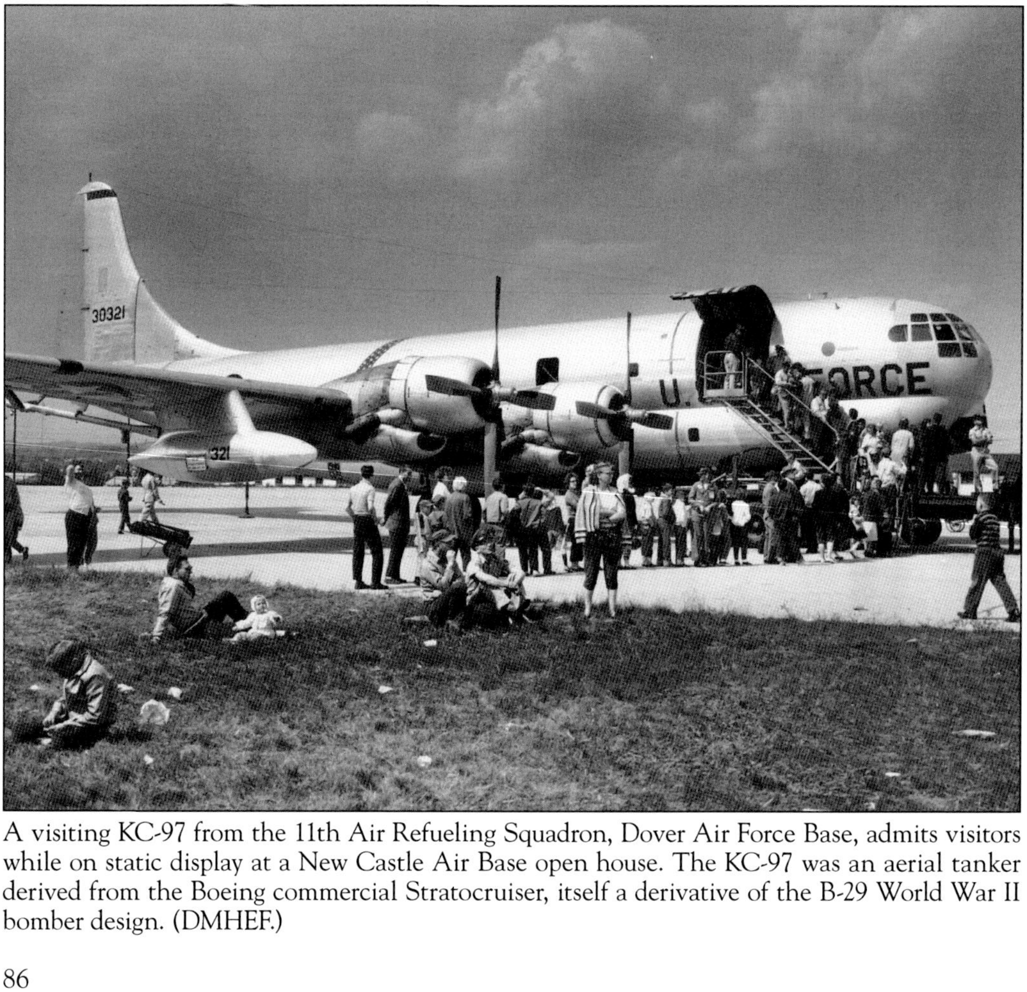

A visiting KC-97 from the 11th Air Refueling Squadron, Dover Air Force Base, admits visitors while on static display at a New Castle Air Base open house. The KC-97 was an aerial tanker derived from the Boeing commercial Stratocruiser, itself a derivative of the B-29 World War II bomber design. (DMHEF.)

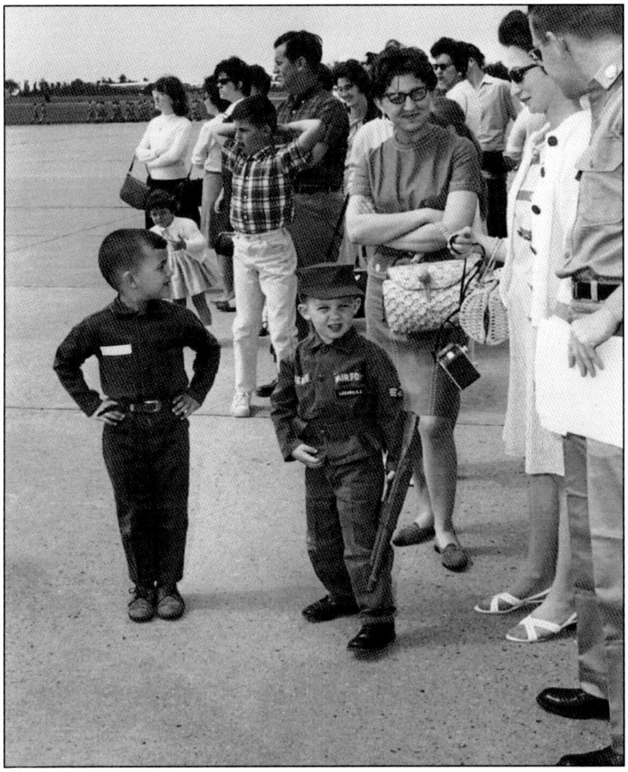

A pair of youngsters celebrates Independence Day at Operation Firecracker, the annual air show and open house at New Castle Air Base. The air show was followed by a huge firecracker display, sponsored by a local service organization. (DMHEF.)

A waiting line forms as curious attendees queue to see the cockpit of a Delaware Air National Guard F-86H during the base's annual open house. At the time, the F-86H fighter-bomber was top-line equipment, and the Delaware Air National Guard was considered a crack outfit. (DMHEF.)

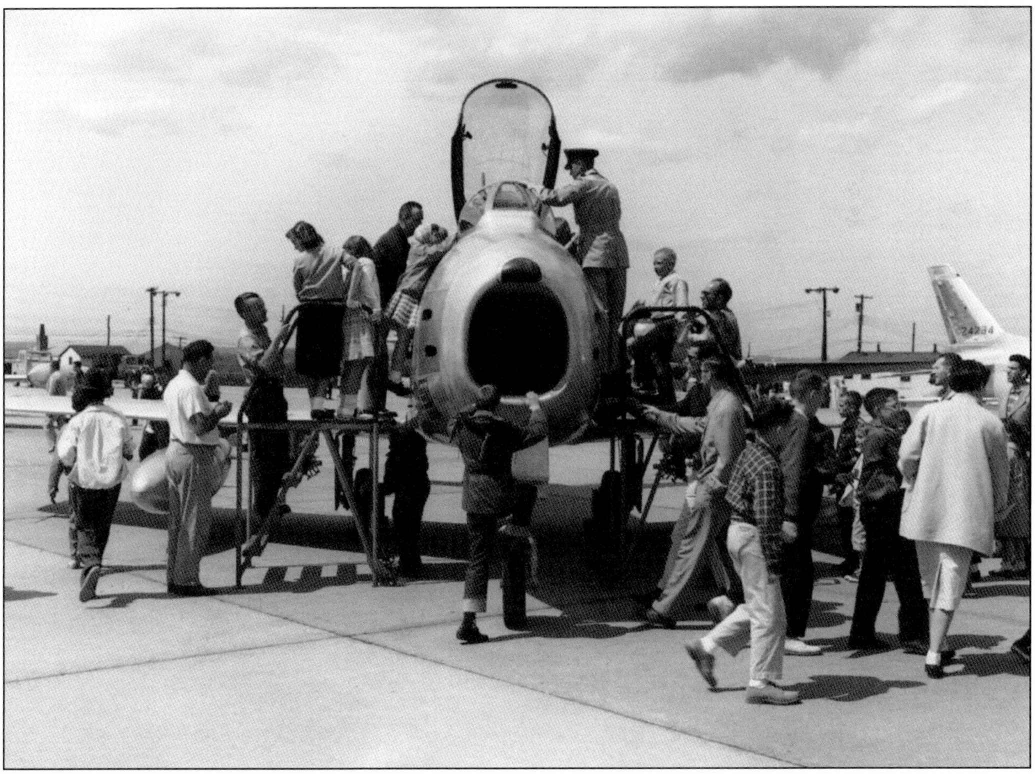

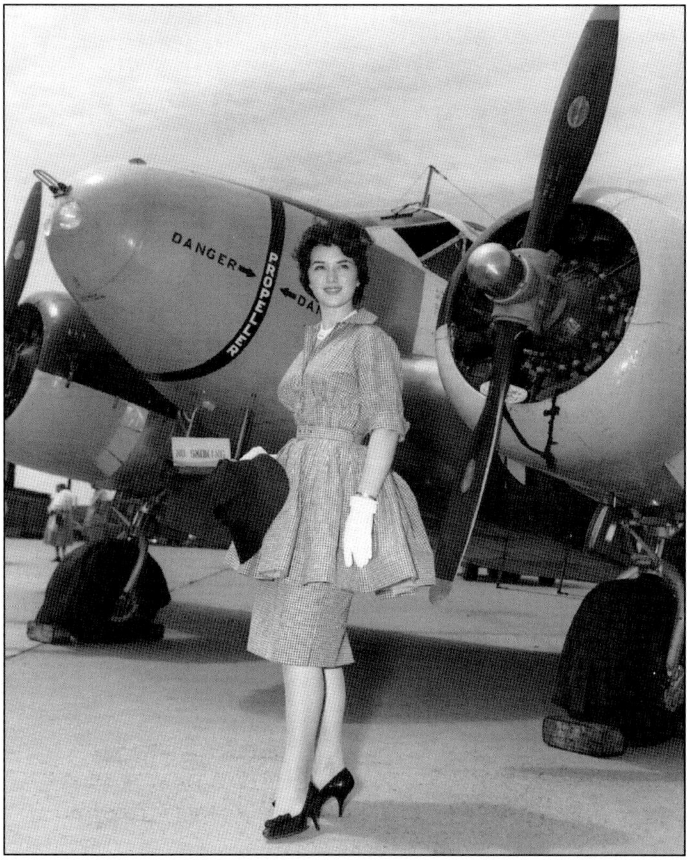

Esther Olney of Newark, Miss Delaware 1959, poses before a Delaware Air National Guard C-45 transport during the annual open house and air show at New Castle Air Base. Miss Olney, 18 years old, was a Newark resident whose Miss America talent was vocals. (DMHEF.)

Grumman F-11F Tiger fighters of the US Navy Bluc Angels aerial demonstration team are parked on the ramp at New Castle Air Base for the open house and air show, Operation Firecracker, on July 4, 1957. (DMHEF.)

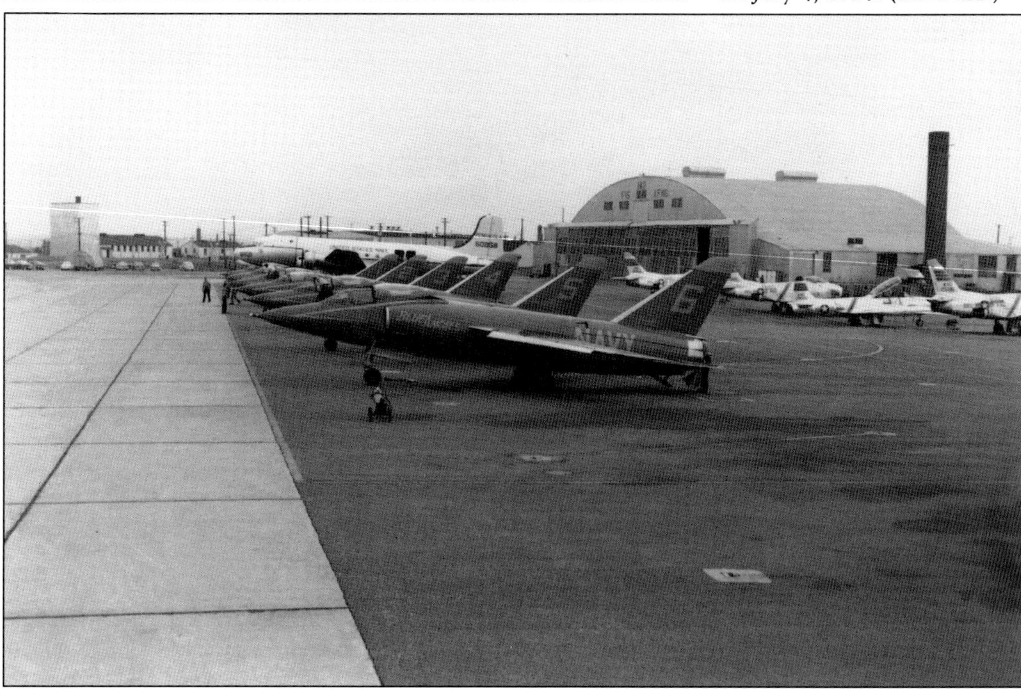

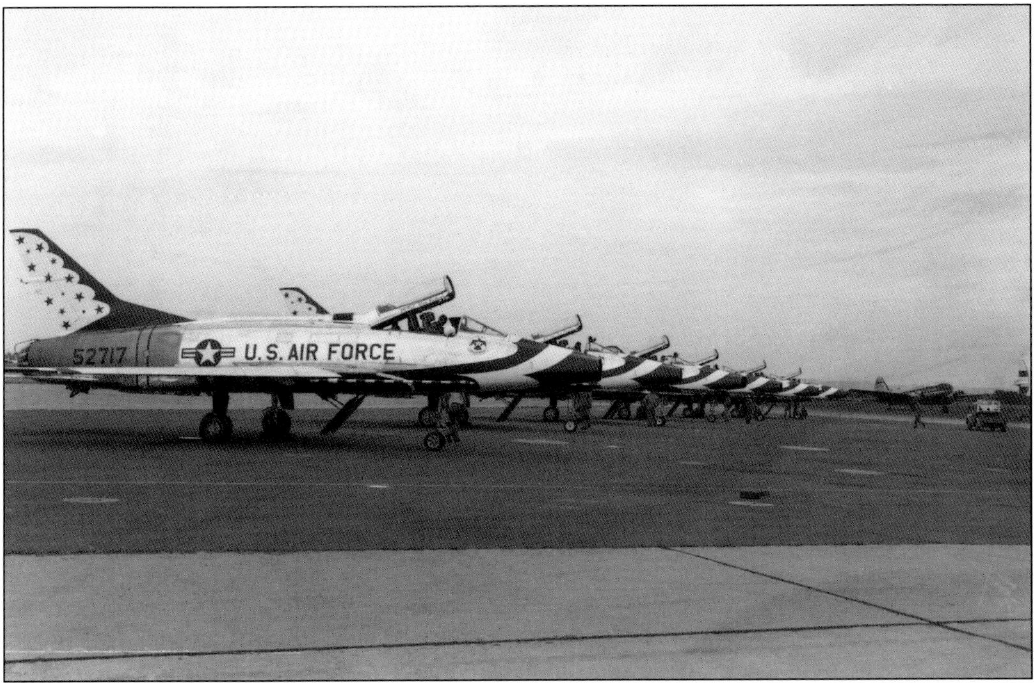

F-100 Super Sabres of the Thunderbirds Air Force aerial demonstration team are on the flight line at New Castle Air Base for an Independence Day celebration in 1960. The "Ambassadors in Blue" flew the *Hun* from 1956 to 1962. (DMHEF.)

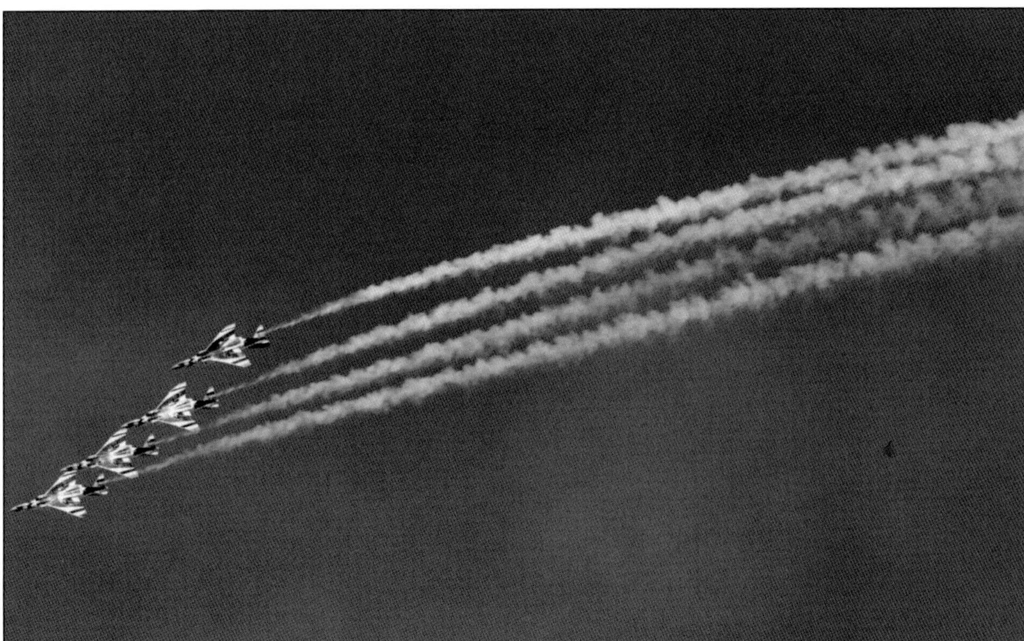

The US Air Force Thunderbirds aerial demonstration team demonstrates its precision flying skills, flying F-4 Phantom II jets, at an open house at Dover Air Force Base. The Thunderbirds were activated on May 25, 1953, as the 3600th Air Demonstration Team at Luke Air Force Base, just west of Phoenix. (AMC.)

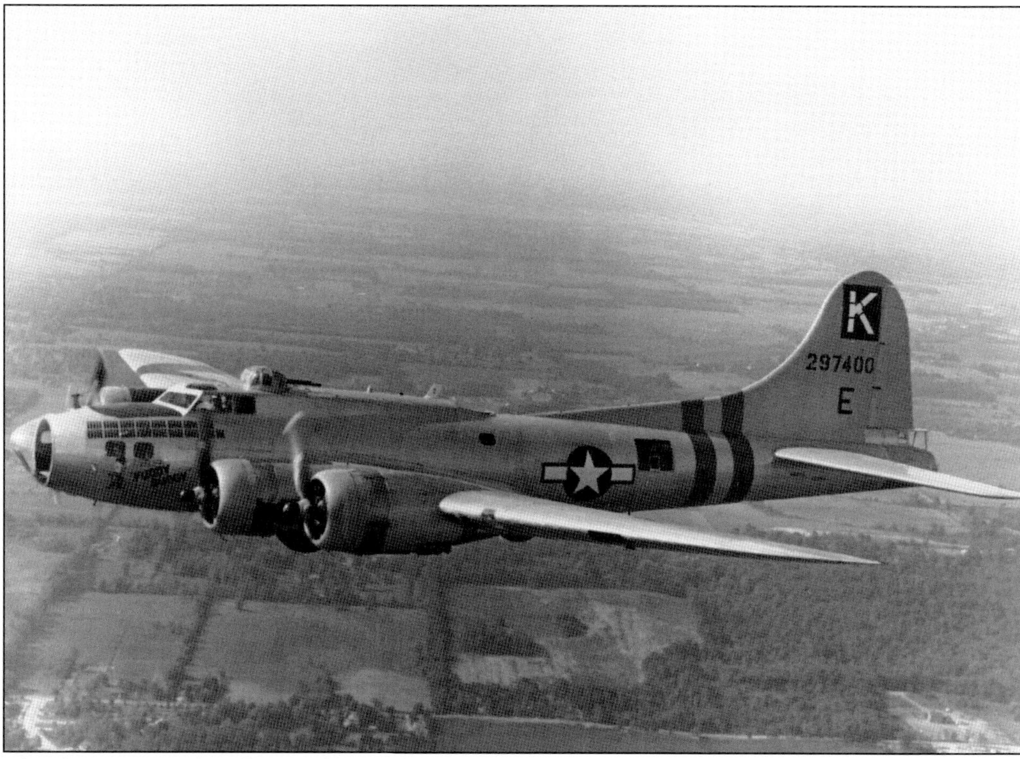

The famous B-17 bomber *Fuddy Duddy*, owned by the National Warplane Museum, is shown approaching New Castle for an air show. The four-engine bomber was restored to what it would have looked like in World War II. It played an important part in the war in Europe during the invasion. (JC.)

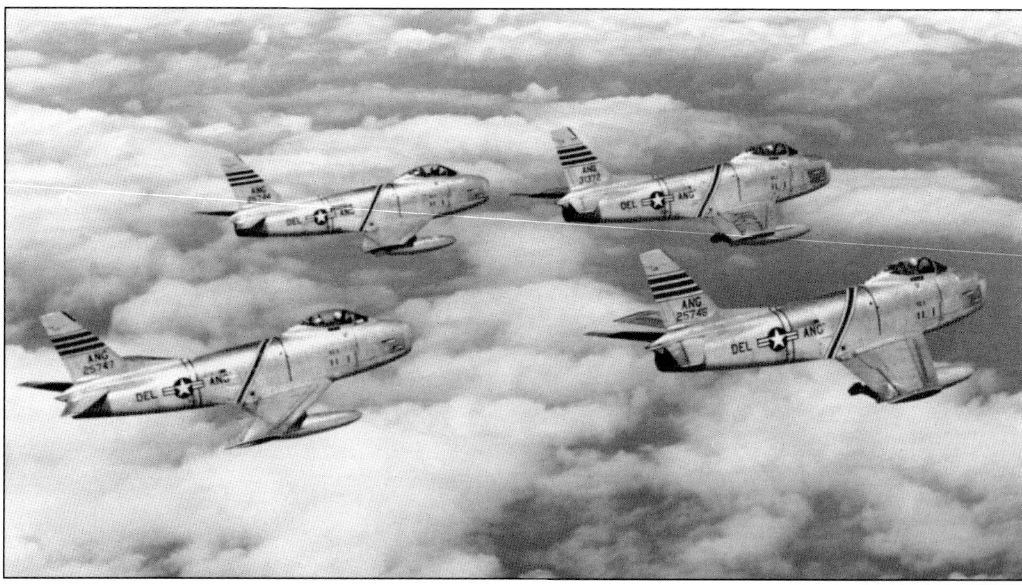

The Delaware Diamond 16-ship formation of the Delaware Air National Guard F-86 fighter jets flies over the crowd at an open house at New Castle Air Base. This formation was a favorite of Lt. Col. David McCallister, the squadron commander who gave it its name. (DMHEF.)

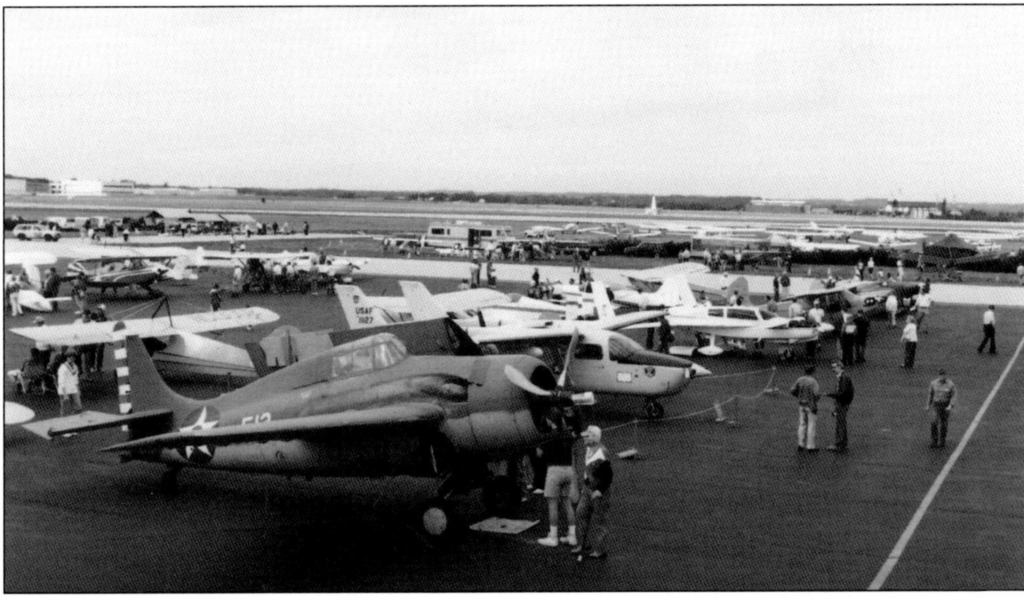

In 1994, the ramp at New Castle County Airport was covered with airplanes for the East Coast Fly-in. The Wildcat fighter in the foreground was flown in by owner Alexis duPont. The Grumman F4F Wildcat carrier-based fighter first entered service in 1940. It served in the Pacific theater in World War II. (JC.)

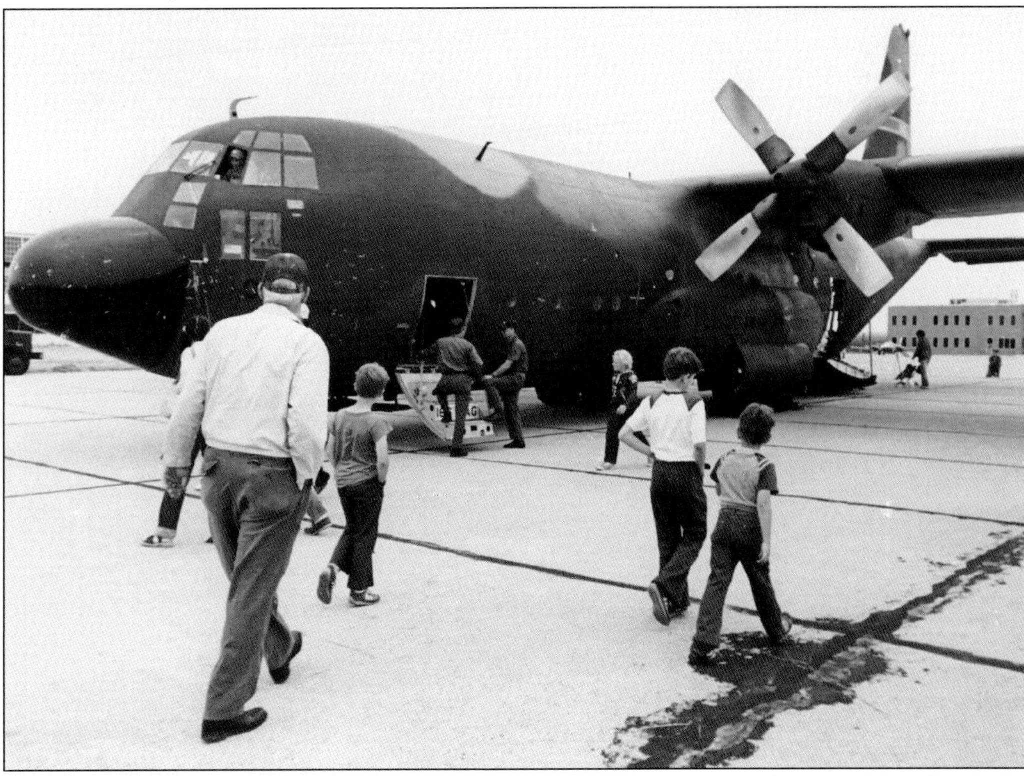

A Delaware Air National Guard C-130 attracts visitors during an open house at New Castle Air Base. (DMHEF.)

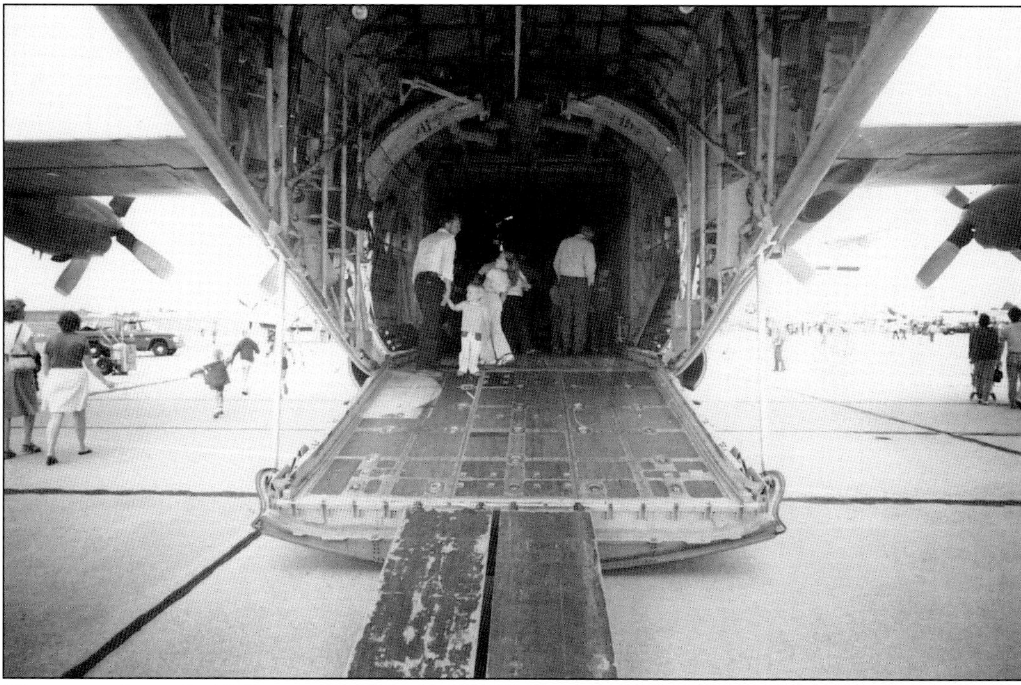

The cargo bay of a Delaware Air National Guard C-130 Hercules transport is shown to good advantage as attendees clamber aboard during the base open house at New Castle Air Base. Capable of using unfinished runways for takeoffs and landings, the C-130 was designed as a troop medical evacuation cargo transport aircraft. (DMHEF.)

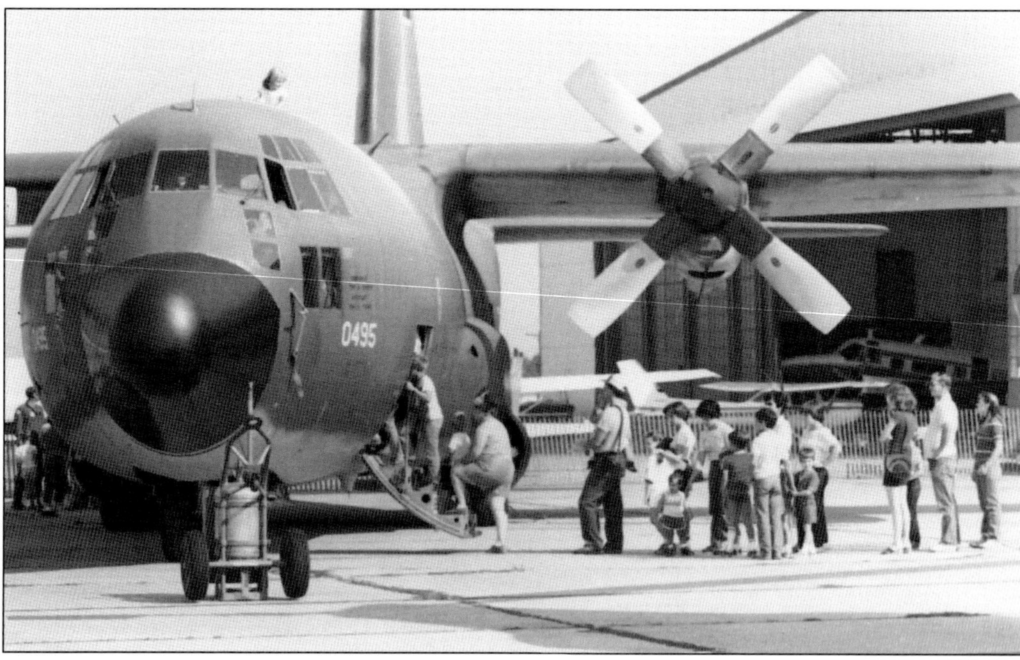

Visitors queue to board a Delaware Air National Guard C-130 during an open house at New Castle Air Base. Delaware received its first C-130A in 1971. These original ships were replaced by new C-130H model aircraft in 1985, which still serve today with the Air National Guard. (DMHEF.)

On March 16, 2004, commercial pilots Jan Churchill and Carol Timmons (present-day brigadier general of the Delaware Air National Guard) visit the veterans hospital to speak to the patients about their aviation experiences. (JC.)

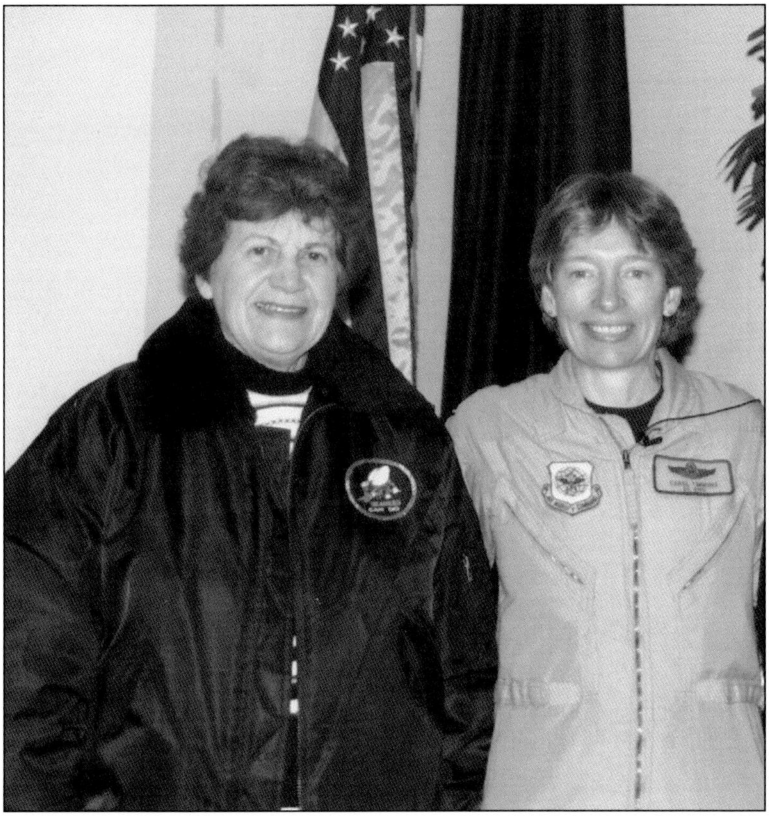

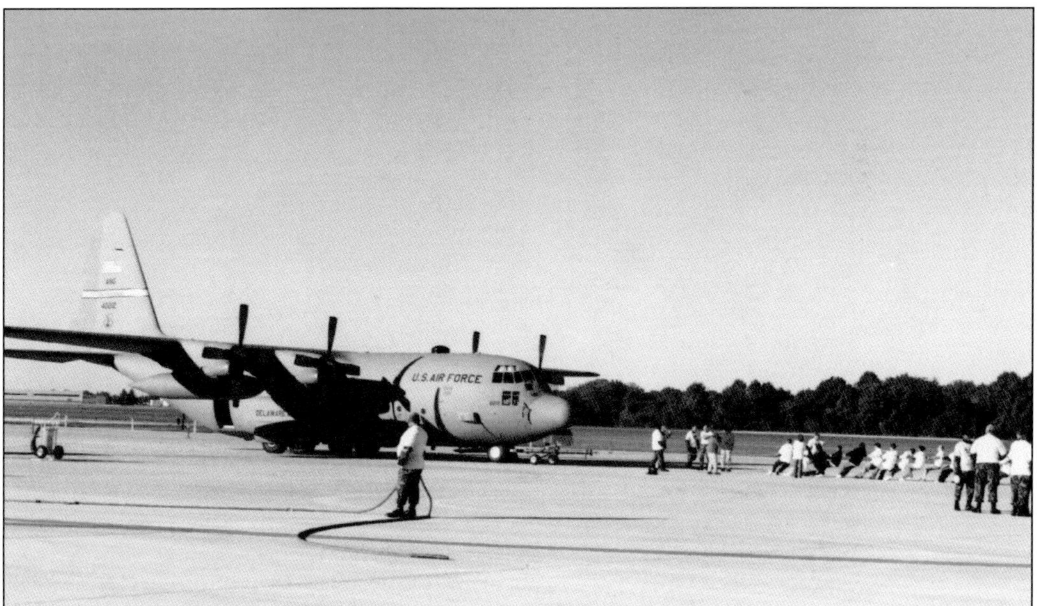

A team of plane pullers competes in the annual fundraising event for Delaware Special Olympics. The Delaware Air National Guard event was hosted 13 times in 15 years, during which 344 teams raised more than $250,000 for Special Olympics Delaware. (DMHEF.)

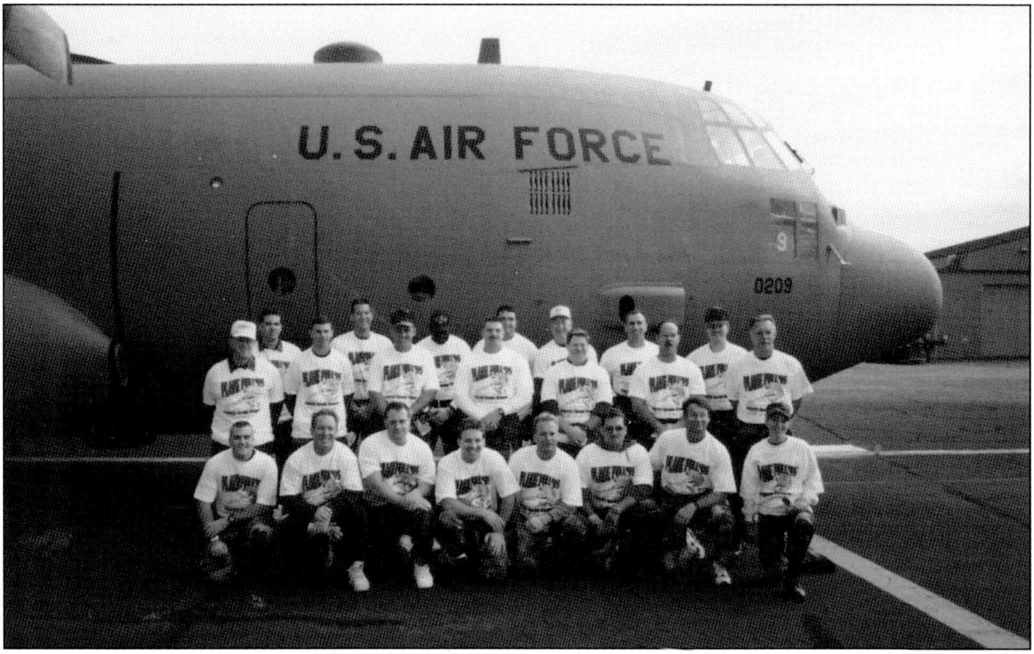

A plane-pulling team poses before a C-130H *Hercules* transport during the annual fundraising event for Special Olympics Delaware. This annual tug-of-war event consists of 20-member teams competing in the timed event to see which team can pull a 100,000-pound C-130 aircraft the fastest. (DMHEF.)

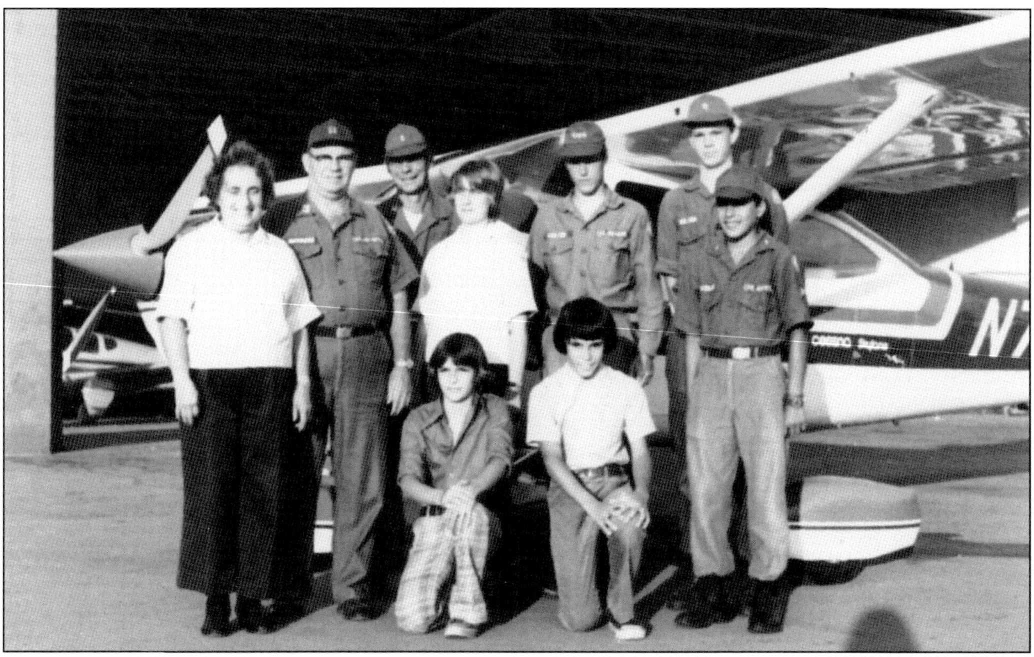

Civil Air Patrol cadets and senior leaders pose before Jan Churchill's Cessna 182 at Summit Airpark. The cadets had orientation rides throughout the summer in this airplane. The adults in this image are, from left to right, Lieutenant Colonel Hammond, Captain Hammond, and Lieutenant Fox. (JC.)

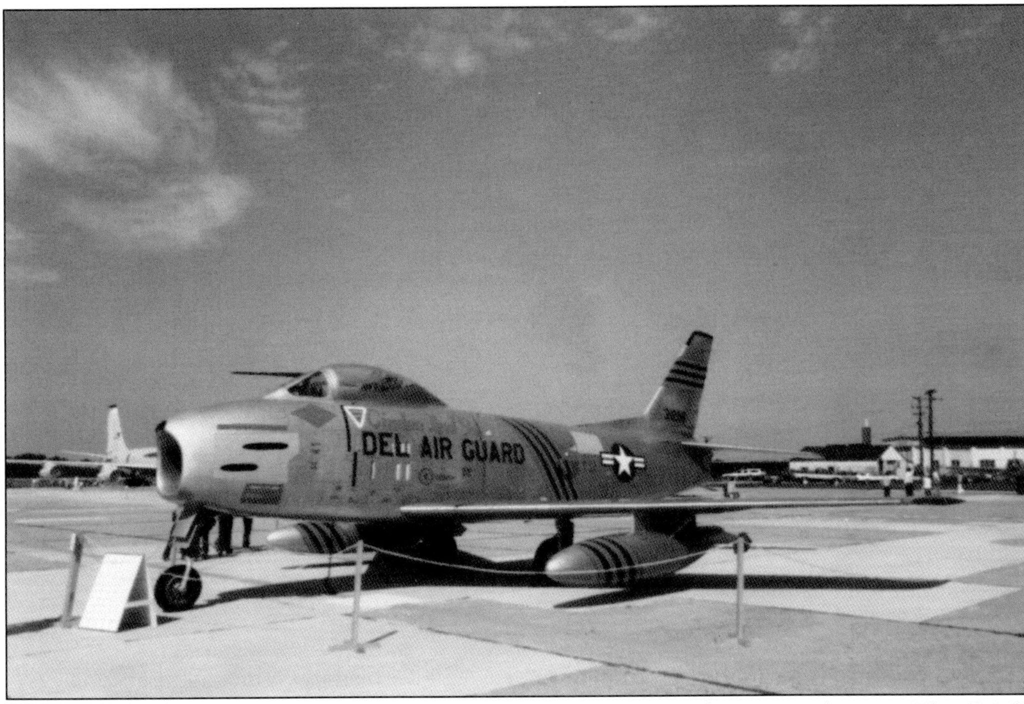

Cindee Lind 9th is on static display at an open house at New Castle County Airport. This F-86H Sabre jet was the mount of Lt. Col. David F. McCallister. The airplane is displayed today in a place of honor near the entrance to the Delaware Air National Guard Base in New Castle. (JC.)

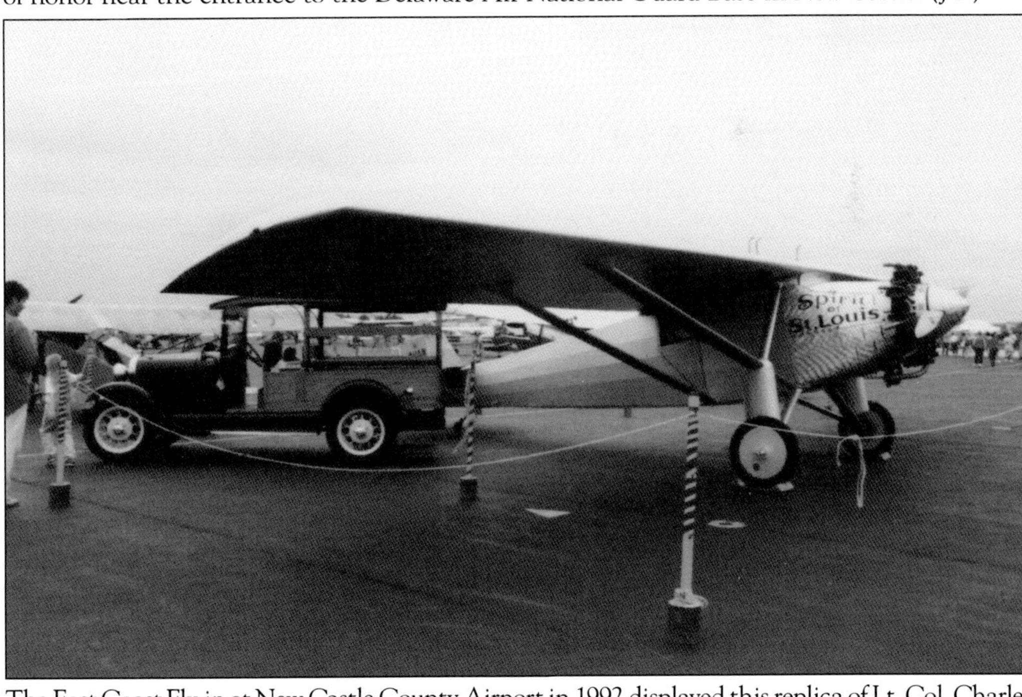

The East Coast Fly-in at New Castle County Airport in 1992 displayed this replica of Lt. Col. Charles Lindbergh's famous *Spirit of St. Louis*. The replica was built and flown by David Cannavo. The replica was an exact copy, and so the pilot had to fly looking only out the side window. (JC.)

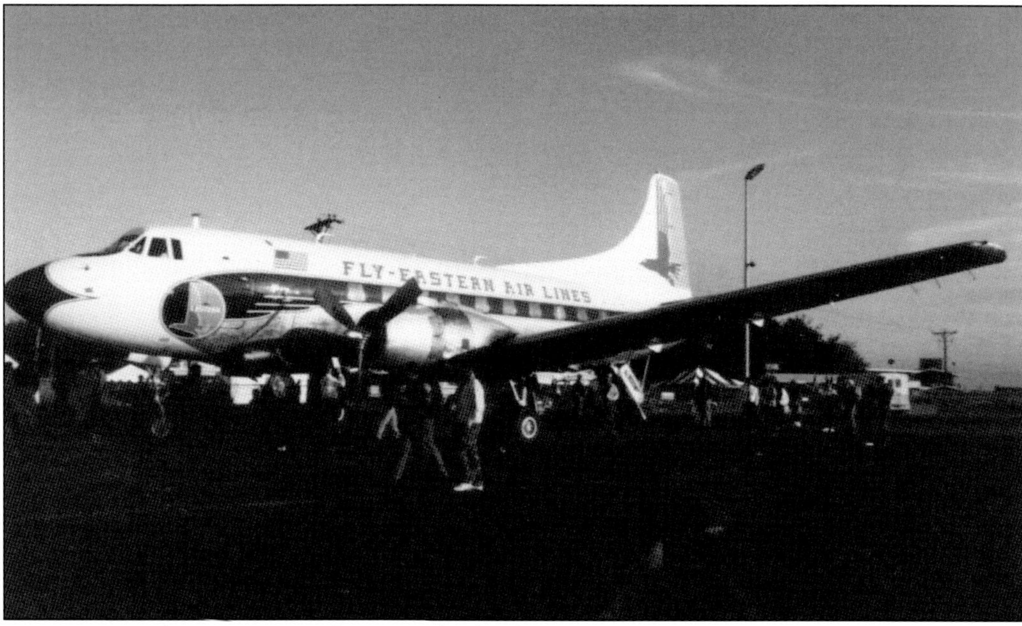

An Eastern Airlines Convair is shown on display during an air show at New Castle County Airport. By November 1974, Eastern had discontinued service at the Greater Wilmington Airport. This type of airplane was built to replace the Douglas DC-3 with a more modern design. (JC.)

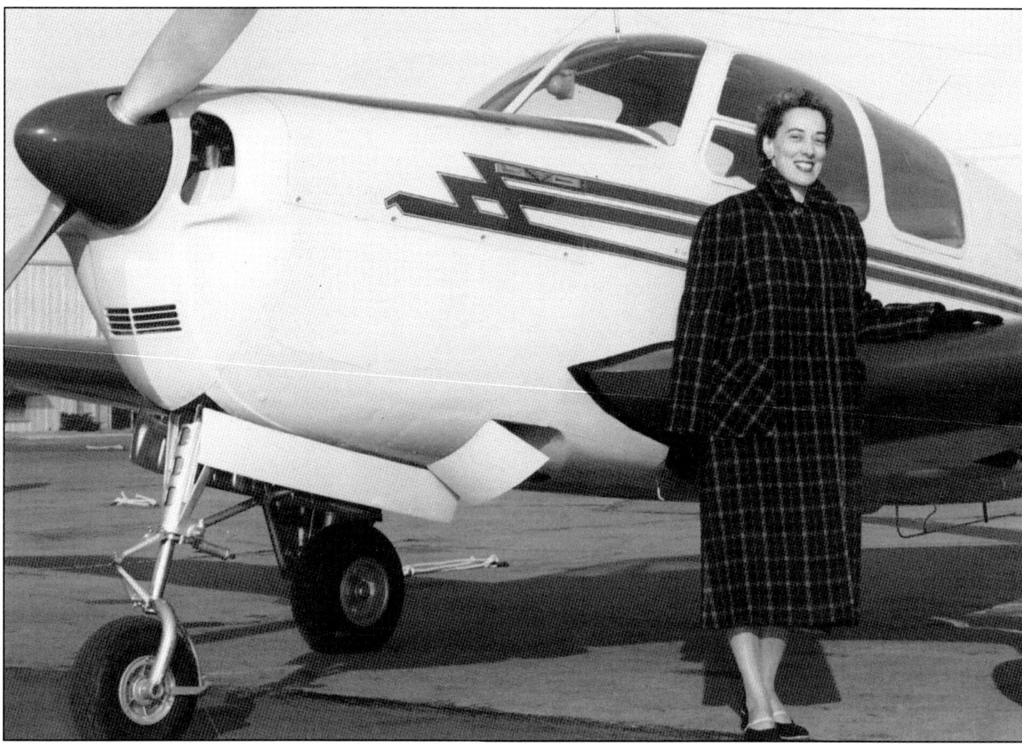

Pilot Adelaide Tinker has just landed in her new Beechcraft Bonanza airplane, which she delivered from the factory in Kansas to DuPont Airfield on December 19, 1952. The Bonanza was a high-performance, single-engine airplane. (AT.)

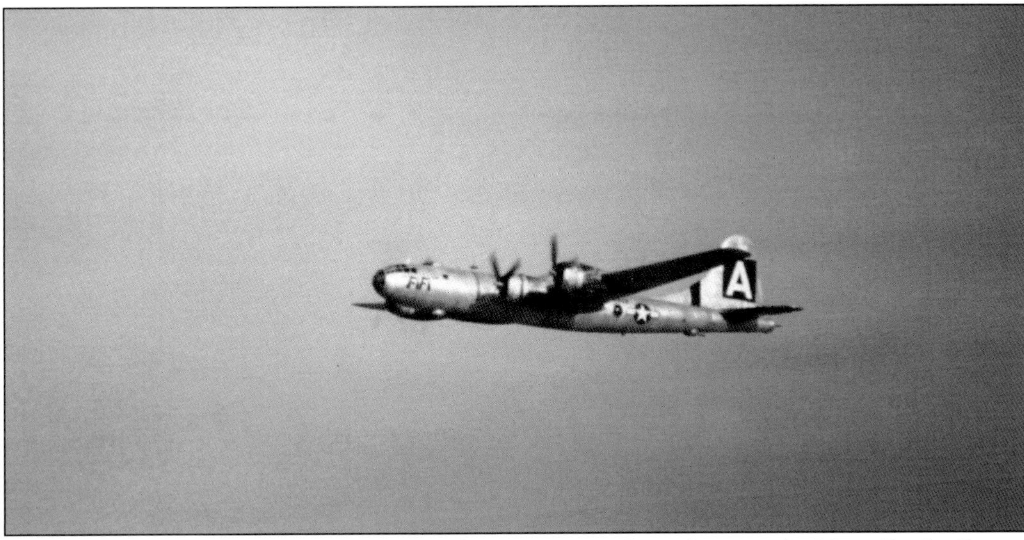

The Confederate Air Force's B-29 *Fifi* is shown arriving for a fly-in at the New Castle County Airport in 1990. This Superfortress came from Harlingen, Texas. In wartime, it flew with a crew consisting of a pilot, copilot, navigator, engineer, radio operator, bombardier, and three gunners. (JC.)

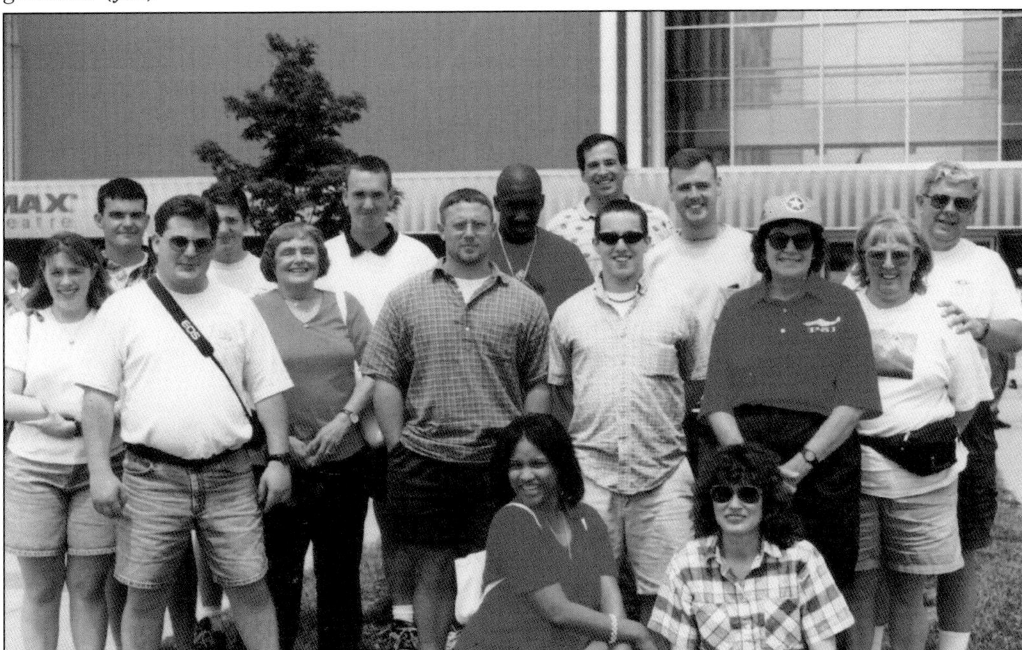

In May 1998, students from Wilmington College went on an aerial trip to the National Museum of the US Air Force in Dayton, Ohio, as part of the aviation program that offered degrees in many fields of aviation. Local pilots used their personal airplanes to fly the group to and from Ohio. In this image are, from left to right, (first row) two unidentified; (second row) Dawn Avanzato, Chris Course, Anne Eriksen, Claudio Shardonofski, Joseph Moore, Jan Churchill (pilot), Mary Lou Hagen (pilot), and William Hagen (pilot); (third row) unidentified, Michael Minner, Mark Dorsey, Napoleon Brown, Peter Bailey (pilot and course instructor), and Andrew Sides. (JC.)

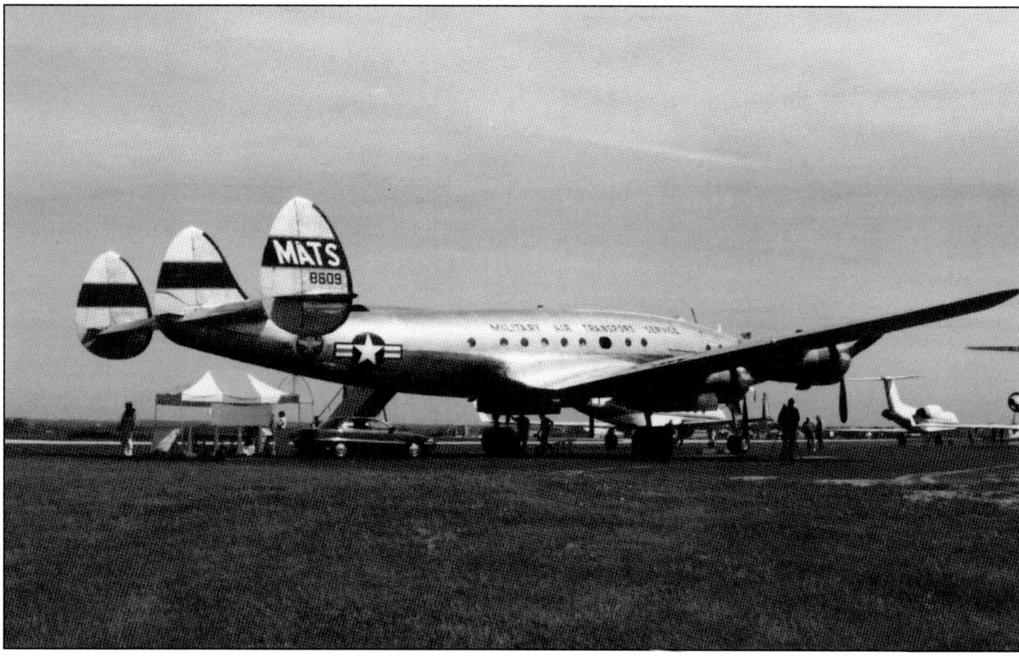

Another air show favorite was the Lockheed C-121 Constellation, which flew for the Military Air Transport Service (MATS). The fuselage was shaped like an airfoil to provide lift. The first C-121 started service on January 9, 1943, after the Army took over production and development in 1942. It was retired from military service in 1978. (JC.)

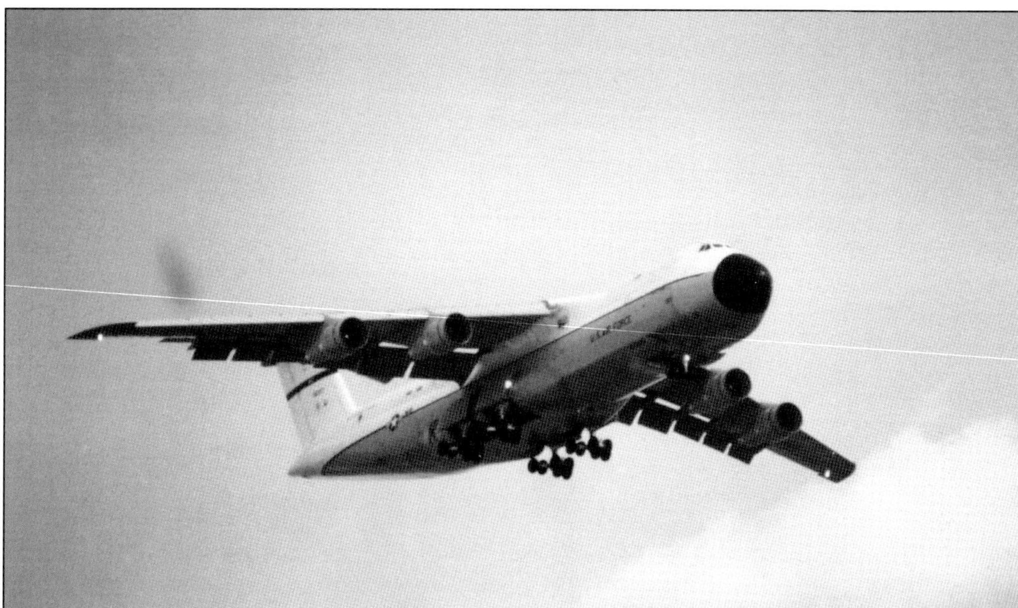

Here, the C-5 Galaxy transport arrives from Dover Air Force Base for an open house at New Castle County Airport. The C-5s were based at Dover Air Force Base where the Military Airlift Command used them. The C-5 was the largest transport used by the military for its missions; it also took equipment and men to areas in the United States where forest fires were being fought. (JC.)

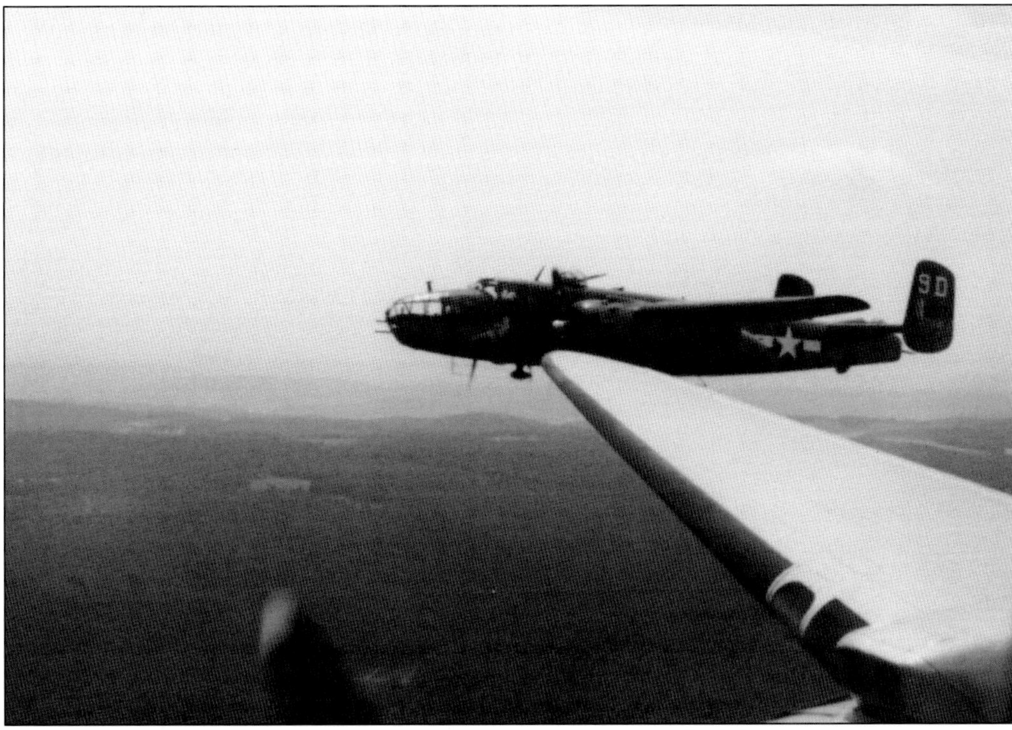

The Mid-Atlantic Air Museum's prize-winning B-25 medium bomber *Briefing Time* is depicted flying off the starboard side of the museum's R4D on its way to New Castle County Airport for the Boy Scout Air Show on June 10, 1984. (JC.)

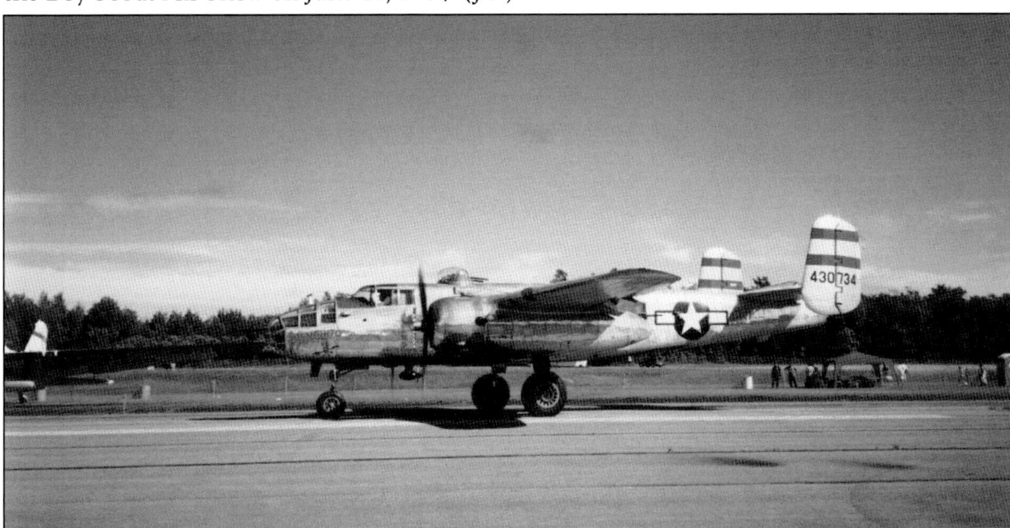

This World War II B-25J bomber *Panchito*, assigned to the 396th Bomb Squadron, 41st Bomb Group, 7th Air Force was flown to an air show in New Castle by owner-pilot Larry D. Kelley. Stationed in the Central Pacific in 1944–1945, this plane was responsible for bombing shipping and land-based targets and the Japanese mainland. A wartime pilot named it after his favorite Disney character, Panchito, one of *The Three Caballeros*. This B-25J is based at the Delaware Aviation Museum at Georgetown Airport in Sussex County. (JC.)

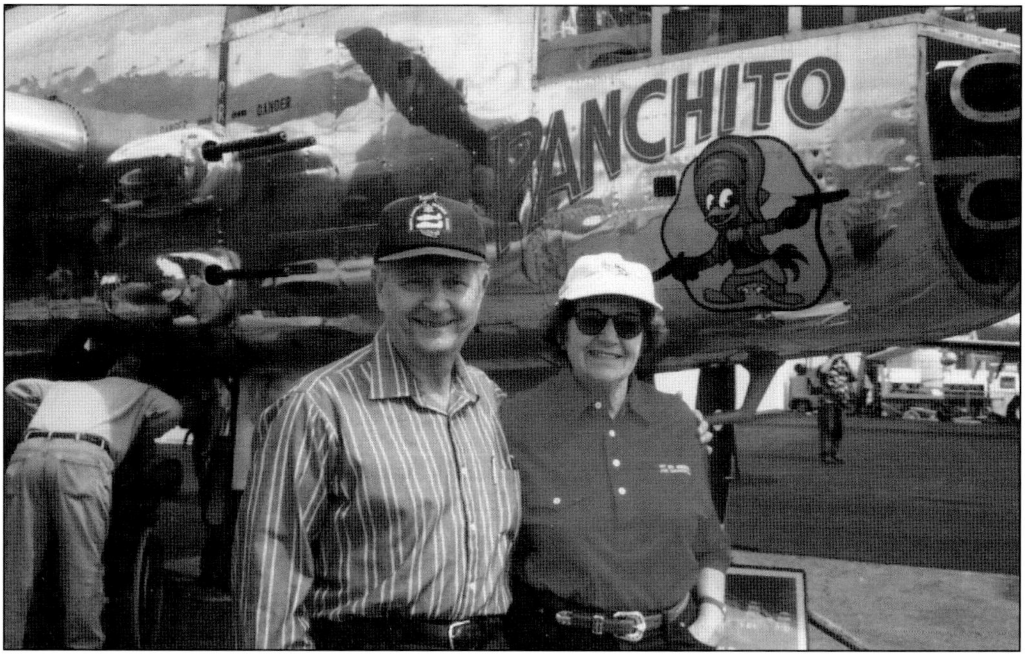

This image shows Walter Ohlrich, founder of EAA Warbirds of America, with Jan Churchill; both persons are qualified to fly a B-25. Note the wonderful nose art on the B-25 as well as its guns. Warbirds of America consisted of pilots who restored retired military aircraft to their original configuration for displays at air shows and in museums. (JC.)

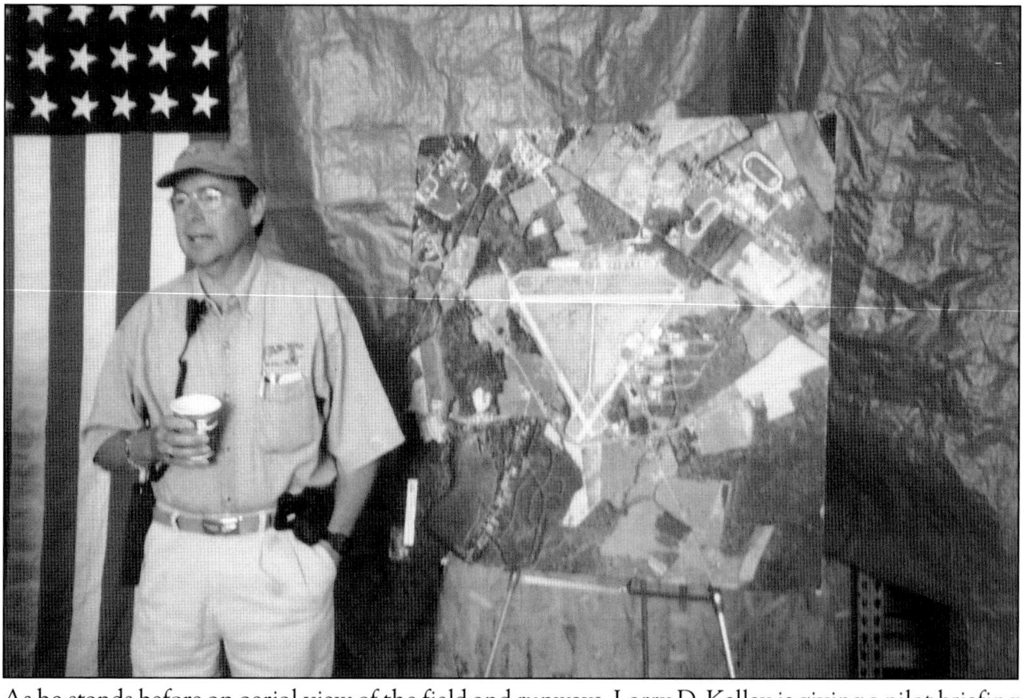

As he stands before an aerial view of the field and runways, Larry D. Kelley is giving a pilot briefing prior to an air show at Georgetown Airport. Kelley is the chairman of the Delaware Aviation Museum Foundation, located at the Georgetown Airport. (JC.)

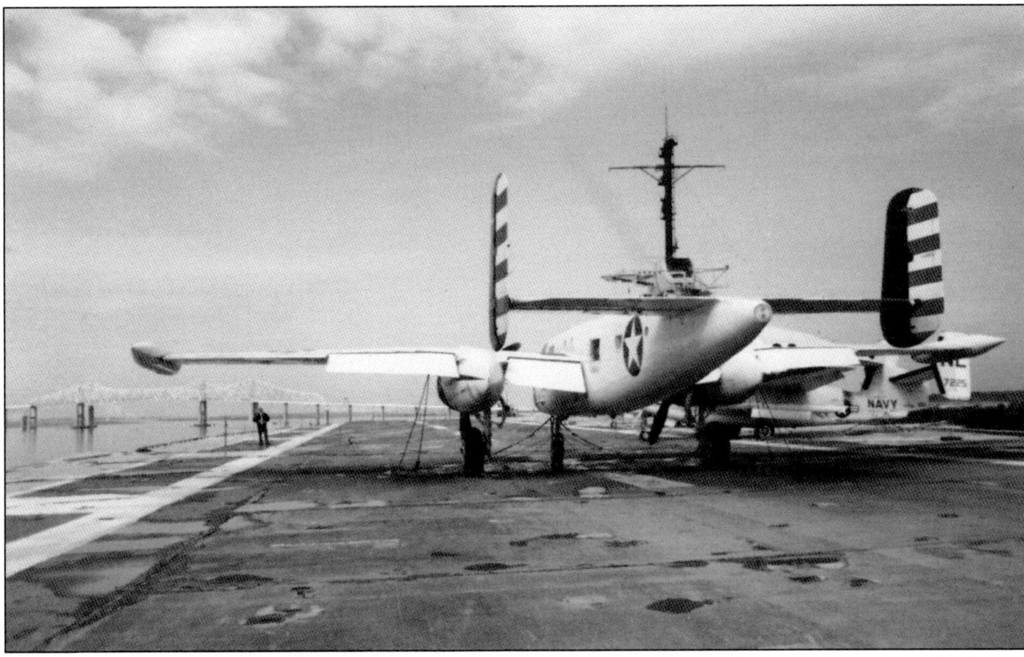

This image depicts Richard duPont's B-25 bomber *Fertle Turtle* on the aircraft carrier *Yorktown* at the Patriots Point Naval and Maritime Museum near Charleston, South Carolina, in 1943. DuPont based his B-25 at Summit Airpark for many years before donating it to the museum to honor the famous Doolittle Raid on Tokyo, Japan, April 18. 1942. (JC.)

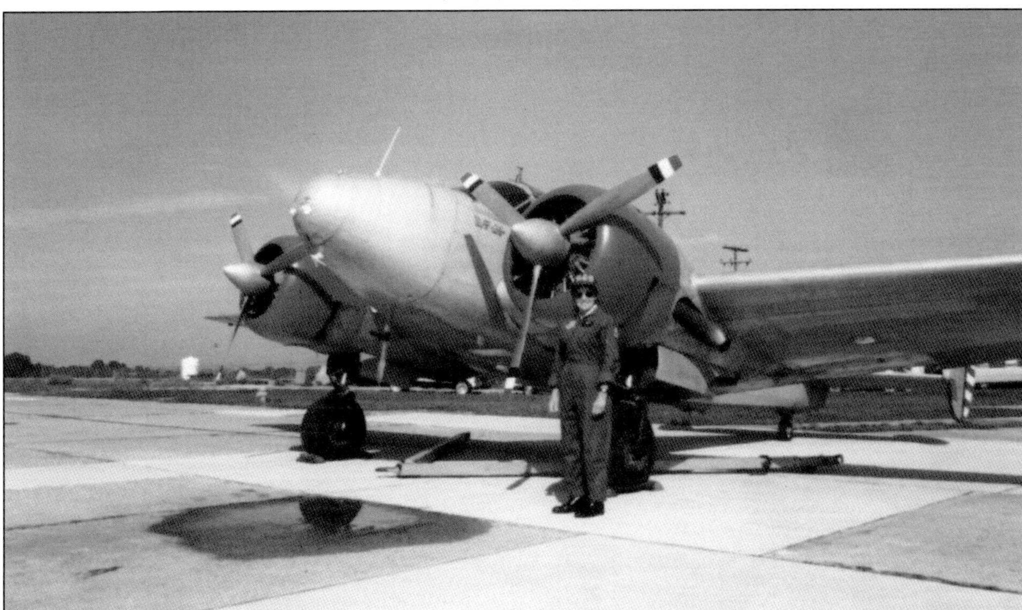

In 1986, Jan Churchill stands before this 1942 Beechcraft AT-B-18-71, S/N 1461, twin-engine airplane seized in a major drug bust on October 6, 1985, by the US Customs Service at New Castle County Airport. The pilot diverted to New Castle from his intended destination in Pennsylvania due to poor weather. Eventually, the plane was donated to the Travis Air Force Base Museum in California. (JC.)

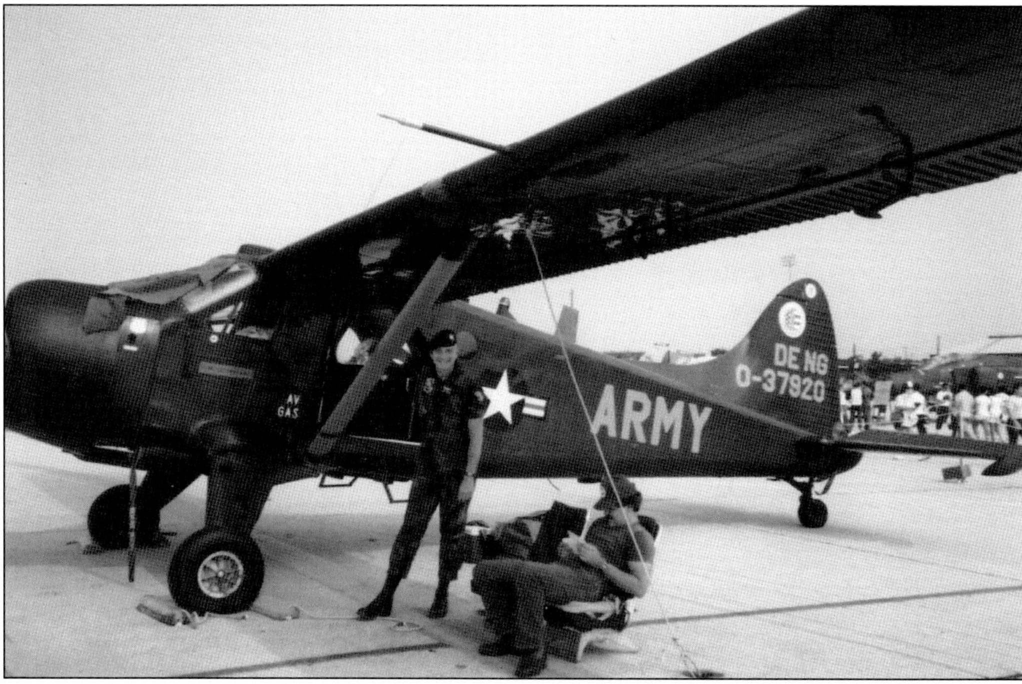

Owner-pilot Stephen J. Roberts displays his U-6A Beaver airplane at an East Coast Fly-in at New Castle County Airport. Built by deHavilland, Canada, this STOL (short takeoff and landing) airplane was used by the Army to reach remote areas. It also towed gliders at the US Naval Test Pilot School. (JC.)

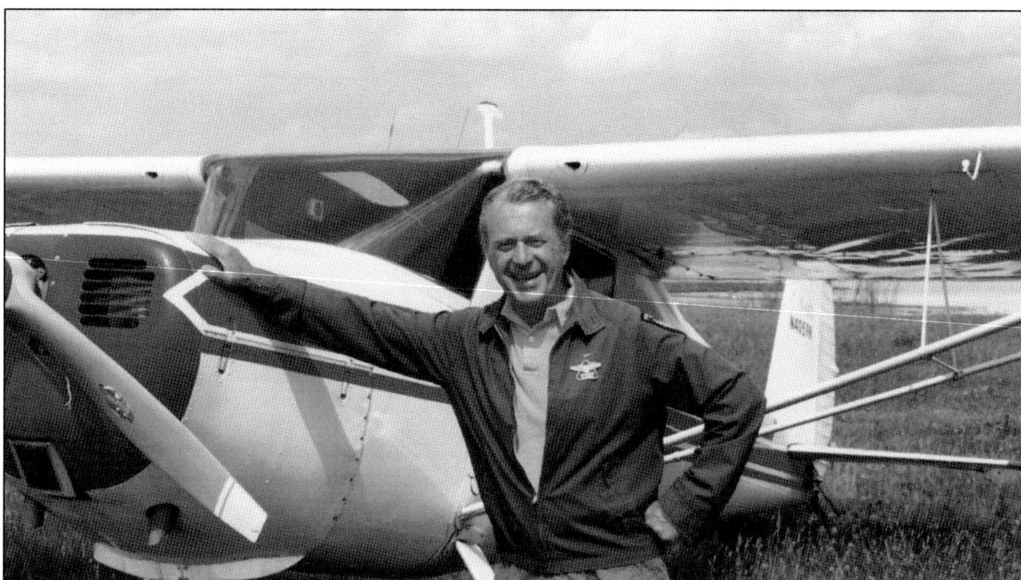

Hugh Horning is shown with his 1947 Cessna Taildragger in 1996. On March 4, 2012, Horning was awarded the Federal Aviation Administration (FAA) Wright Brothers Master Pilot Award for 50 consecutive years of accident-free flying and for having participated significantly in a variety of general aviation organizations and activities. This 87 year-old, in 2014, continues to fly in his C-120. (HH.)

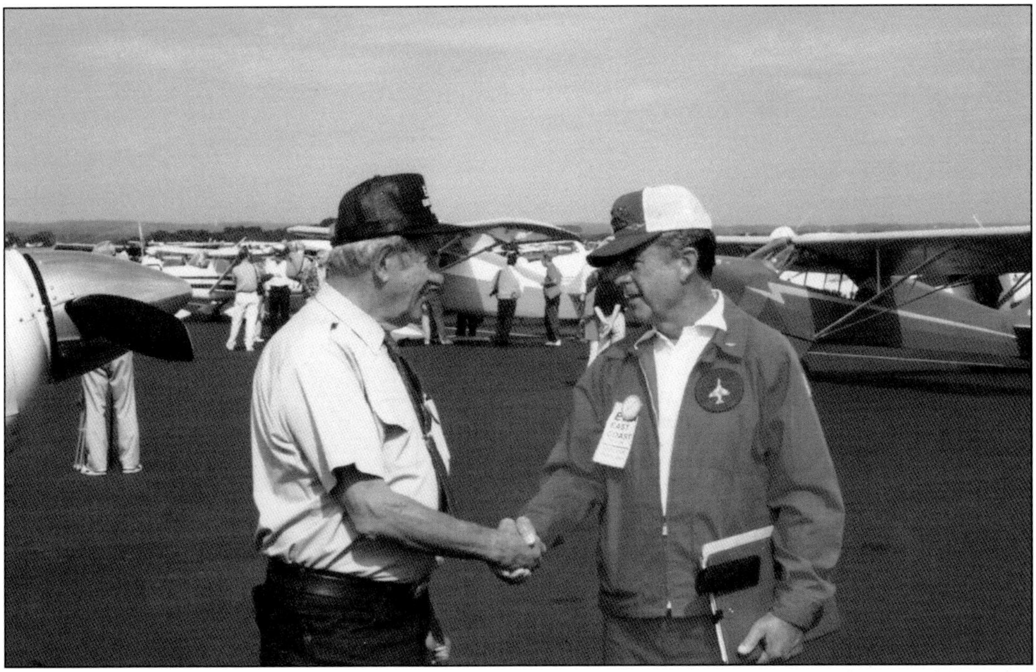

This photograph shows Experimental Aircraft Association (EAA) president and founder Paul Poberezny being welcomed to the 1991 East Coast Fly-in by master of ceremonies Hugh Horning. (HH.)

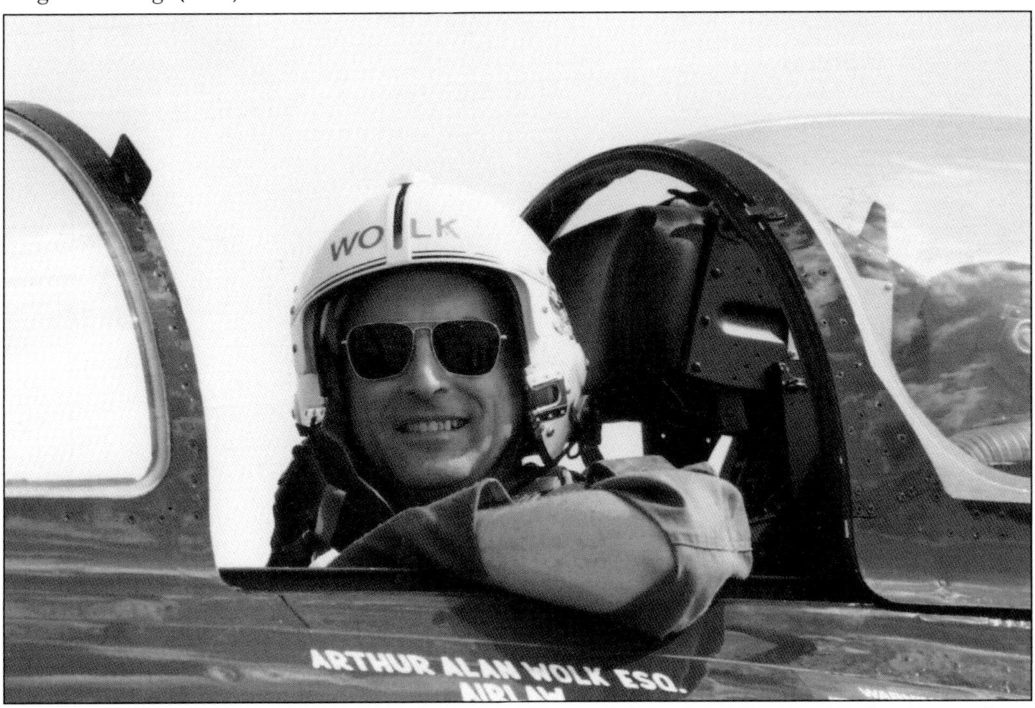

Attorney Arthur Alan Wolk flew in his F9F Panther jet fighter for a New Castle Air Show where he performed a solo routine. This was Grumman's first jet fighter aircraft. The Navy and US Marine Corps used it as a primary jet fighter and ground-attack aircraft in Korea. (JC.)

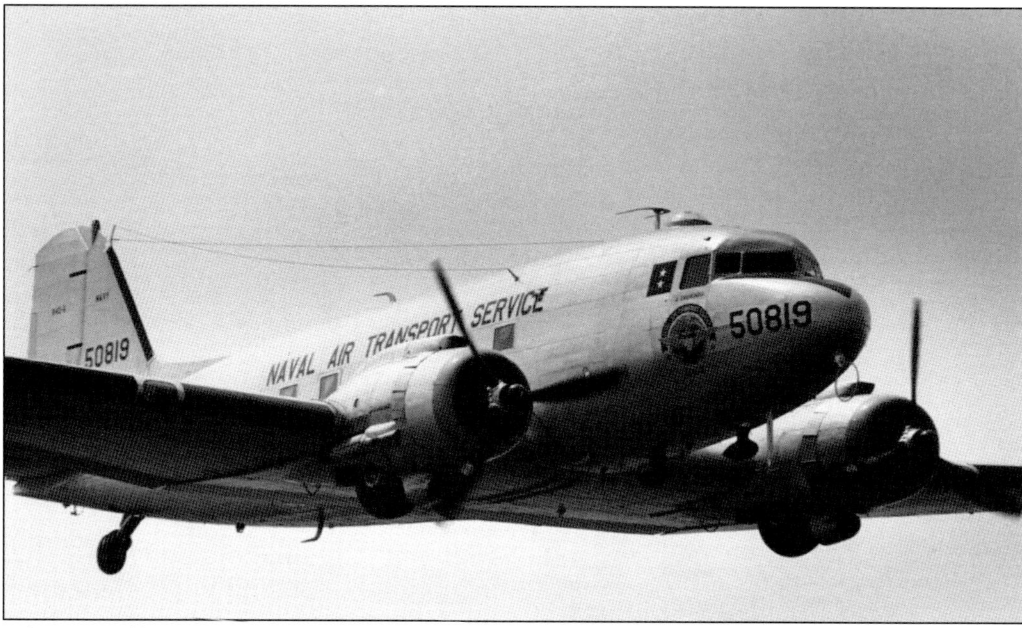

Pilots Russell Strine and Jan Churchill are seen flying the Mid-Atlantic Air Museum's Douglas R4D in the 1994 East Coast Fly-in. In 1983, this airplane was Grand Champion Warbird at the huge Oshkosh, Wisconsin, air show. It was restored by the museum exactly the way it looked in World War II when it was part of the Naval Air Transport Service. (NATS.)

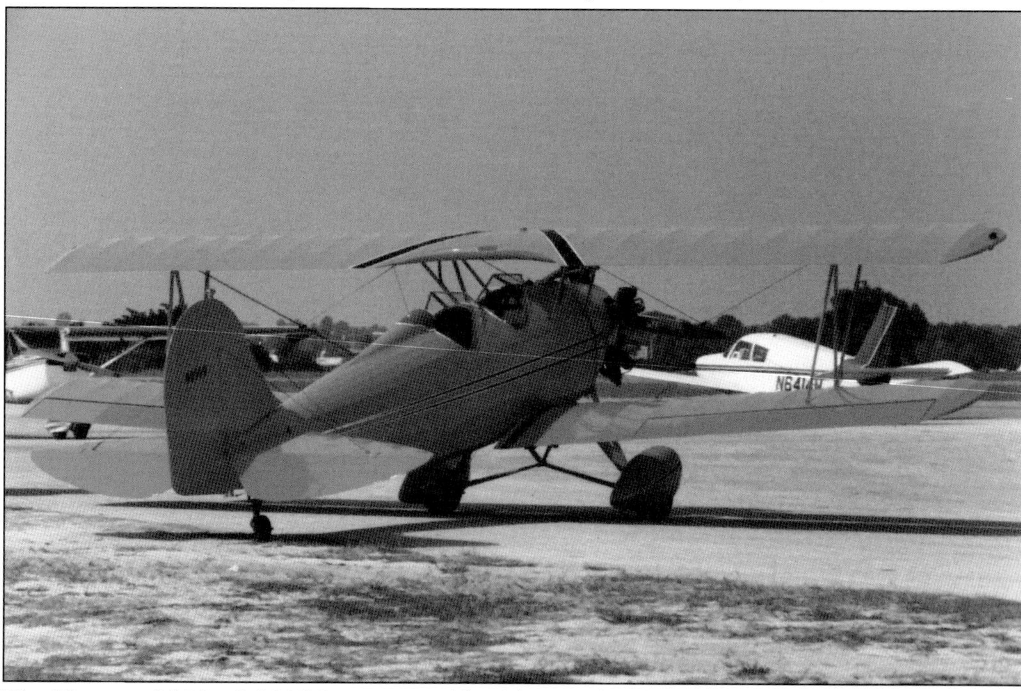

The Fleet model No. 9, N66V, was owned by Alexis Felix duPont Jr. Designed by Maj. Reuben Fleet, it was a robust primary trainer built by Consolidated Aircraft, of which Fleet was a subsidiary. Lieutenant Colonel duPont flew combat missions with the Troop Carrier Command in the Far East Air Force in World War II. (JC.)

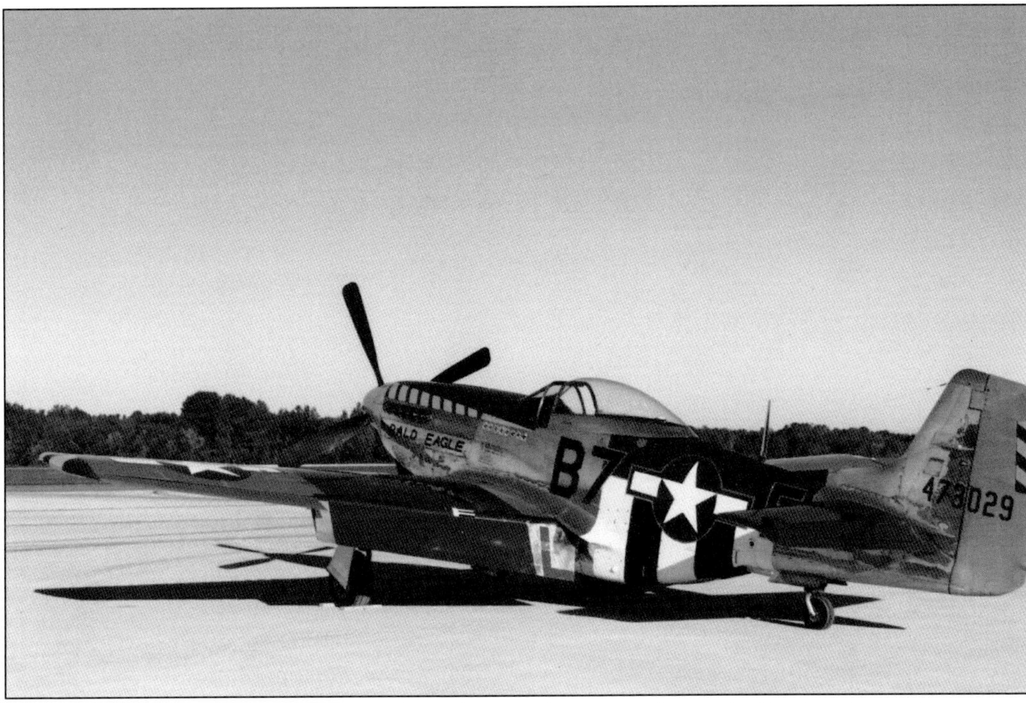

The P-51 Mustang, named *Bald Eagle* and flown by owner James E. Beasley, is on display at a Delaware Air National Guard open house. This popular World War II fighter airplane served in World War II and Korea. (JC.)

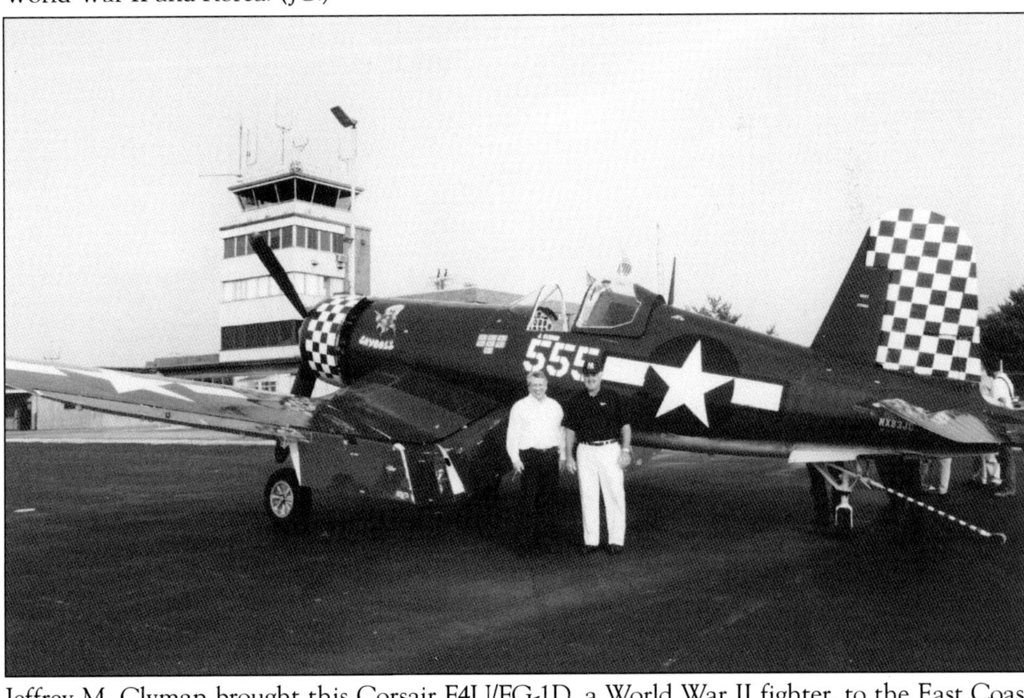

Jeffrey M. Clyman brought this Corsair F4U/FG-1D, a World War II fighter, to the East Coast Fly-in at New Castle County Airport in 1995. Clyman (right) is pictured with air show enthusiast Gene Smith. (JC.)

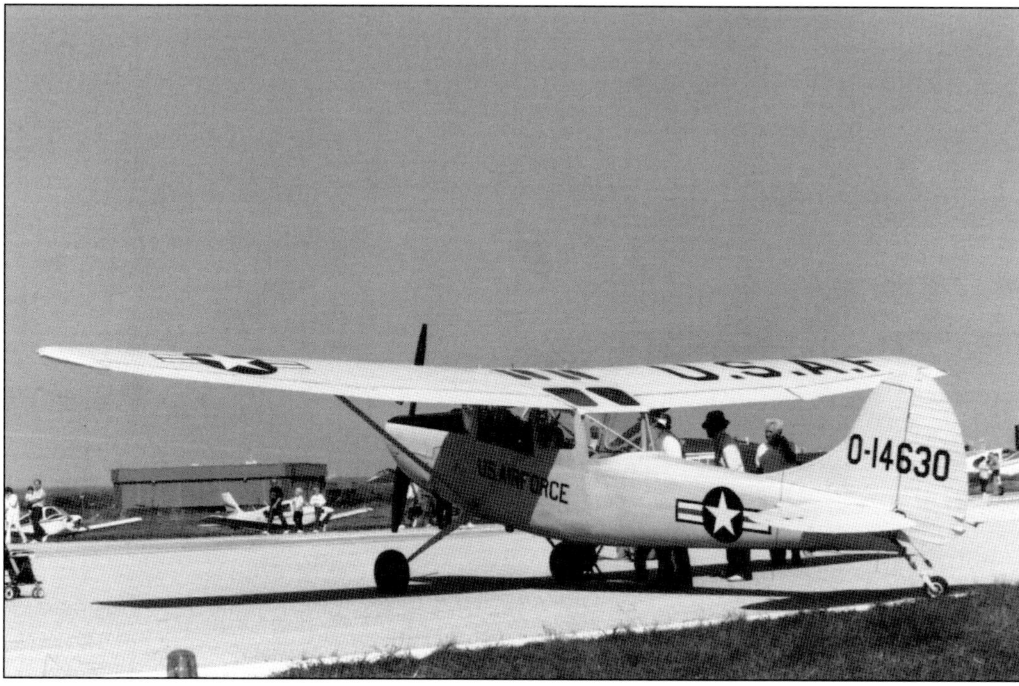

On display at many air shows is Jan Churchill's Cessna O-1 Bird Dog. Churchill restored this airplane to its original military configuration with gun racks, as it would have looked when flown in Vietnam. (JC.)

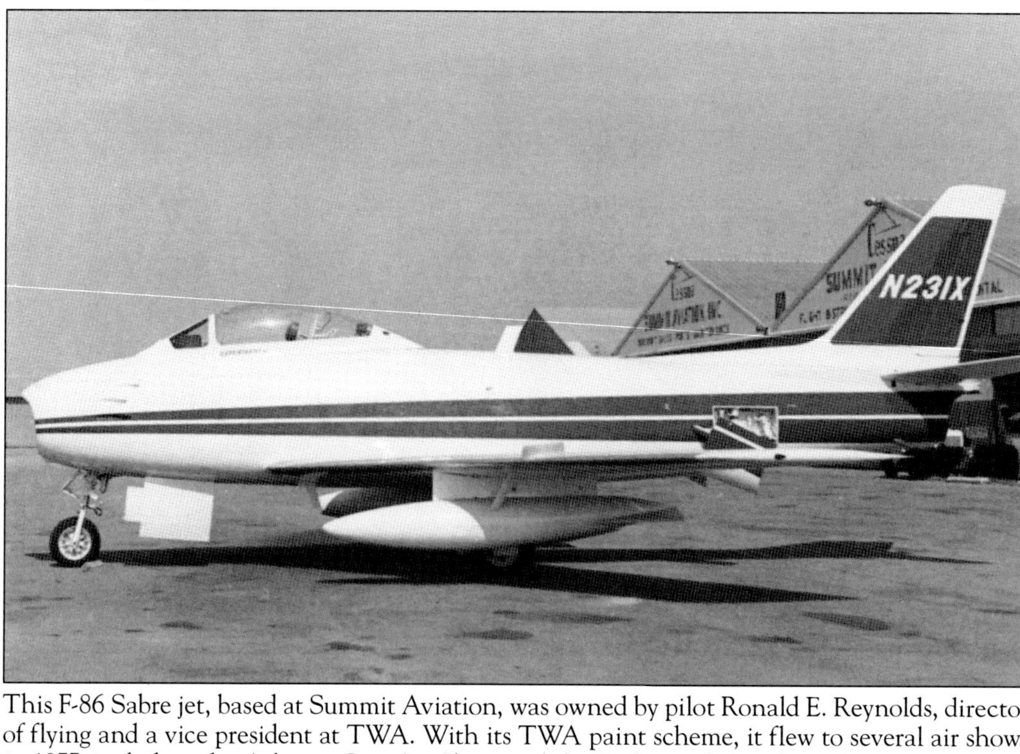

This F-86 Sabre jet, based at Summit Aviation, was owned by pilot Ronald E. Reynolds, director of flying and a vice president at TWA. With its TWA paint scheme, it flew to several air shows in 1977, including the Atlantic City Air Show and the Richmond Air Show. (JC.)

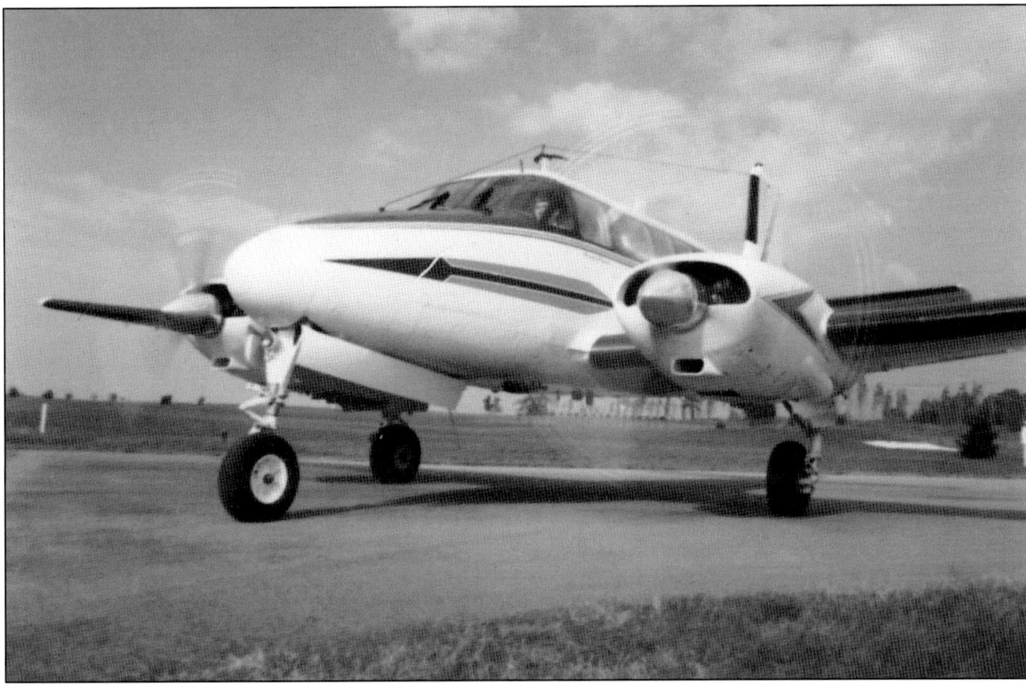

This Beechcraft BE-65 Queen Air, owned by famous harness-racing driver Stanley Dancer, was often seen picking up his veterinarian, Dr. Edwin A. Churchill, at Summit Aviation in Middletown. This airplane, N738SD, was white with blue-and-yellow trim, Dancer's racing colors. (JC.)

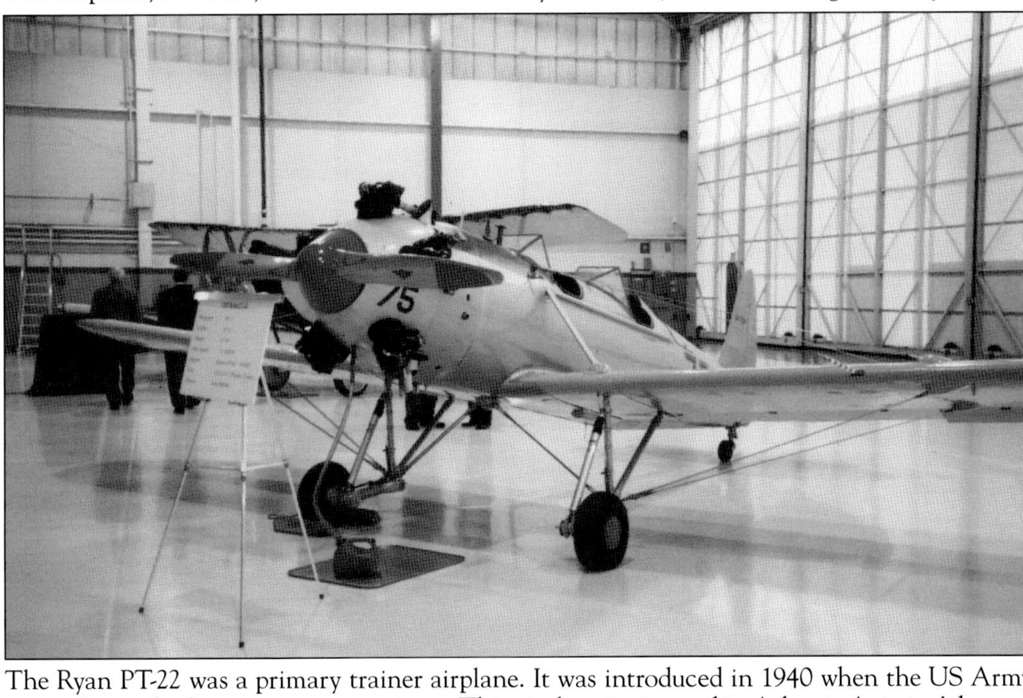

The Ryan PT-22 was a primary trainer airplane. It was introduced in 1940 when the US Army stopped using biplanes as primary trainers. This airplane is pictured in Atlantic Aviation's hangar at New Castle County Airport for the first Delaware Aviation Hall of Fame Banquet in October 2000. (JC.)

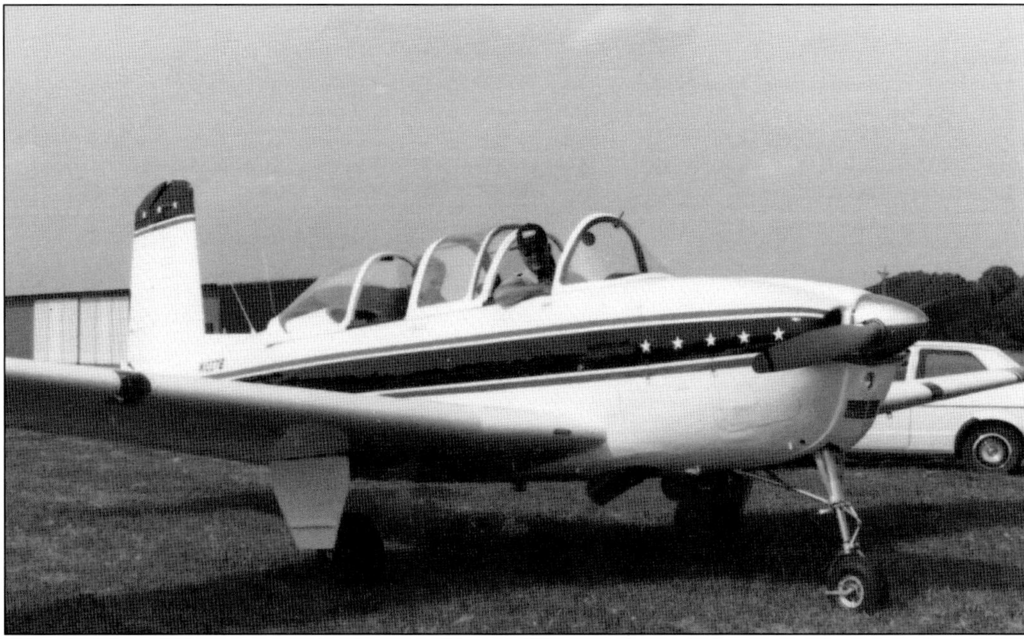

This photograph of a two-seater Beechcraft T-34 shows owner-pilot Joseph Cael, a TWA international pilot, as he taxies out for a flight from Summit Airpark in Middletown in 1980. Joseph Manion was a passenger in the rear seat. (JC.)

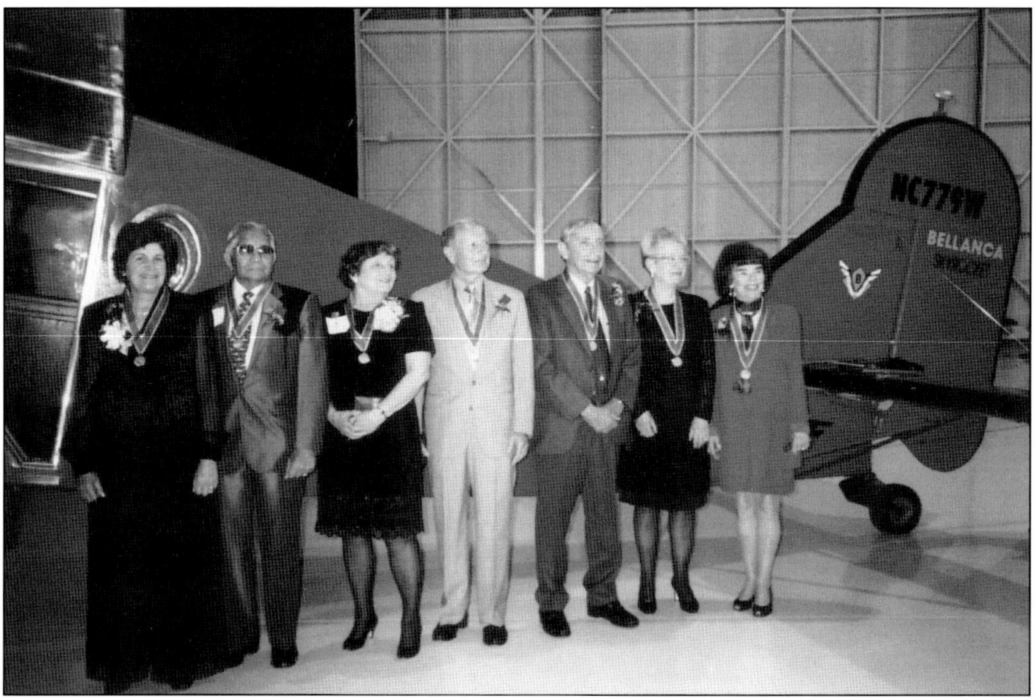

The first inductees into the Delaware Aviation Hall of Fame are pictured on October 21, 2000, in Atlantic Aviation's hangar. From left to right are Jan Churchill, Floyd H.L. Durham, Anne C. Eriksen, James R. Sulpizi, and family members of deceased honorees Guiseppe Mario Bellanca (1886–1960), George P. Durney (1923–1998), and Richard H. Ellis (1919–1989). (JC.)

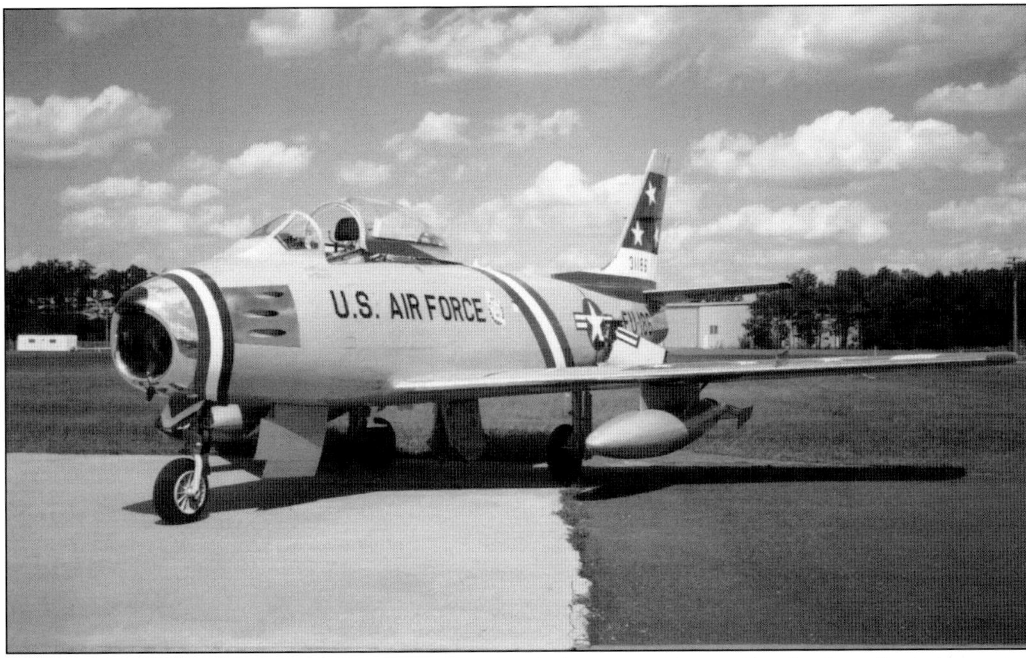

This F-86 Sabre jet fighter was flown to New Castle by owner Steven Snyder for a fly-in honoring men who were fighter pilots in Korea in this type of airplane. This was America's first swept-wing fighter-interceptor and fighter-bomber. F-86s continued in US service with the Air National Guard until 1970. (AK.)

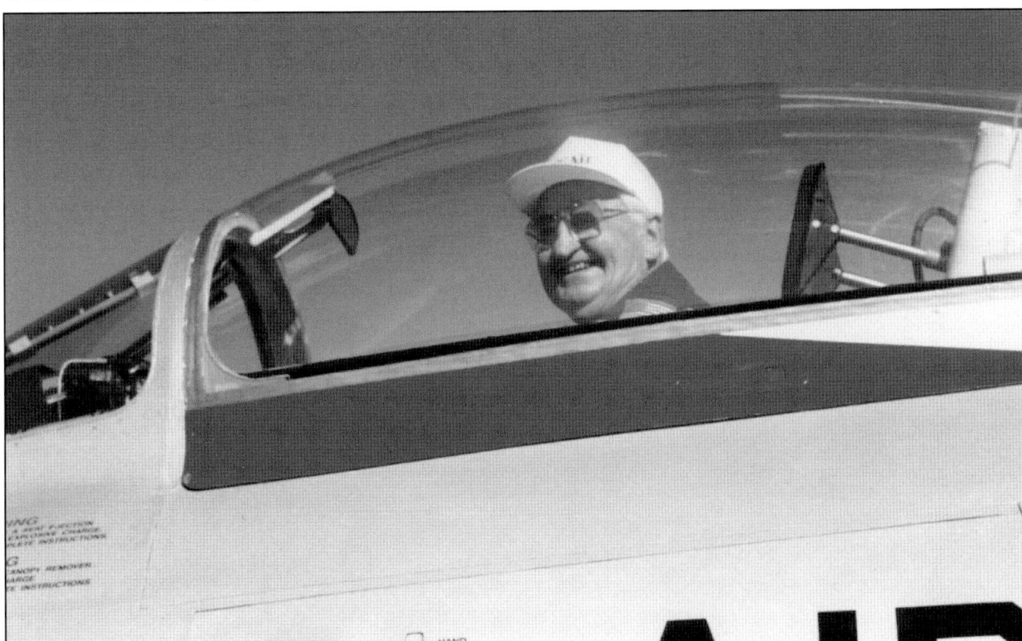

Col. Francis "Gabby" Gabreski, known as the "Ace of Aces," enjoys sitting in this F-86, owned by Steven Snyder. Gabreski's exploits as a fighter pilot in World War II and Korea were legendary. Gabreski flew F-86s in Korea where he scored 6 ½ victories, making him one of the few pilots to obtain "ace" status in two wars in propeller and jet aircraft. (JC.)

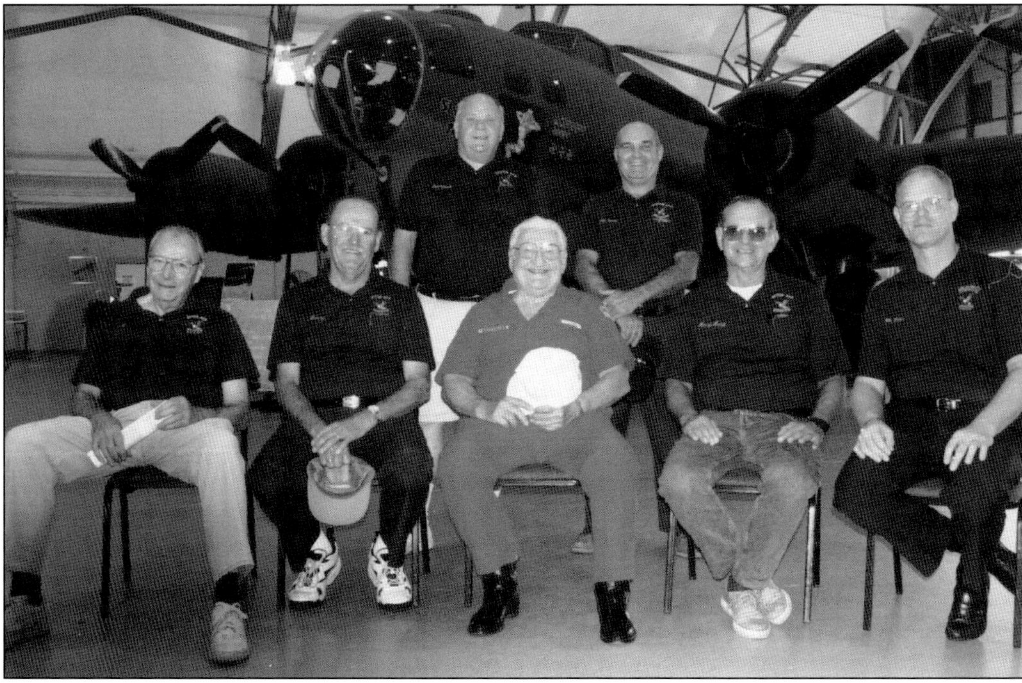

Col. Francis "Gabby" Gabreski (center) sits with docents at the Air Mobility Command Museum at Dover Air Force Base. Seated at far right is Michael Leister, director of the museum. The plane in the background is a B-17 Flying Fortress four-engine bomber. (JC.)

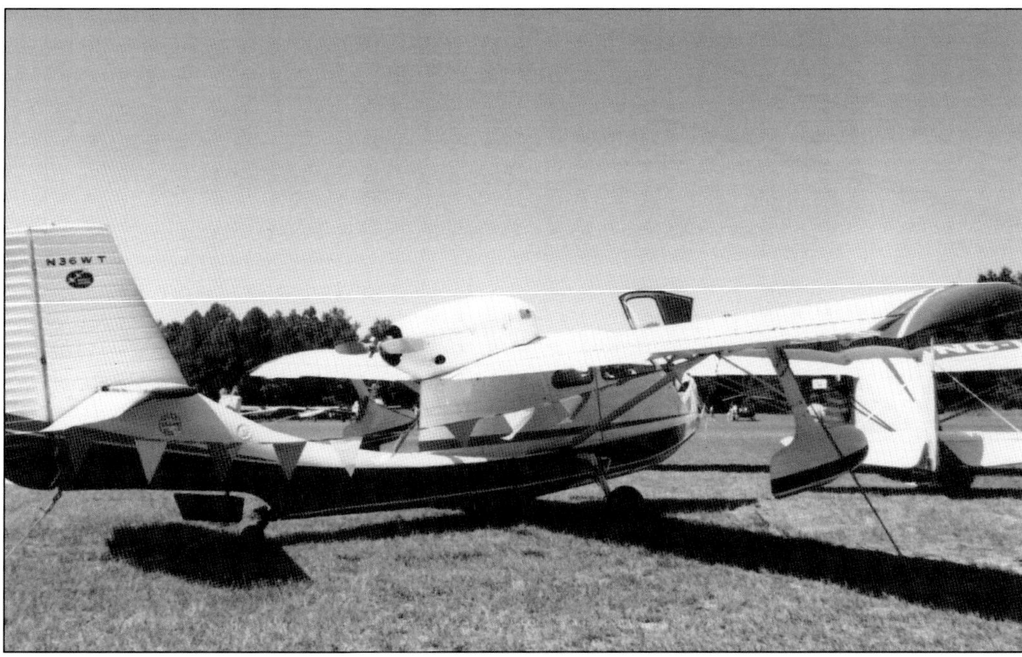

This is a Republic Seabee amphibian plane, owned by Lee Clark, at a fly-in at Summit Airpark in Middletown. Note the engine is high enough on the wing to avoid water splashing as the main cabin floats in the water. There are sponsons under the wings for stability in water. The wheels retract for water landings. (JC.)

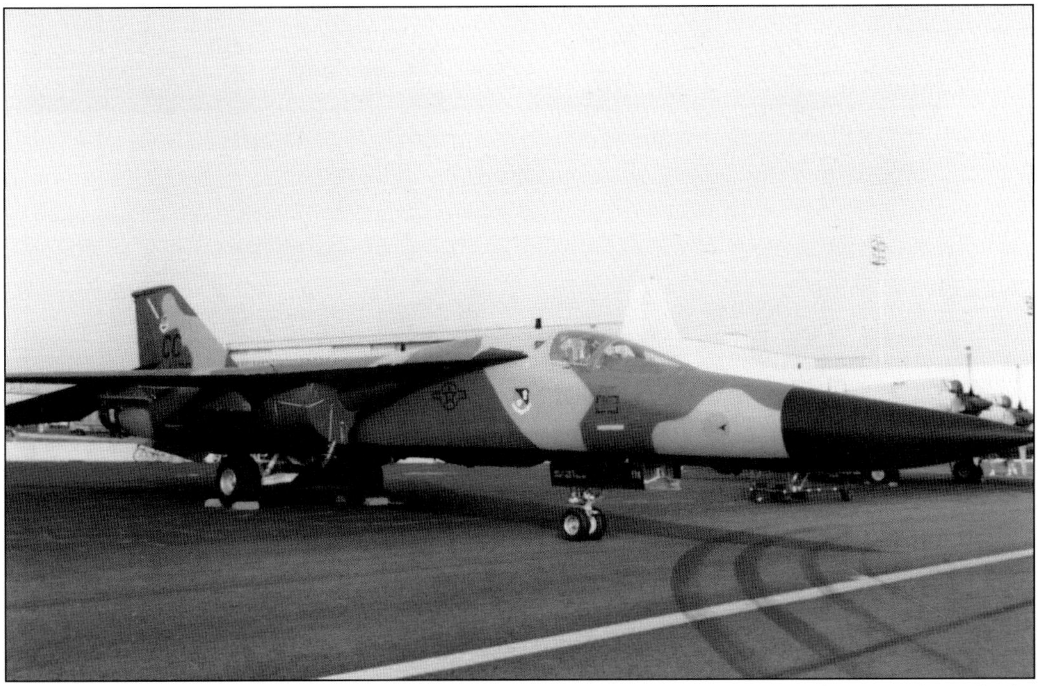

General Dynamics FB-111 Aardark long-range medium interceptor and strike aircraft, with the swept-wing platform, is at the open house at Dover Air Force Base in 1991. The FB-111 was retired in 1996 from active service with the US Air Force. (JC.)

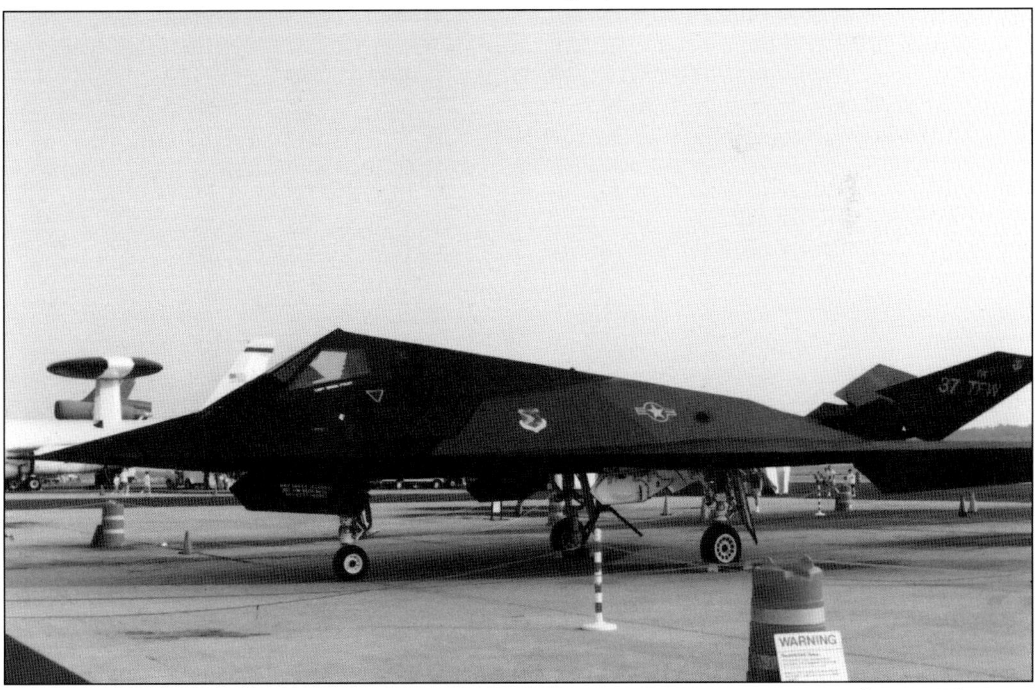

An F-117A Nighthawk stealth fighter is at the 1991 Dover Air Force Base open house. This was the world's first operational stealth aircraft used only for nighttime missions. The surfaces and edge profiles are optimized to reflect hostile radar. (JC.)

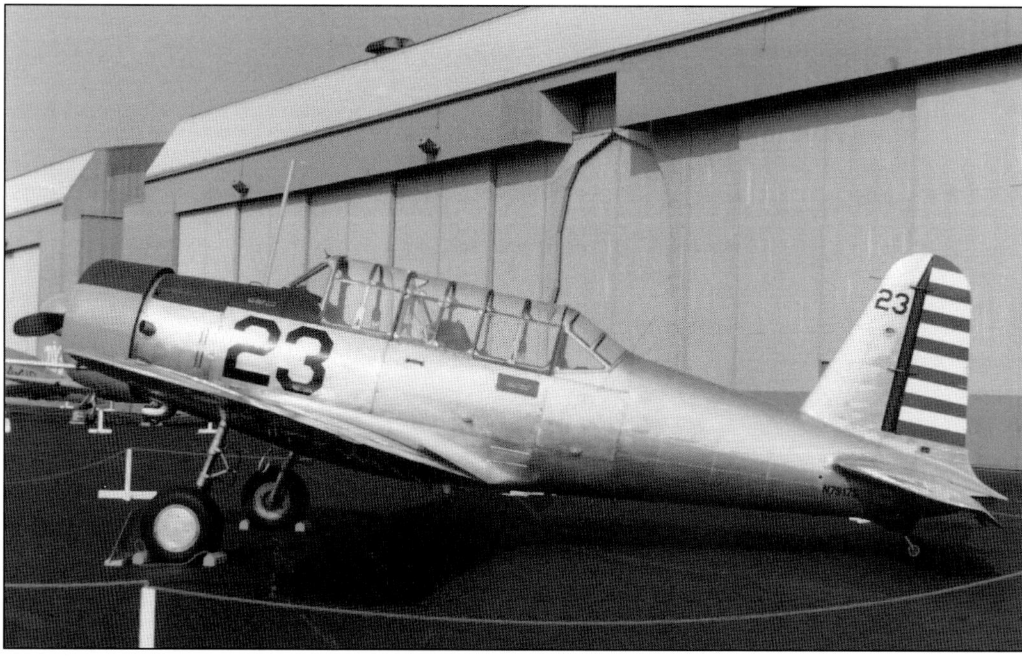

A Vultee BT-13 Valiant, owned by North Canaan Aviation, is seen on display at the Dover Air Force Base open house in 1991. After initial primary pilot instruction, many aviation cadets during World War II transitioned into a BT-13 for basic training, aerobatics, and instrument training. (JC.)

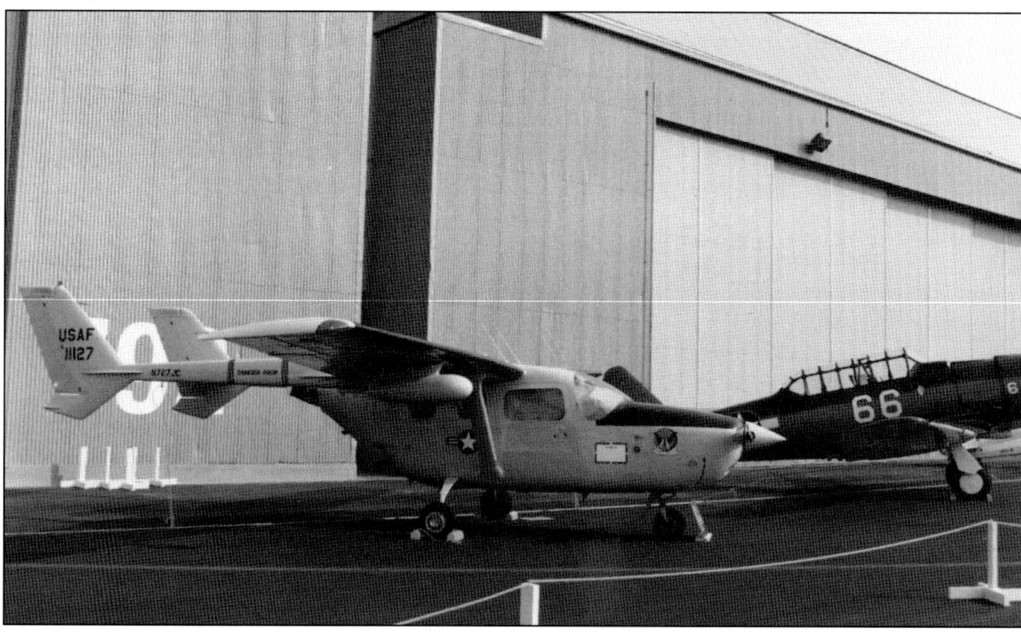

A Cessna O-2 Skymaster, owned by Jan Churchill, and a North American AT-6 trainer, flown in by Jeffrey Ethell, a prominent aviation writer, were at the Dover Air Force Base open house on July 6–7, 1991. The O-2, sometimes called "Oscar Deuce" by the military, was built to replace the O-1 Bird Dog. The O-2 and O-1 were used for forward air control in Vietnam. The AT-6 was an advanced trainer. (JC.)

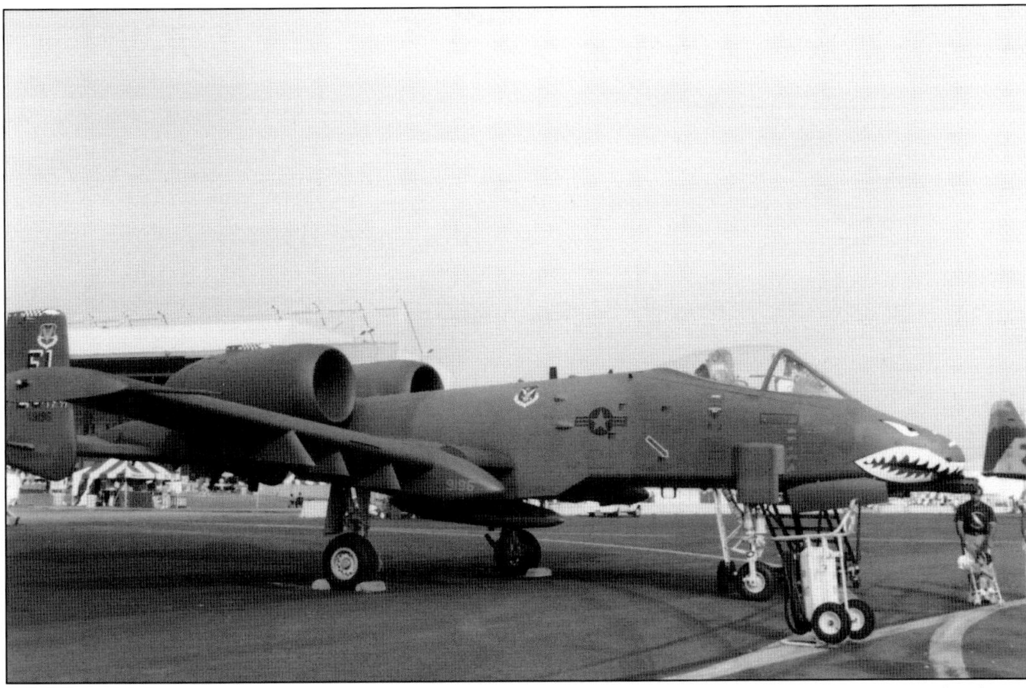

A Fairchild A-10 Thunderbolt II "Warthog" from the Maryland National Guard is on display at the Dover Air Force Base open house in 1991. The A-10 was designed in the early 1970s as close air support for ground forces and forward air control. It had superior mobility at low speeds and altitudes and could operate from primitive forward airfields. (JC.)

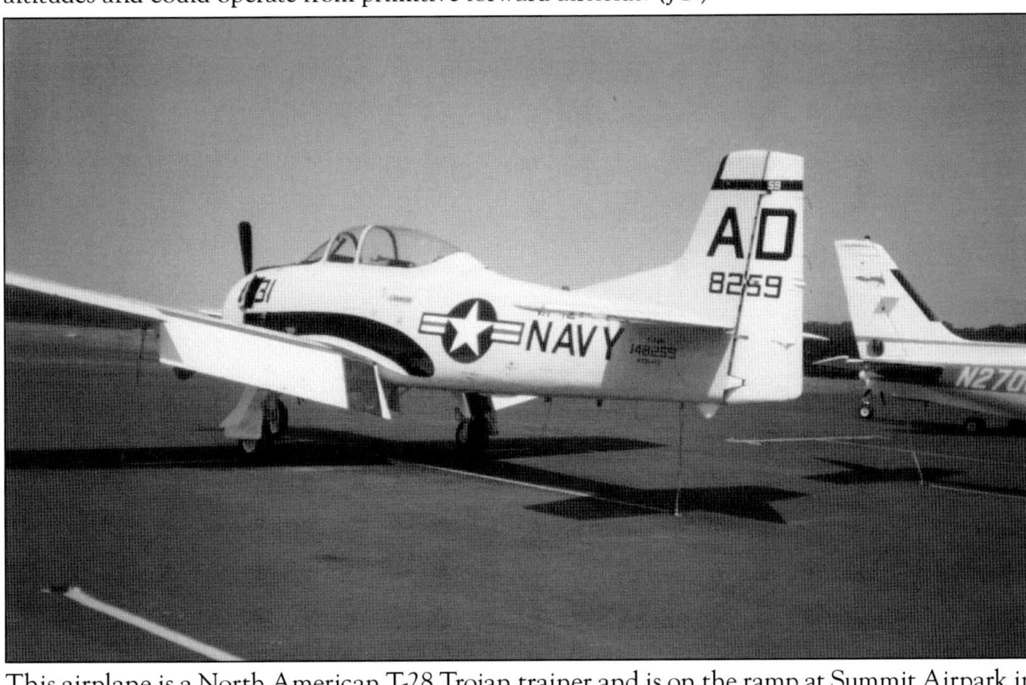

This airplane is a North American T-28 Trojan trainer and is on the ramp at Summit Airpark in Middletown. Beginning in the 1950s, the US Air Force and US Navy used it. It also saw service primarily in the Vietnam War as a counter-insurgency (COIN) aircraft. (CduP.)

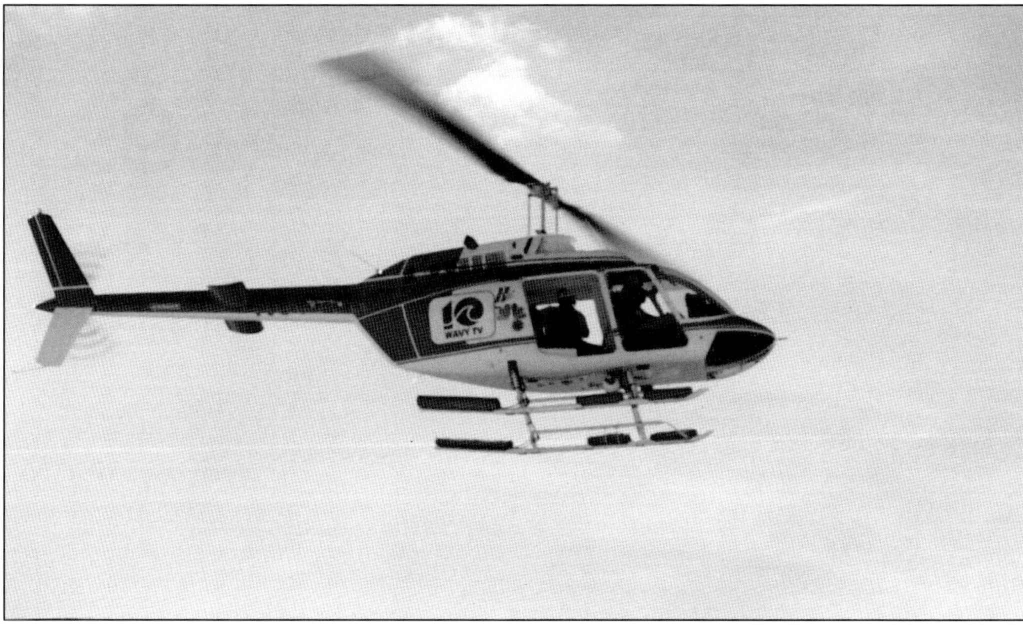

The WAVY News Bell Jet Ranger hovers over New Castle County Airport in 1998. Beginning service in 1967, this became the most successful commercial helicopter. It was also used by the US Army as an observation helicopter, the OH-58 Kiowa. (JC.)

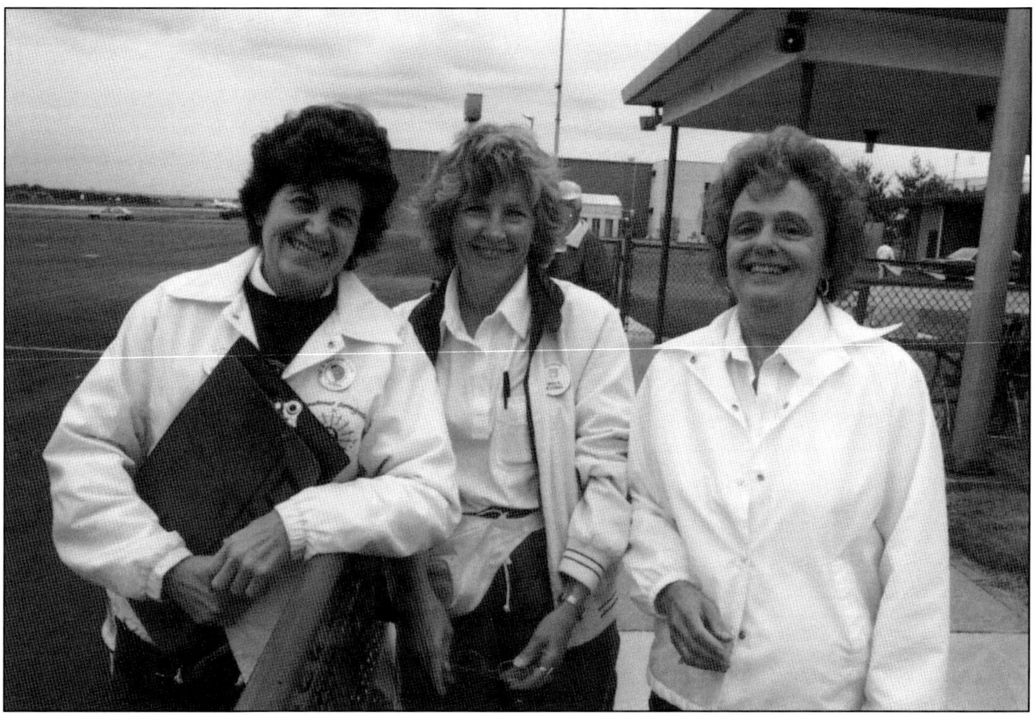

Judges for the NIFA (National Intercollegiate Flying Association) Regional Competition in 1981 were, from left to right, Jan Churchill, Marilyn Alderman, and Anne Eriksen. All pilots, they were members of the Delaware Chapter of the Ninety-Nines, International Organization of Women Pilots. NIFA was formed in 1919; Delaware was in Region VII. (JC.)

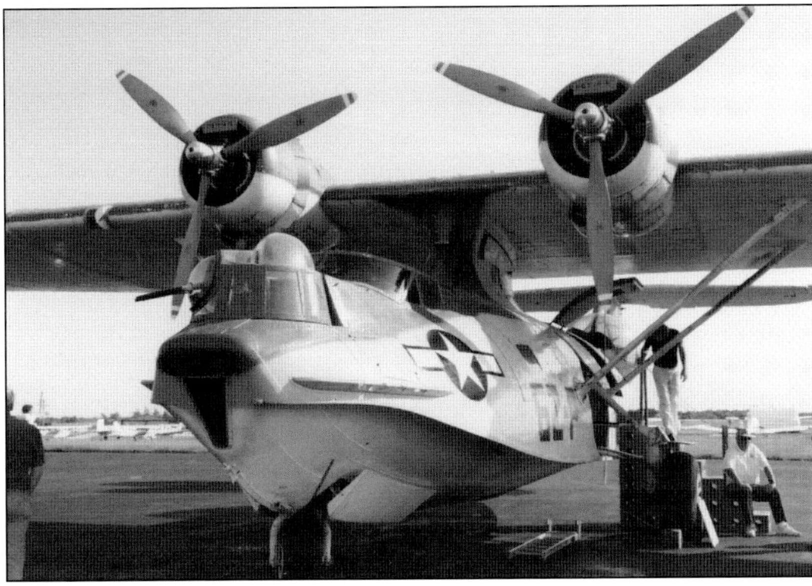

A US Consolidated PBY Catalina flying boat, and later amphibian, is shown visiting New Castle for a regional fly-in in 1992. The PBY was one of the most numerous aircraft of its kind. Its first flight was March 28, 1935. It was not retired from military service until the 1980s. (EAA.)

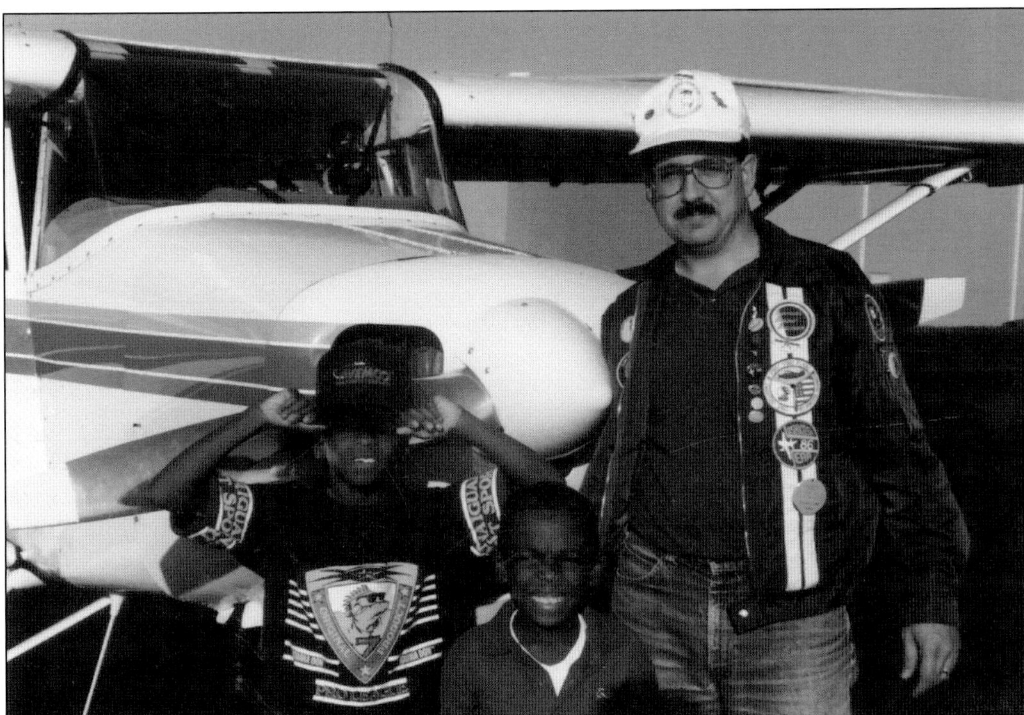

To celebrate the 100th anniversary of the Wright brothers first flight in 1903, EAA began a program asking its members to give airplane rides to one million children by 2003. In this image, pilot Lee Thomas is shown with "Young Eagles" Reggie (left) and William (right) Thompson after their flight. (EAA.)

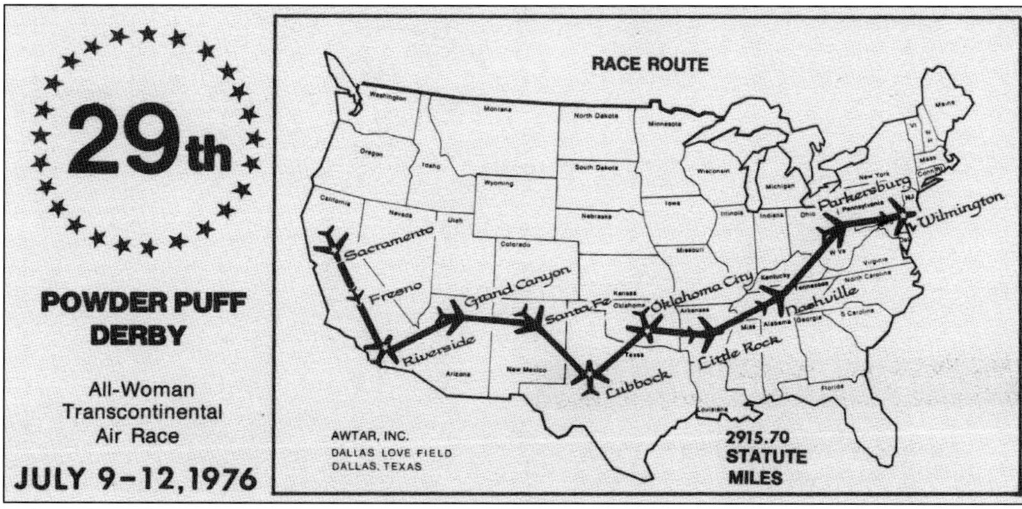

When the All-Woman Transcontinental Air Race (AWTAR) officials announced that the 1976 race, known as the Powder Puff Derby, would be the last AWTAR race, they limited the field to 200 airplanes, the largest race ever. This image shows the route, and its stops, from Sacramento, California, to Wilmington, Delaware, a distance of 2,915.70 miles. (JC.)

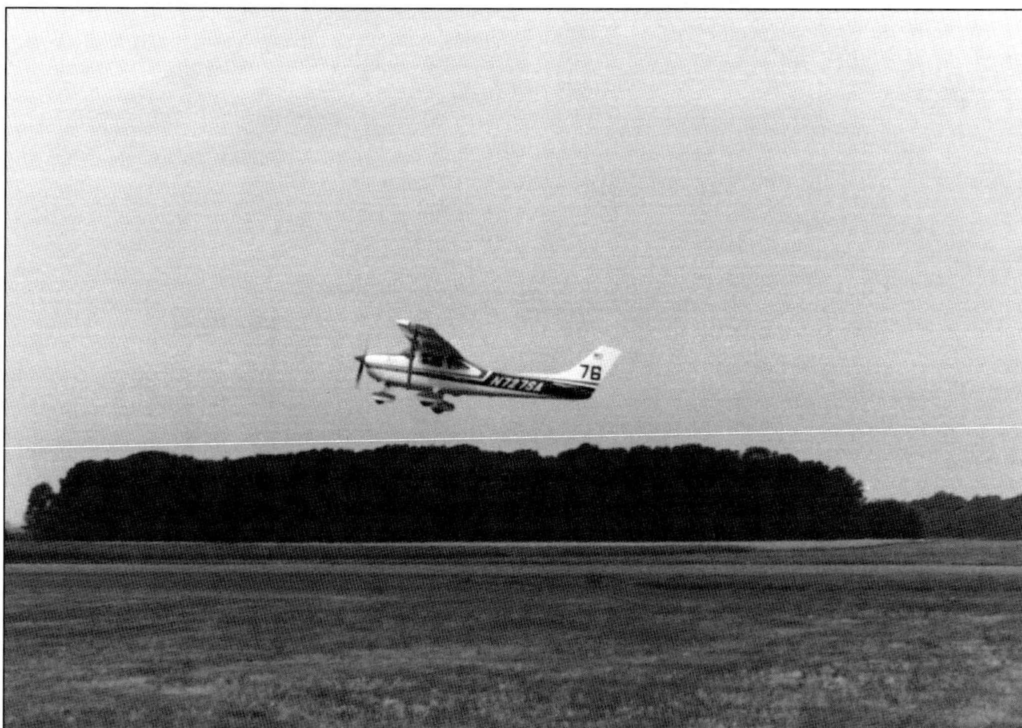

This image shows AWTAR competitor No. 76 departing Summit Airpark, Middletown, for California, for the start of the race. The Cessna 182, sponsored by Summit Aviation, with Jan Churchill, pilot, and Dorothy Miller, copilot, was assigned No. 76 because it was the first plane from Delaware to enter the race during the United States' bicentennial year. Summit Aviation purchased a new C-182. Churchill flew it from Kansas to Delaware where Summit Aviation installed the latest in avionics. (JC.)

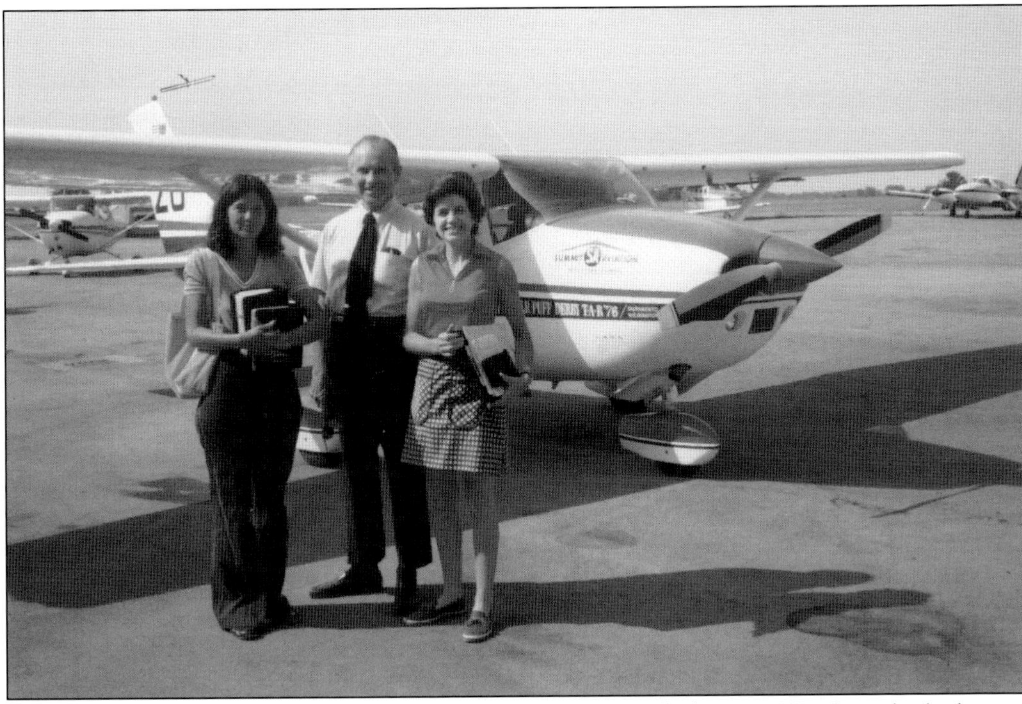

The AWTAR officials decided to have a 30th anniversary flight in 1977, after which the race trophy was retired to the Smithsonian Museum in Washington, DC. This image shows Caroline duPont (left) and Jan Churchill (right) with John McChesney Morgan, Summit Aviation's manager, and Churchill's Cessna 182, which was sponsored by Summit Aviation. This image is at Summit Airpark before the race pilots departed for California. (JC.)

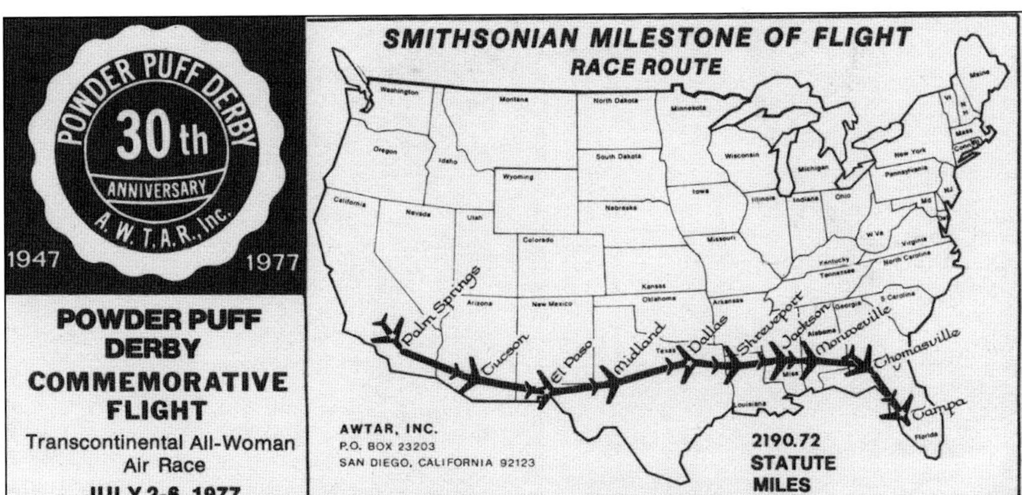

The commemorative flight went from Palm Springs, California, to Tampa, Florida. This race ended the Powder Puff Derby, which lasted from 1947 to 1977. Leaving Palm Springs on an extremely hot day, contestants had to fly through several difficult weather systems before reaching the East Coast. Flying at very low levels, they had wonderful views of the countryside. (JC.)

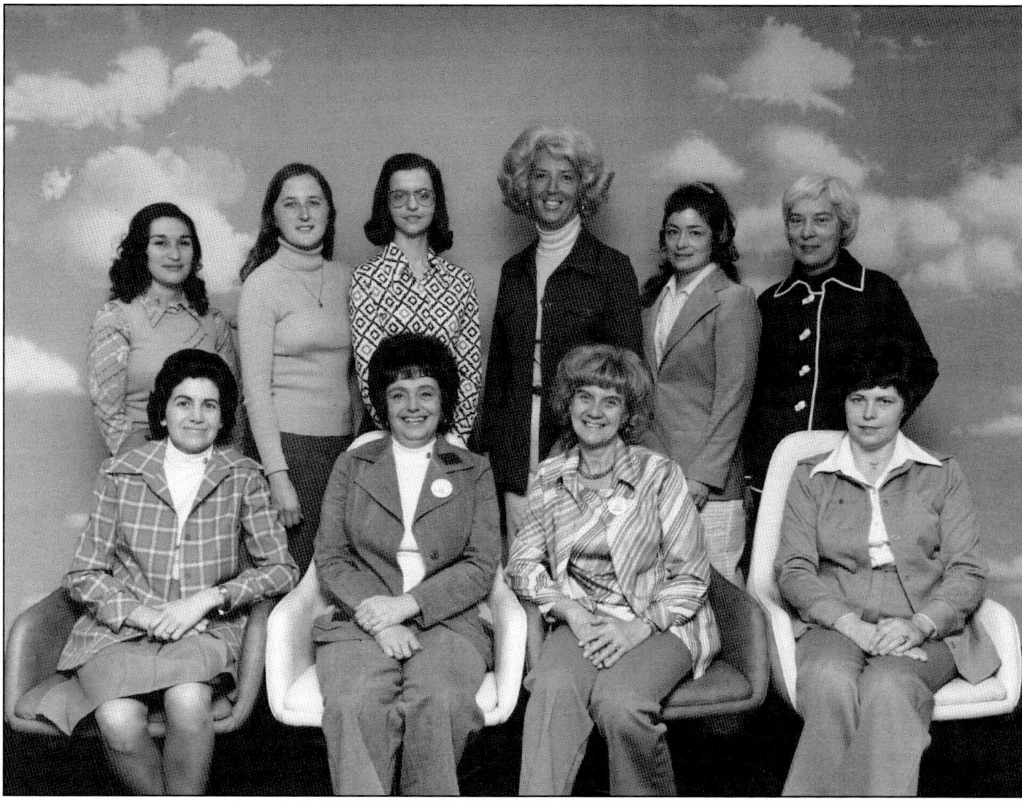

This photograph shows the 1976 terminus committee for the Powder Puff Derby. Pictured are, from left to right, (sitting) Jan Churchill, Anne Eriksen, Kate Macario, and Beverly Howett; (standing) Pepi Eskin, Lori Robb, Mary Ann Gorski, Gail Lingo, Julie Jones, and Adelaide Tinker. This image was taken in the terminal building at manager William Comer's office at New Castle County Airport. (JC.)

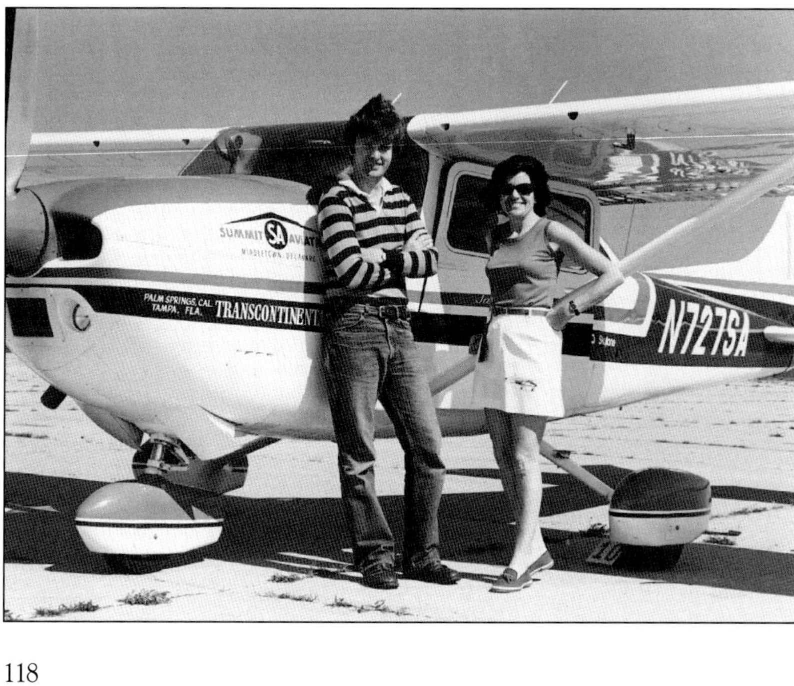

This race team competed in the Garden State 300 in 1978. Jan Churchill, pilot, and Steven Seningen, copilot, are standing by Churchill's C-182 at Summit Airpark in Middletown. (JC.)

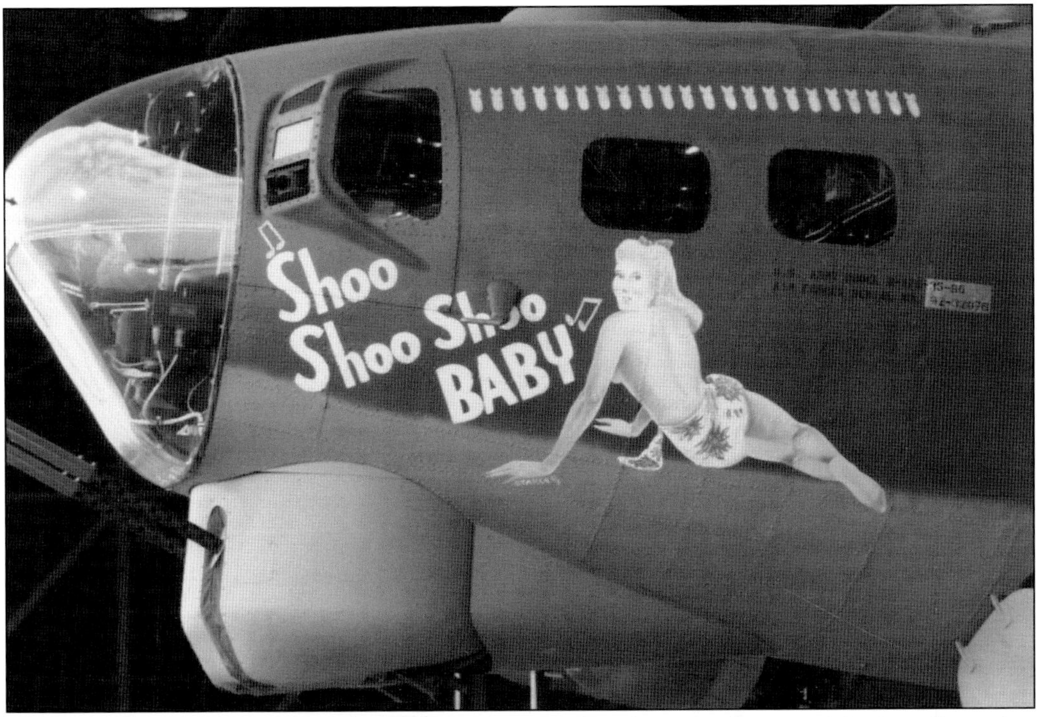

This B-17 Flying Fortress, *Shoo Shoo Baby*, was painstakingly restored to its original configuration by military personnel and civilian volunteers at Dover Air Force Base. It is now on display at the National Museum of the US Air Force in Dayton, Ohio. (AMC.)

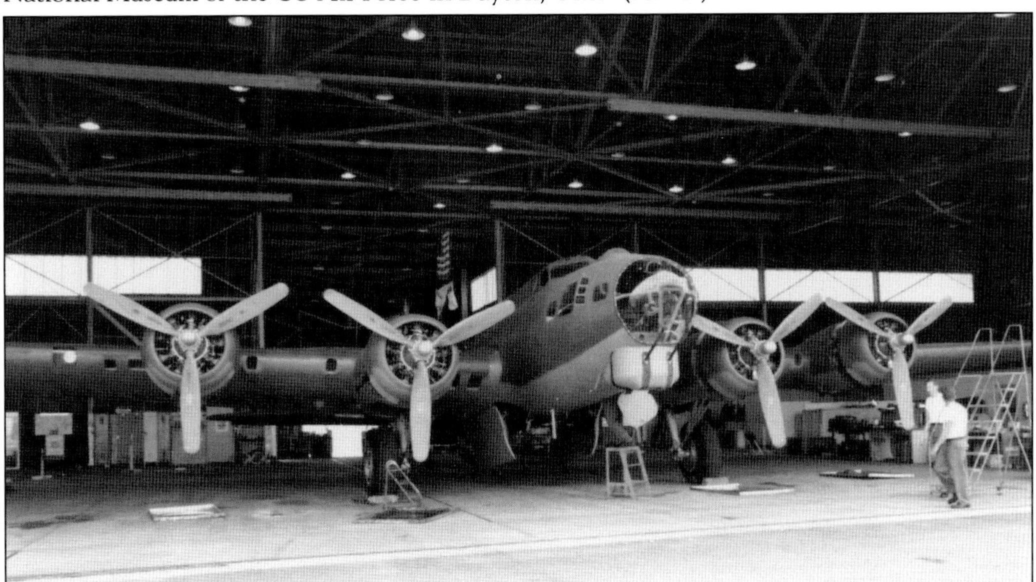

Shoo Shoo Baby is in the hangar at Dover Air Force Base during its restoration. From 1978 to 1988, the 512th Military Airlift Wing and civilian volunteers restored this B-17G, which entered service on January 19, 1944, using over 60,000 man-hours. In 1981, Tony Starcer re-created his original nose art. The B-17G was flown to Dayton, Ohio, on October 13, 1988, for display at the National Museum of the US Air Force. (JC.)

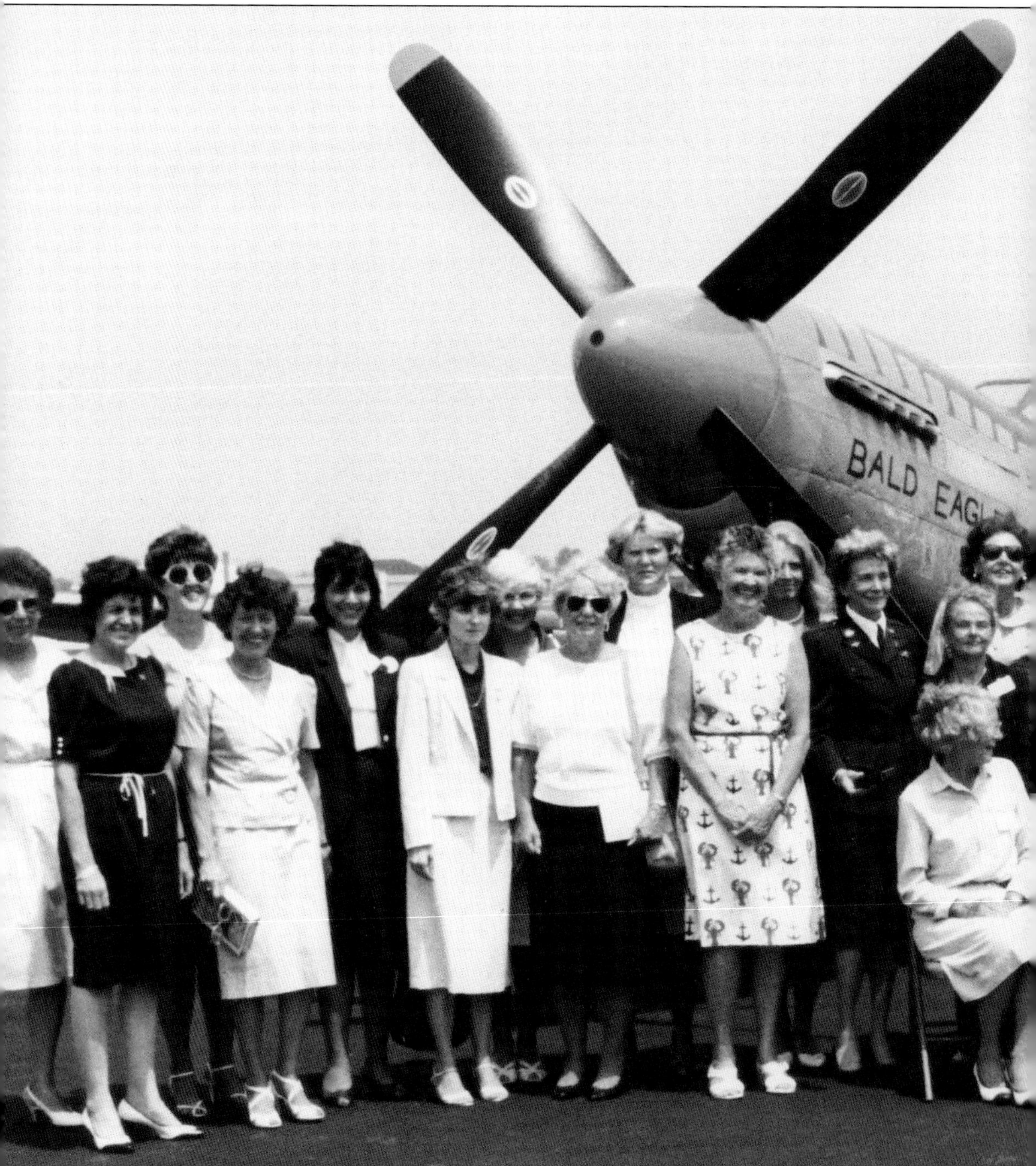

The WASPs returned to New Castle for the first time since World War II when they served as military pilots at New Castle Army Air Base. Joining them for the dedication of a bronze plaque honoring their service were women pilots from the Delaware Chapter of the Ninety-Nines, International Organization of Women Pilots. Some of the WASPs are seated in front of James E. Beasley's P-51 fighter airplane. Pictured are, from left to right, (sitting) Nancy Batson Crews, Betty H. Gillies, Adela Scharr, Kathryn "Sis" Bernheim, Teresa James, Barbara Poole Shoemaker, and

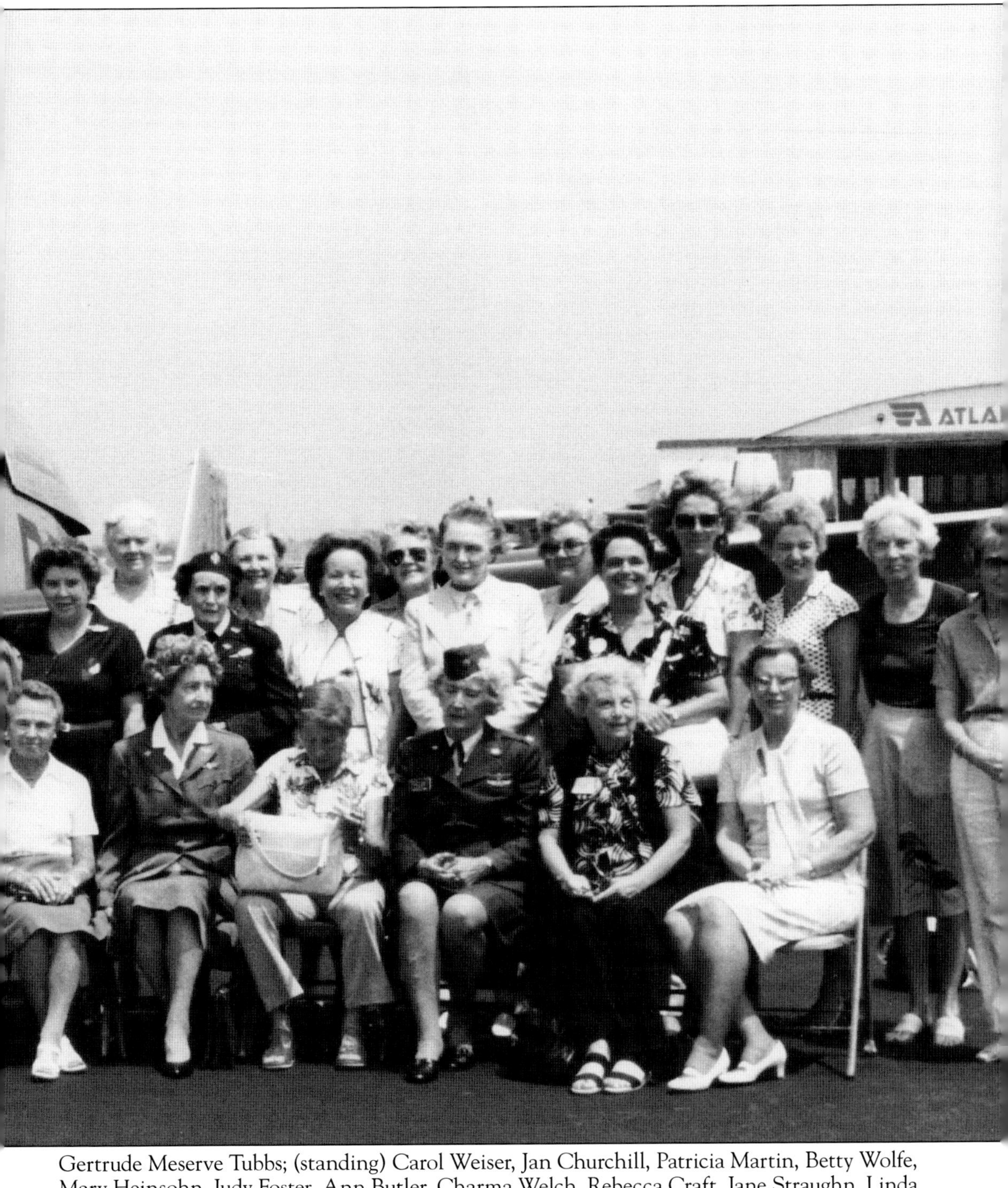

Gertrude Meserve Tubbs; (standing) Carol Weiser, Jan Churchill, Patricia Martin, Betty Wolfe, Mary Heinsohn, Judy Foster, Ann Butler, Charma Welch, Rebecca Craft, Jane Straughn, Linda Luchs, Bernice Falk Haydu, Jane Thomas Campbell, Kay Brick, Sadie Honan, Elizabeth Gilman, Frankie Yearwood, Nancy R. Johnson, Vivian Gilchrist Nemhauser, Elizabeth Sullivan, Ann Shields, Helen M. Schaeffer, Anne Eriksen, Virginia Batzel, Renne O'Leary, Adelaide Tinker, Midge Oliver, and Darlene Wolf. (JC.)

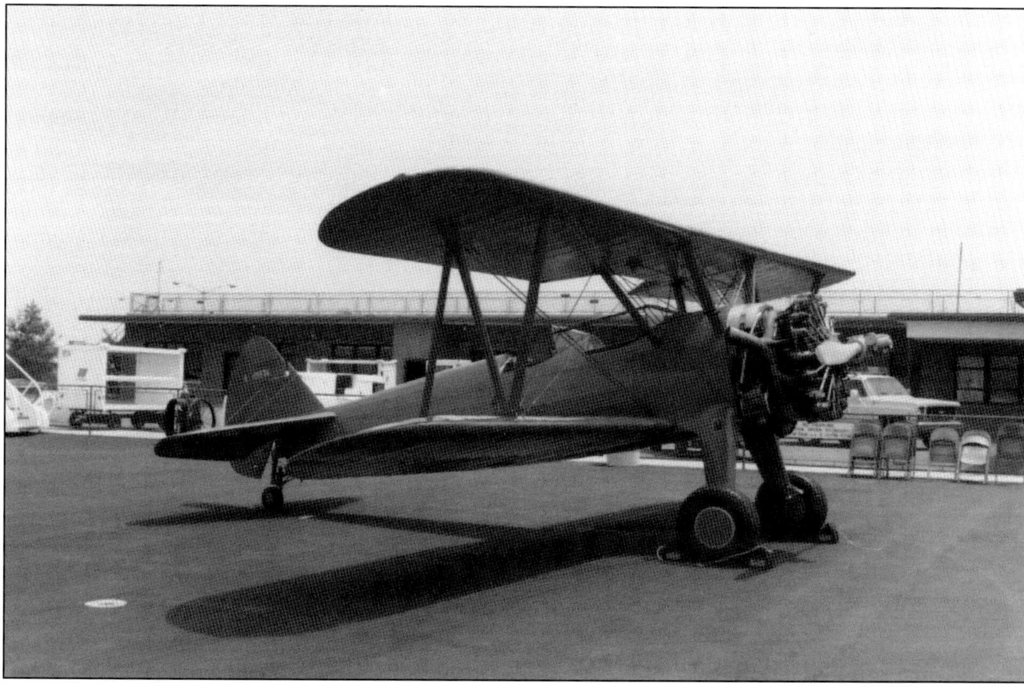

This image shows a PT-17 Stearman biplane, owned by Frederick G. Krapf III and Jan Churchill, on the ramp at New Castle County Airport for the WASP plaque dedication in 1985. The Boeing-Stearman model No. 75 was a military trainer. It was popular after the war with civilian pilots. Many were displayed at air shows for aerobatics and wing walking. (JC.)

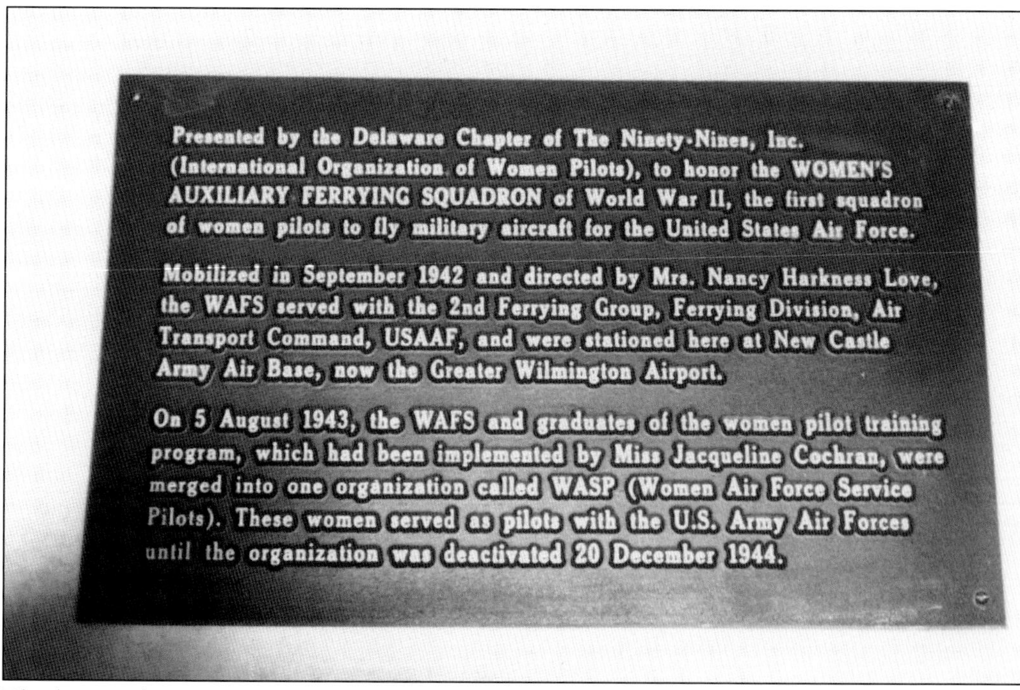

This bronze plaque is seen in the terminal building at New Castle County Airport. It honors the first women to fly for the US military; they began their service at New Castle Army Air Base. (JC.)

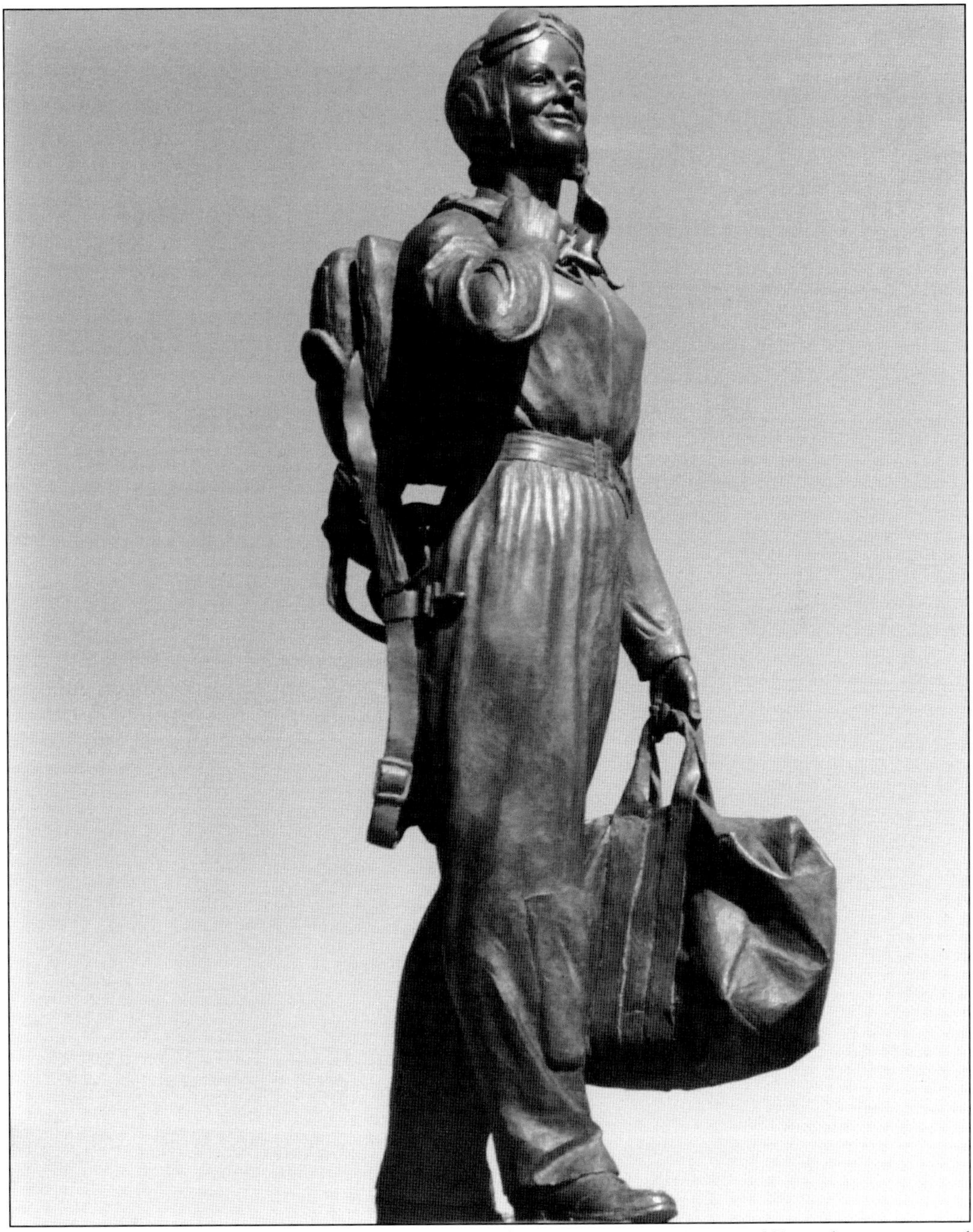

Sculptor Charles Cropper Parks, thanks to the Delaware Aviation Memorial Foundation, created this life-size bronze statue, named *To the Flightline*, of a WAFS/WASP with her parachute and B-4 bag. A special dedication ceremony took place at New Castle County Airport on October 7, 1995, as part of the World War II Victory Air Show, sponsored by the EAA East Coast Fly-in. (JC.)

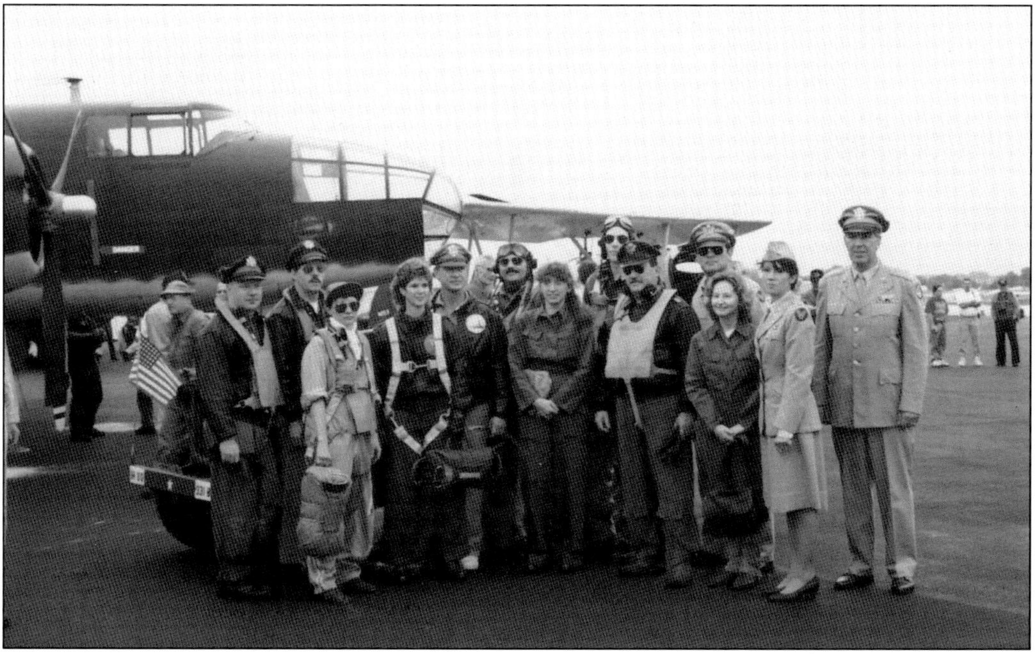

In October 1995, reenactors gathered in front of a B-25 World War II bomber for the dedication of the WASP statue at New Castle County Airport. Reenactors displayed original uniforms and brought history to life to educate the public at air show displays to honor veterans who had served. (JC.)

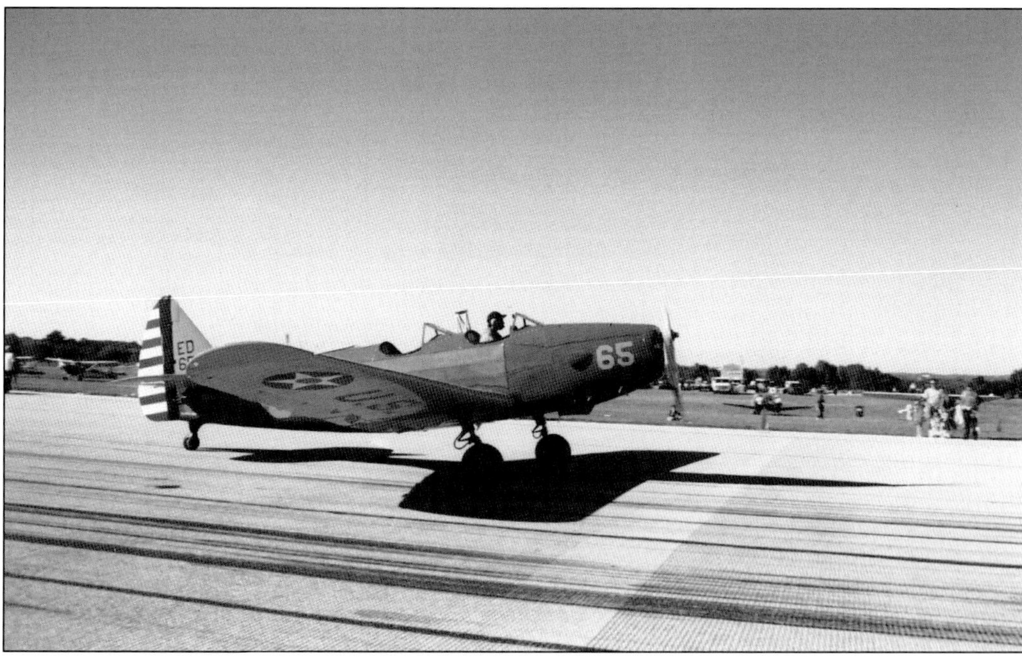

Pilot Michael Denest is arriving at New Castle in his award-winning PT-19, after flying the Missing Woman formation at the dedication of the WASP statue, *To the Flightline*, on October 7, 1995. At air shows, a tribute to those killed is flown by a formation of similar airplanes, with one pilot pulling up and away to honor those who gave their lives. (JC.)

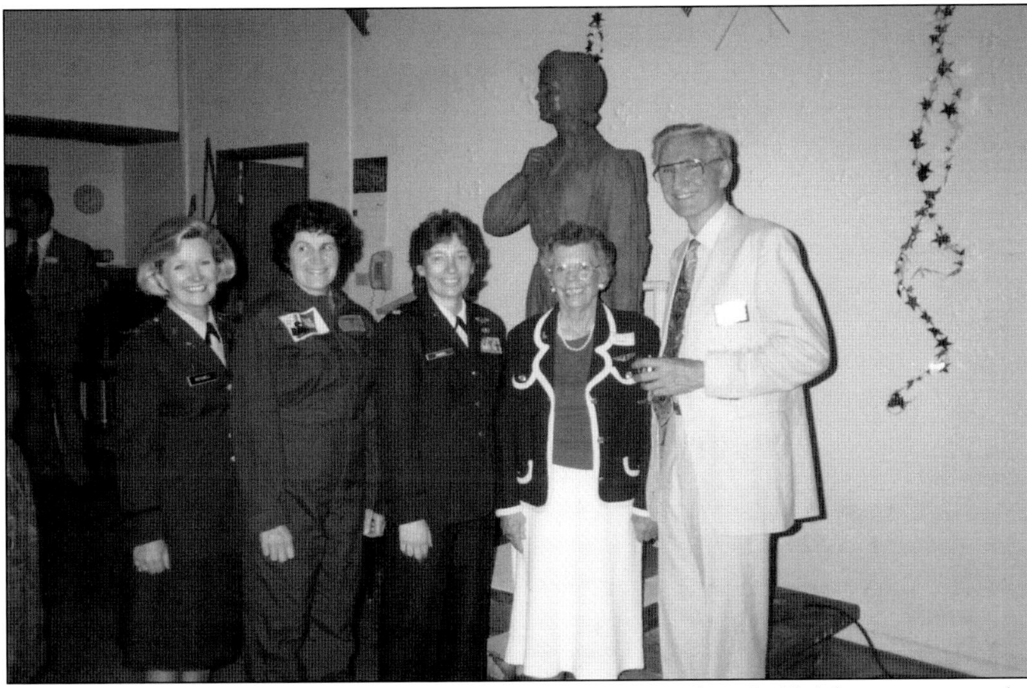

Charles Cropper Parks shows the clay model of the statue, named *To the Flightline*, to guests at his studio for a fundraiser. From left to right are Brig. Gen. Carol Mitchell, US Coast Guard aircraft commander Jan Churchill, Brig. Gen. Carol Timmons, WASP Faith P. Richards, and Parks. (JC.)

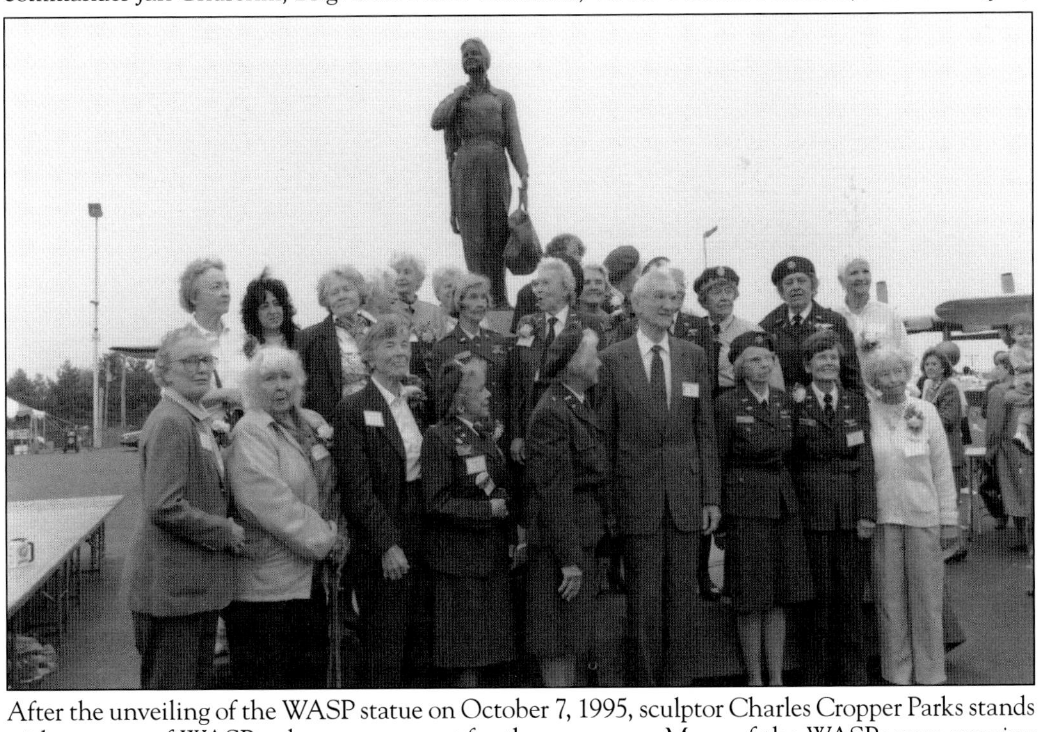

After the unveiling of the WASP statue on October 7, 1995, sculptor Charles Cropper Parks stands with a group of WASPs who were present for the ceremony. Many of the WASPs were wearing their original World War II uniforms. (JC.)

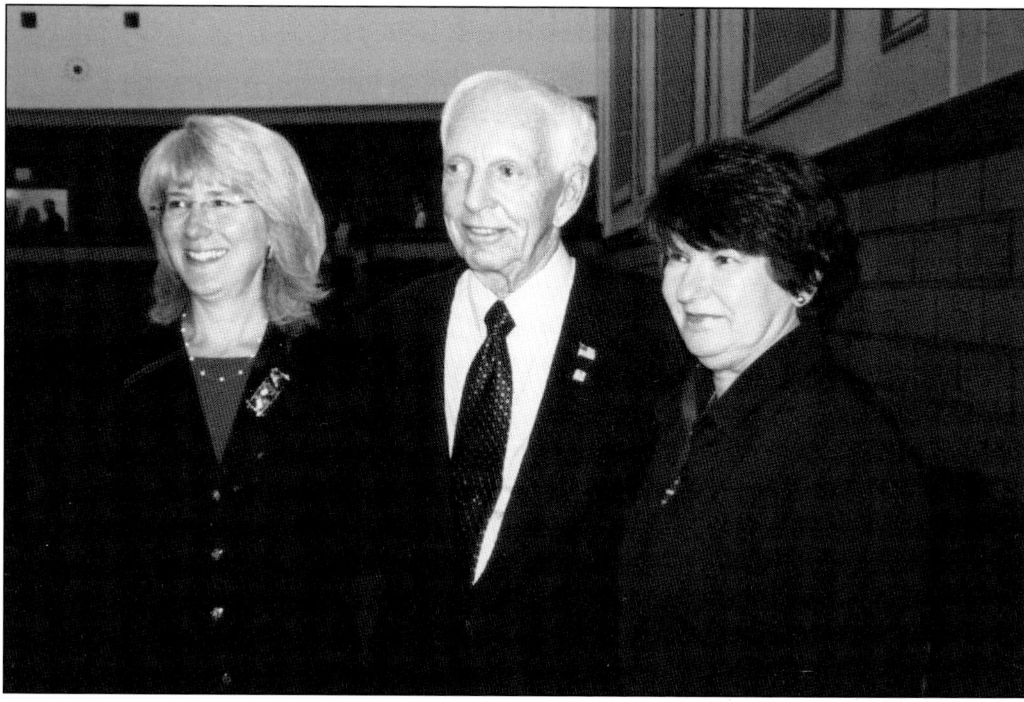

In 2003, aviation enthusiasts attended a lecture at William Penn High School, New Castle, to hear airline pilot Alfred C. "Al" Haynes speak about his miraculous landing in 1989 in a crippled DC-10. Although there were 112 fatalities, 185 passengers survived. Pictured to Haynes left is Nancy Rohr from the Delaware Ninety-Nines, and to his right is FAA Safety manager Eileen Iandola. (JC.)

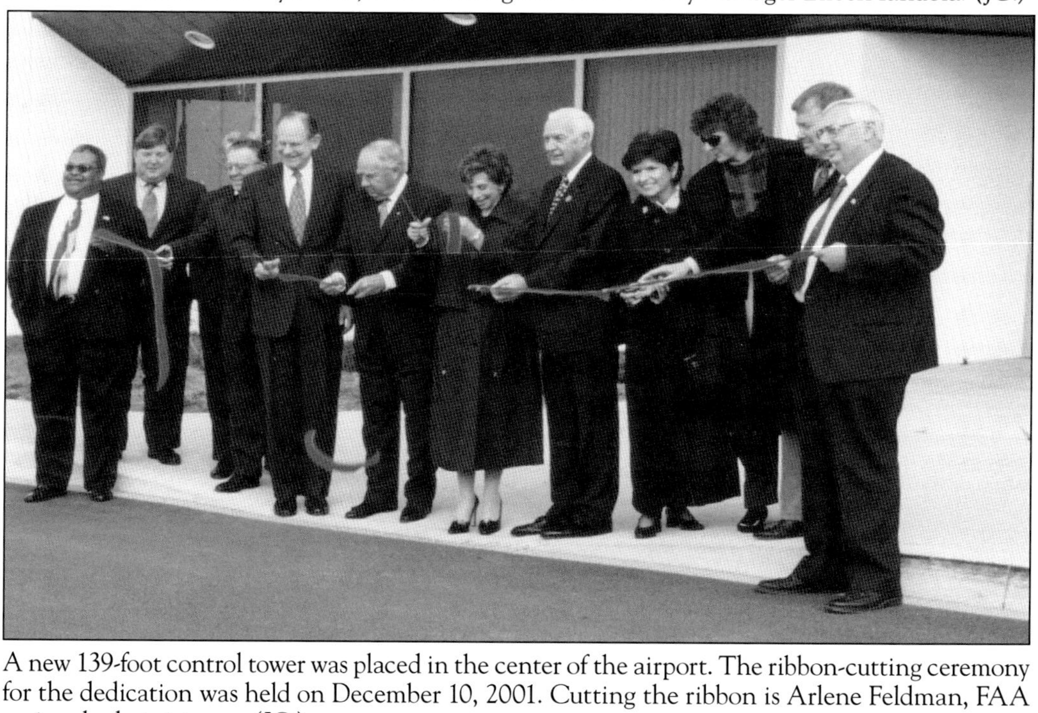

A new 139-foot control tower was placed in the center of the airport. The ribbon-cutting ceremony for the dedication was held on December 10, 2001. Cutting the ribbon is Arlene Feldman, FAA regional administrator. (JC.)

Bibliography

Abel, Alan, and Drina Welch Abel. *The Golden Age of Aviation Series: Bellanca's Golden Age.* Brawley, CA: Wind Canyon Books, 2004.

Churchill, Jan. *From Delaware to Everywhere: New Castle Army Air Base and New Castle County Airport.* New Castle, DE: J. Churchill Publishing, 2007.

———. *On Wings to War.* Manhattan, KS: Sunflower University Press, 1992.

Conner, William H., and Leon deValinger Jr. *Delaware's Role in World War II, Vo. I and II.* Dover, DE: Public Archives Commission, 1955, 2003.

Delaware National Guard 1946–1986, 40th Anniversary. Dallas, TX: Taylor Publishing, 1986.

Delaware National Guard 1946–1996, 50th Anniversary. Dallas, TX: Taylor Publishing, 1996.

Delaware National Guard, 1946–2006, 60th Anniversary. Dallas, TX: Taylor Publishing, 2006.

Frebert, George J. *Delaware Aviation History.* Dover, DE: Dover Litho Printing Company, 1998.

Lewis, W. David, and William F. Trimble. *The Airway to Everywhere, History of All American Aviation, 1937–1953.* Pittsburgh, PA: University of Pittsburg Press, 1998.

Matz, Onas P. *History of the 2nd Ferrying Group.* Seattle, WA: Modet Enterprises, 1993.

Wiggins, Kennard R., Jr. *Delaware Air National Guard.* Charleston, SC: Arcadia Publishing 2008.

———. *Delaware National Guard.* Charleston, SC: Arcadia Publishing, 2010.

———. *Dover Air Force Base.* Charleston, SC: Arcadia Publishing, 2011.

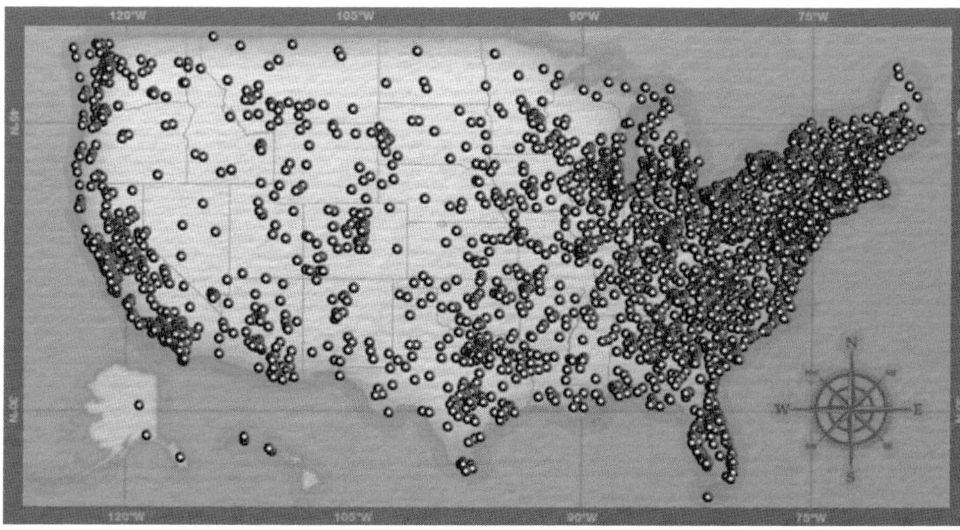